100 THINGS
SENATORS FANS
SHOULD KNOW & DO
BEFORE THEY DIE

100 THINGS
SENATORS FANS
SHOULD KNOW & DO
BEFORE THEY DIE

Chris Stevenson

TRIUMPH
BOOKS

Library of Congress Cataloging-in-Publication Data

Names: Stevenson, Christopher John, author.
Title: 100 things Senators fans should know & do before they die / Chris Stevenson.
Other titles: One hundred things Senators fans should know and do before they die | Hundred things Senators fans should know and do before they die
Description: Chicago, Illinois: Triumph Books LLC, [2018]
Identifiers: LCCN 2018015281 | ISBN 9781629373669
Subjects: LCSH: Ottawa Senators (Hockey team)—Miscellanea. | Hockey—Ontario—Ottawa—Miscellanea. | Ottawa Senators (Hockey team)—History. | Hockey—Ontario—Ottawa—History.
Classification: LCC GV848.O89 S74 2018 | DDC 796.962/640971384—dc23
LC record available at https://lccn.loc.gov/2018015281

This book is available in quantity at special discounts for your group or organization. For further information, contact:
Triumph Books LLC
814 North Franklin Street
Chicago, Illinois 60610
(312) 337-0747
www.triumphbooks.com

Printed in U.S.A.
ISBN: 978-1-62937-366-9
Design by Patricia Frey
Photos courtesy of AP Images unless otherwise indicated

To Senators fans everywhere

Contents

1 Bring Back the Senators

Colonel E.R. Bradley was a self-described "speculator, raiser of race horses and gambler," so it was fitting that the saloon in West Palm Beach, Florida, that bore his name was where the supporters of the Bring Back the Senators campaign gathered on a sultry night— December 5, 1990.

Gamblers is a fitting word to describe the men behind the bid to bring NHL hockey back to Ottawa: Terrace Investments Inc.'s president, Bruce Firestone, a brash 39-year-old entrepreneur; vice president, Randy Sexton; and COO, Cyril Leeder.

Firestone had come up with the idea to bid for an NHL expansion franchise over a dressing room beer with Sexton and Leeder after a pickup game of hockey at the old Lions Arena in Westboro. "He said to us, 'I think the NHL is going to expand,' and we took another swig of beer and said, 'Okay, Bruce,'" Sexton told me a few years ago. He continued, "Then he said, 'And I think Ottawa would support a team,' and we nodded and said, 'Okay, Bruce.' And then he said, 'I think we're the guys to do it,' and we spit our beer out on the floor."

Going into stealth mode, Terrace Investments quietly went about assembling the land they needed for a rink. They announced their plans to Bring Back the Senators in a fax (I still have it) to newsrooms in Ottawa on a June day in 1989. The reaction was: "Who?"

So there we were on that night in Florida, in a saloon, on the 542nd day after the Terrace bid, with excitement and anticipation high. The Terrace group had made their presentation earlier that day, spending 63 minutes in front of the NHL's board of governors at the posh and stuffy Breakers resort in Palm Beach. They had presented their case for why Ottawa should be chosen from the remaining field of seven candidate cities to be awarded an NHL expansion franchise to begin play in 1992–93.

Most people were still overwhelmingly skeptical about whether NHL hockey would return to Ottawa following a 58-year absence after the original Ottawa Senators, pummeled by the Great Depression, had picked up and left for St. Louis. There remained legitimate questions about whether Terrace had the $50 million franchise fee and the wherewithal to build a state-of-the-art arena, to be called the Palladium. At that point the rink was nothing but 100 acres of cornfield in the city's West End that was, at that moment, getting dumped on in the winter's first major snowfall. Who knew if the Ontario Municipal Board (OMB) would even allow the land to be rezoned to allow the building of a rink?

Nobody was even sure the NHL governors would get the answers they wanted from the bidders and award *any* franchises. "I have a lot of experience dealing with the board of governors," Cliff Fletcher of the Calgary Flames told me on the eve of the meetings. "When they meet, it's not like dealing with the board of directors of a big corporation. It's more like the meeting of an oil cartel. Everyone has his own distinct and separate associations and, quite frankly, everyone has his own particular ox to gore."

There were twists and turns in the hours before the presentations. The morning of the presentations it was announced the OMB had shuffled its schedule to allow for a quick hearing into the zoning for the Palladium, to be built in the West End community of Kanata. The average wait was 16 months. The Terrace request was fast-tracked to March. That was good news.

The Tampa bid, fronted by Hall of Famer Phil Esposito and backed by Japanese investors, was dealt a blow when it was announced Hillsborough County commissioners voted 5–2 against spending $30 million of public funds on a $96 million rink for

Tampa. "I don't know what to say," said Esposito, for the first time in his life.

Houston had withdrawn the week before, and Seattle bowed out just before the board of governors was to meet. That left Hamilton, Miami, Tampa Bay, St. Petersburg, San Diego, and Anaheim in the mix. They made their presentations throughout that day.

The Terrace boys were confident. They had painstakingly worked the room. They had produced an impressive leather-bound bid book. They knew the names of every governor's wife, girlfriend, and child. Birthday cards were hand-delivered. The paying of respects had been done in trips across North America. They had a theme song—Tom Petty's "I Won't Back Down"—and the backing of Frank Finnigan, the last surviving member of the original Senators. These guys knew how to market and knew how to sell the sizzle, even if they didn't have any steak. "It's crunch time, and we're more prepared than any other bid," Sexton said. "We have more civic, corporate, and political support than anybody else."

About 100 people had gathered at E.R. Bradley's to assess Ottawa's chances over a drink and rehash the day's events. Ottawa had had by far the most visible and noisy support of the eight cities that remained from the 11 that had originally put in bids for the NHL's sixth plan of expansion.

Hamilton, backed by doughnut czar Ron Joyce and his Tim Horton's chain, was viewed as the favorite if the NHL decided to give another franchise to Canada. St. Petersburg, backed by the computer company Compuware (owned by future NHL owner Peter Karmanos) and fronted by Karmanos's hockey guy, Jim Rutherford, was also seen as a front-runner.

The sunny, warm day started ominously for the Ottawa bid. The red-clad Ottawa Fire Department Band broke into a brassy rendition of Canada's "Centennial Song" at 9:30 AM outside the

Breakers and moved into a bouncy version of "This Land Is Your Land"—the Canadian version, of course.

About 50 supporters hefted placards attached to hockey sticks and chanted, "We want a franchise," giving the gathering the feel of a political rally. It wasn't exactly the kind of noise the blue-rinse, polo-playing patrons of the Breakers were used to experiencing along with their morning coffee. "We were told by hotel security that if the band struck up one more tune, we'd be physically removed," said Gary Thom, an insurance broker who was part of Kanata's chamber of commerce. "We came here with the interest of showing our support for the bid. We were looking forward to giving Ottawa a good positive image. We're disappointed. We're not here trying to create a stir."

"We couldn't hear anything through the band playing," said Godfrey Wood, who was president of Miami Hockey Inc. "And I've got a pretty good idea whose band it was."

When Firestone walked into the meeting room, Bruce McNall, then the owner of the Los Angeles Kings, barked "Is that your goddamned band?" In his book *Don't Back Down: The Real Story Behind the Founding of the NHL's Ottawa Senators*, Firestone wrote that he replied, "No, it's his," and gestured with his thumb to Ottawa's mayor, Jim Durrell, who was following him in.

Security inside was tight. The NHL's director of security was positioned menacingly outside the men's room closest to the boardroom where the governors were meeting. He was poised to prevent any media types from getting a story through a leak.

In the boardroom, there were six members for the Ottawa bid: Firestone, Sexton, Leeder, Durrell, former U.S. attorney general Elliot Richardson, who was their U.S. lawyer, and accountant Gary Burns. They made their presentation, which included a six-minute video, and took questions.

In the evening, the governors and the bidders gathered at the home of Boston Bruins owner Jeremy Jacobs. The Terrace bidders worked the room to get a sense of where their bid stood. They needed the support of 16 of the NHL's 21 governors. "You're close, but you're not there," they were told by governors who liked what they had heard from Firestone and his group. "Get out there and start lobbying."

A few hours later, Firestone and the rest of the Terrace bidders showed up at E.R. Bradley's. Firestone, characteristically optimistic earlier in the day, was now shockingly somber. A governor, who might have been the host, had walked up to him at the reception earlier and told him Ottawa would get an NHL franchise "over my dead body." A threat? Grim reality? A test to see how Firestone would react? Whatever it was, it had left Firestone shaken. "Bruce is kind of white, all this work down the drain," remembered Leeder. "Everybody is partying except us. We're freaked out."

"It doesn't look good," Firestone told me quietly against the noise of the bar. His canvassing revealed 12 governors supported the Ottawa bid, 3 didn't, and there were "2 maybes and 4 wafflers." The ominous words of the governor had cast a pall over the bid. Supporters went to sleep that night thinking an NHL franchise, which had seemed so close hours before, was now heartbreakingly beyond their grasp.

2 Ottawa and Tampa

After being told by NHL governor Jeremy Jacobs that their campaign to bring an NHL expansion franchise to Ottawa was on the rocks, bidders Bruce Firestone, Randy Sexton, and Cyril Leeder left a party for the bid's boosters in West Palm Beach, Florida, and headed back to their hotel.

Firestone, despondent that two years of work had brought them so close but appeared not to be enough, called a meeting with his lieutenants in his suite at midnight. "It's all Randy and I can do to talk him into not withdrawing. What he wanted to do was withdraw," Leeder remembered. "He said, 'We know there are going to be more [expansion] teams; we'll be ready for the next round.' We said, 'We came this far. What have we got to lose?'"

They had made their presentation to the board of governors that day—December 5, 1990—and Sexton had arranged a breakfast meeting for the next morning with Winnipeg Jets governor Barry Shenkarow and Ronald Corey of the Montreal Canadiens. The Terrace group wanted to get a feel for where they stood and to make one last appeal for Ottawa's candidacy.

The word from the governors over bacon and eggs: don't throw in the napkin just yet. "'You've done everything you can; just see what happens,' they said," remembered Leeder. "'Let the governors run their course. You have lots of friends on the inside, lots of people that believe in you guys.' We went back and told Bruce we had to stay in there. That's when he said, 'I'm going to go for a run.'" A little later, the word came down: the NHL wanted to see them. They had to wait for Firestone to come back from his run.

Jim Steel and some other Terrace executives were on the golf course at the Breakers. Everybody was rounded up for what they thought was going to be bad news. The group—Firestone, Sexton, Leeder, Ottawa mayor Jim Durrell, accountant Gary Burns, and former U.S. attorney general Elliot Richardson—was led through the basement at the Breakers and through a kitchen ("The pipes were leaking on us," said Firestone), and finally into a boardroom.

"It had to be a 10,000-square-foot ballroom," Leeder said. "Six of us standing there, and we don't know what's going on. The doors open after what seemed like an hour but was probably 10 minutes, and it's Esposito and the Tampa guys."

Phil Esposito, a Hall of Famer as a player and as a smooth-talking front man for the Tampa Bay bid, had been working to convince people hockey in Florida could work. It was an improbable proposition: hockey in the sunbelt backed by a Japanese golf course operator (don't forget, the Los Angeles Kings were the most southerly franchise at the time). Esposito's bid was viewed skeptically.

"The rumor down there was we had done a good job and Ottawa may be turning some heads," Leeder said. "Espo looks at us and says, 'It's Ottawa! This is the winners' room!' We looked at him and said, '(Bleep), it's Esposito. This is the losers' room.' "He said, 'It's Ottawa. We're getting a franchise,' and we said, 'No, no, we think this is the losers' room, buddy.'"

After standing around, Leeder needed a bathroom break and went down the hall to the men's room. Montreal Canadiens general manager Serge Savard got there at the same time. "We're in there having a leak, and he looks at me, winks at me, and says, 'Way to go. Well done. Congratulations.' I went back to the ballroom, and before I can say anything, they're wheeling us into the room," Leeder said.

As Firestone wrote in his book *Don't Back Down*, "The result was that on December 6th, 1990, I stood next to John Ziegler in the boardroom of the Breakers Hotel in Palm Beach shortly after 1 PM to read on a piece of paper: 'The NHL is pleased and proud to announce today that conditional memberships have been awarded to the cities of Ottawa and Tampa...'"

Over the years, the story has been that the Terrace bidders and the Esposito group got their franchises because they were the only groups that didn't try to change the terms of the expansion deal. They answered yes to every question: "Will you pay $50 million on our terms?" "Yes." "Will you build an 18,000-seat rink?" "Yes."

Ron Joyce, the front man for the Hamilton bid, and other bidders were rumored to have tried to negotiate the terms of

The First to Know

You might have thought the first outside the NHL to know officially that Ottawa had won an expansion franchise was founder Bruce Firestone. You'd be wrong. He looked down and saw the paper NHL president John Ziegler was about to read from at a press conference at the Breakers Hotel; it announced Ottawa and Tampa as the winners. He was at least the second person to know.

In the lead-up to the bid, the guys at Terrace Investments got a call from a fellow named Dave Saunders from Brockville, Ontario, the hometown of Terrace executives Randy Sexton and Cyril Leeder. Saunders was looking for a job. They didn't have anything at that point but offered him a job helping with the then-upcoming bid presentation at the Breakers in Florida.

Here's Cyril Leeder, one of the three men who won the bid, with the story:

> We needed guys to go down to Florida as part of the bid at the Breakers, just to help out, move stuff around. We asked him if he would be interested in going down to Florida. We told him, "We can't pay you much, but if we get the team, you'll be on the inside."
>
> Dave goes into the board of governors' room to help set up our video for the presentation. He goes in, does what he has to do, works with the IT guys from the Breakers, gets everything set up. We go in, it's all working perfectly. Bang, bang, we do the presentation. That night, Saunders goes back to get all our gear out of the room. He goes back in, and there's nobody around. He goes into the room and starts getting our stuff. He looks up on the board and it's got all the cities on the board, the cities that had made their presentations. There's lines through them all, except Ottawa and Tampa are circled and it says "1:00 press conference," so he knew.
>
> *We've got it*, he thinks, and he gives a "Yes!" and just as he does that, the NHL security guy who is supposed to be guarding the door walks in.
>
> "What are you doing in here?"
>
> "I came in to get my gear. There was nobody here, so I walked in."
>
> "If you tell anybody, Ottawa will lose the fucking franchise."
>
> "I won't tell anybody. I'm sorry."
>
> "I'm telling you, you can't tell anybody."
>
> Dave didn't tell anybody.

payment of the franchise fee, which was two payments of $22.5 million to go with the nonrefundable $5 million deposit. Firestone and his guys didn't blink.

As for the "over my dead body" comment made by the governor, Firestone wrote of a later conversation with that same man:

> [That governor said,] "You see me and three members of the board got together. We decided to go up to each bidder and say, 'You will never, ever, ever get a franchise in Tampa, St. Petersburg, Houston, Portland, Ottawa, Seattle, Milwaukee, Hamilton…"
>
> "You did that?"
>
> "We did. And the only two bidders who didn't quit, who kept going, were you and Phil. So we gave the franchises to Ottawa and Tampa. It was a character test."

The Senators passed.

3 Maybe Rome Was Built in a Day

It had seem so improbable just four years earlier, the idea that NHL hockey could again be played in Ottawa after a 58-year absence. Ottawa had become a professional sports backwater with only the pathetically inept Ottawa Rough Riders occupying the landscape, and they were tottering toward bankruptcy.

The bid for an NHL expansion franchise by Terrace Investments, to that point a relatively unknown company working out of the Mallorn Centre on Moodie Dr., had seemed like such an improbable long shot. But here on the night of October 8, 1992, real, live hockey players wearing Ottawa Senators sweaters (that fantastic so-called 2-D logo of the Centurion in profile on their chests) skated out through the dry-ice fog amid faux Roman columns that had unfurled from the ceiling.

Across from them was the most storied franchise in hockey and maybe all of professional sports: the Montreal Canadiens, in their iconic red uniforms, la Sainte-Flanelle incredibly juxtaposed against the new white sweaters of the upstarts.

It was happening: the NHL was living again in Ottawa, though the predictions for the Senators were not good. They were a team of castoffs, draft busts, and aging veterans discarded by their teams. In their first training camp, one of their best players had been former NHLer Larry Skinner, then working in the circulation department of the *Ottawa Sun*, who had taken part in camp to write a daily diary of his experiences for the newspaper.

But Canadiens coach Jacques Demers was wary. He was behind the bench of the 1979–80 Quebec Nordiques for their debut in the NHL after being absorbed from the defunct World Hockey Association, and they had beaten the Canadiens in their first meeting. "We beat Montreal, and for us it was like winning the Stanley Cup," he said.

Demers reminded his team about the 1976–77 Canadiens, perhaps the greatest team of all time, which lost but eight games that season, one of them to the Colorado Rockies, perhaps one of the worst teams of all time. "This is like a Stanley Cup game for them," Demers told his players. "[Don't] take anything for granted. [The Senators] have a lot of pride. Some of them are getting their second or third chance to make it, and they will want to make the most of it."

The 10,449 fans in the building greeted their new team with a five-minute standing ovation. There had been a pent-up demand for this moment. As part of their bid to prove NHL would be a success in Ottawa, the Terrace bidders had sold 15,000 "personal registration numbers" that gave fans the right to line up and buy season tickets. The personal registration numbers were sold for $25 each, and each holder got a certificate and a bumper sticker.

When Terrace won the franchise, the holders lined up to select their tickets and pumped about $20 million in cash into the franchise. There were times, at the end of the day, when there would be $5 million in cash sitting on a boardroom table.

Fans had slapped down their money, and now it was time for the show. *Hockey Night in Canada* and Ron MacLean and

Near Beer

One of the best behind-the-scenes stories of opening night at the Civic Centre came from owner and founder Bruce Firestone in his memoir of the early Senators days, *Don't Back Down*.

The Senators had a long and profound battle with the New Democratic government of Ontario, which threw up every manner of bureaucratic red tape, from minor to major. The culmination was a series of battles over the zoning of the land to build the proposed Palladium that went before the Ontario Municipal Board, followed by having to pay for the interchange to allow access to the site from the Queensway.

There were all manner of slights, such as making the Senators wait uncomfortably for their liquor license so they could sell beer at the Civic Centre. As the clock clicked down inside of an hour until the puck drop on October 8, 1992, the Senators still did not have the license to open the coolers and fridges and allow hockey fans to partake of a Molson product.

According to Firestone's account, the minister of consumer and corporate affairs made Senators lobbyist Rick Anderson wait the entire day outside of his office before he signed the license at 5:00 PM at Queen's Park. A police escort brought Anderson from the airport to the Civic Centre, and the duly signed license was posted at 7:00 PM.

Wrote Firestone: "Everyone who got a beer between gates opening and 7 [PM] got a phony [one]—you know, [an] insipid dealcoholized version. Sorry about that."

Don Cherry were in town. There were figure-skating Centurions weaving around the ice. Canadian figure-skating champion Brian Orser skated out, and despite specific orders not to do his trademark backflip (there was fear his landing would chip the ice), he did it anyway. Young Ottawa singing star Alanis (she would add Morissette and several million dollars in sales to her résumé a few years later with her album *Jagged Little Pill*) sang "O Canada."

The Senators were welcomed with what would become their theme song, which started with a trumpet and then was followed by a thumping bass line. The opening trumpet was played by Carmelo Scaffidi, who passed away in January 2016 after a battle with brain cancer. The song was composed by Ottawa musician Andrés del Castillo of the band Eight Seconds.

The Senators honored Frank Finnigan—who had played for the last Senators Stanley Cup team in 1927 and had been part of the Bring Back the Senators campaign—by raising his No. 8 to the rafters. After that, referee Kerry Fraser dropped the puck, and then the Senators beat the Canadiens.

After a scoreless first period, Neil Brady, a former first-round draft pick of the New Jersey Devils, took a pass from Jody Hull and scored the first goal in Senators history. It came on the power play 26 seconds into the period.

Doug Smail scored for the Senators at 11:04, and when Montreal's Mike Keane scored 32 seconds later, there was a feeling of "Here come the Habs." But Ottawa defenseman Ken Hammond got another one before the second period was over for a 3–1 Senators lead.

Each time the Canadiens scored, the Senators had an answer. Montreal's Vincent Damphousse made it 3–2 early in the third, but ex-Hab Sylvain Turgeon scored with 2:09 left in the game. It got tense when Brian Bellows scored with 29 seconds left to make it a one-goal game, but Smail added an empty-net goal with 15 seconds left. That last 15 seconds as the clock wound down were a joyous celebration of the NHL's return and a great moment in Ottawa history.

The Senators won despite finishing the game with just four defensemen after Brad Shaw left the game with a concussion after a hit into the glass by Montreal's Kirk Muller, and Hammond was kicked out halfway through the third for a kneeing penalty that was judged by Fraser to be an attempt to injure.

"I remember reading the papers before we started, and the media were picking us to win maybe eight, nine games," goaltender Peter Sidorkiewicz reminisced to the *Ottawa Citizen* years later. "After the first game, when we beat Montreal on *Hockey Night in Canada*, I think I was with Ken Hammond and Brad Marsh. We were standing in front of the mirror shaving; we looked at each other and said, 'Those reporters have to be crazy; we'll win 10 games by Christmas!' We went on and lost our next 21, so I guess you guys were right." (They actually went 0–20–1, but who's counting?)

"I was a part of 13 other opening nights in my career," the Senators' first captain, Laurie Boschman, said on the night of that magical first win, "and I never once saw one that made the impact like [this] one did. [This] was a real treat."

If I know the newspaper business, headline writers, in keeping with the Senators' Roman theme, no doubt had their banner ready to go for what they surely anticipated would be an inevitable loss to the mighty Canadiens: Rome Wasn't Built in a Day.

After the unexpected victory, there was a nice bit of stick handling: Maybe Rome Was Built in a Day.

4 By the Book

When it came to winning an NHL expansion franchise for Ottawa, the men from Terrace Investments, to quote Vancouver Canucks executive Brian Burke at the time, wrote the book on it. Much of the Senators' successful bid centered around their impressive leather-bound, 704-page bid book, personalized for each member of the NHL's board of governors and the members of the NHL's front office. The book really summed up the Senators' approach to bidding for an NHL franchise: pay attention to detail, do everything first-class, and schmooze like crazy.

The bid book was undertaken by Terrace executives Cyril Leeder and Jim Steel. Leeder was a chartered accountant and a meticulous student of hockey. Assembling a document like that was an area of expertise for Steel, who had a background in printing before joining Terrace. Senators founder Bruce Firestone has referred to the bid book as "Cyril's PhD thesis." Dedicated to the 1926–27 Stanley Cup champion Ottawa Senators, the last Ottawa team to win the Cup, it was an incredibly detailed document that not only mapped out why Ottawa deserved to have the NHL return to Canada's capital, but went into an appreciation of NHL history and its record of expansion. It mapped out the structure of the Ottawa Senators Hockey Club from its founding and included detailed biographical information on local ownership, financial information, and a capitalization plan. There was a large section on the proposed Palladium, the new home of the Senators, and the associated development. The Senators hockey operations and team management was mapped out, along with a philosophy of team-building. There was even an extensive explanation of Ottawa's economy and why the market was poised to support the return of NHL hockey to the city, along with details about community support and the media landscape.

When it came time to deliver the books, Firestone didn't trust FedEx or Purolator to ship the precious books to the NHL's headquarters in New York. That would be boring. He had Terrace president Randy Sexton and Steel pile into a limousine and personally deliver the cargo. It was another indication of the show Terrace put on when it came to grabbing attention for their bid. There were cameras waiting for them when they pulled up in front of the NHL HQ.

Along with the bid books to be distributed to the governors, Sexton and Steel brought with them another gift, which was in keeping with their style of creating memorable interactions with the powers that be…which is to say, they knew how to suck up in style.

The Senators commissioned artist Bruce Garner, of Plantagenet, Ontario, east of Ottawa, to create a brass sculpture titled *He Shoots, Il Lance*, which depicted a player taking a slap shot. Garner—whose *Dagain* sculpture soars above the Bell Media building in Ottawa's ByWard Market—created the illusion of the stick whipping through the puck by creating six sticks in stop-action style. Sexton and Steel unloaded all their gifts from the limo, including a two-foot-high aluminum maquette of Garner's work, and made their way to the office of NHL vice president Gil Stein.

"We went into his office to present this statue and drop off the books. We were in the office and I go to open it, show him what we [had there]," Steel said of the box containing the maquette. "I open[ed] the top of the box and [couldn't] see the statue; it [was] all that popcorn, Styrofoam packing stuff. I [tried] to pull it out little by little and let them drop off. That wasn't going to work, so I figured [I'd] just clean up after, so I pull[ed] the statue out."

Steel pulled the statue out of the box, spilling the packing in Stein's office.

"It's the summertime, June or July. He's got the air-conditioning going, and [the packing material was] all along the walls, under the window overlooking the Avenue of the Americas, and there [were] hundreds of these popcorn things flying in his window," Steel said. "Randy [was] giving me these glares, like I could do anything about it, and Gil Stein [was] looking at Randy and me like we [were] idiots."

The bid books and the statue were hits. The popcorn show, not so much, but it obviously wasn't enough to pop the Senators' balloon. Said Burke: "If you're assessing how these guys have handled expansion, they should publish a textbook on it."

They did.

Thank the Smartest Guy in the Room

It's not hyperbole to say that if Rod Bryden hadn't gotten involved with the Ottawa Senators, the team wouldn't be around today. Founder Bruce Firestone was the philosophical visionary, and he seemed to tire of the process once the improbable had been made probable and the vision was a reality.

Rod Bryden, who grew up on a farm in New Brunswick without electricity, having made and lost millions for himself and others, in his impeccably tailored corporate uniform, had a plan. And he wouldn't let go. He was Daniel Alfredsson before there was Daniel Alfredsson—coming from somewhere in the background, smart, relentless, tireless, making the most of what God gave him.

"He didn't sleep. He [was] a shark. Constantly moving," said John Owens, who worked as Bryden's PR consultant for 11 years and was the Senators' vice president of communications in their early days. "He'd send me memos at 2:30 in the morning," Owens added.

Making the Senators happen, from paying the $50 million franchise fee (which neither Firestone nor Terrace Investments had) to coming up with the $240 million it was going to take to build the Palladium—which nobody in Ottawa was interested in doing—Bryden, the serial entrepreneur, took it on.

It never seemed to be about, "Hey, look at me. I own an NHL team. I'll call a radio station because my words are important." It was a chance to do something that would endure here, in his adopted town. It was the tight knot that defied his fingernails. It had to be undone, so he turned it over and attacked another part.

That it happened to be about hockey, well, I'm not sure Bryden knew much more about hockey than anyone in Canada can't help but know. "Not a bit," Owens said. "He looked upon it as a cultural achievement. A business opportunity and a cultural achievement for his beloved Ottawa. There was no swagger at all. When you think of the hundreds of millions of dollars he made for himself and others, you'd think you'd see a hint of swagger. Not a fucking hint. He bought a house in Rockcliffe. But a small one."

Rod Bryden is a smart man. He was a smart kid. In sixth grade, he had the best results in province-wide tests, according to a piece in the *Toronto Globe and Mail* in 2003, when he was building another intricate plan to buy the team back out of bankruptcy. He got a scholarship to Mount Allison University, then to the University of New Brunswick to study law, followed by a master's at the University of Michigan. He became a professor of law at the University of Saskatchewan, recruited by Otto Lang, who would then involve Bryden to run his Liberal campaign for a federal seat. They won, of course, and Bryden came to Ottawa. He swept through government departments learning how government and business worked. His entrepreneurial spirit won out, and he embarked on making and losing millions with Systemhouse.

His holding company, Kinburn Corp., dropped the bag on $831 million in debt.

When Firestone had his "Oh, we got the franchise. Now what do we do?" moment, Bryden stepped in. There was the knot—tight, impenetrable. But in a somewhat Matrix-like movement, Bryden spun it around, stopped it here, sped it up there, looked, and prodded. He found the money to pay the expansion fee, including a few bucks from Ogden, the arena manager, and from the McCains,

The Phoenix Senators

Senators owner Rod Bryden faced a lot of financial challenges to secure the Senators financing for both the franchise fee, which was $50 million, and the Palladium, which was coming in at around $240 million.

Probably nobody would have blamed him if he had packed it in and moved along. The environment in Canada wasn't particularly hospitable for NHL teams. The Canadian dollar was starting its tank against its U.S. counterpart. NHL players' salaries were spiraling upward (between 1992, when the Senators started play in the NHL, and 2002, the Senators' payroll went from $6.5 million CDN to $54 million US, according to Senators founder Bruce Firestone).

In Ontario the NDP government was doing everything it could to deter NHL hockey in Ottawa, such as sticking Bryden with the $24 million tab for the interchange on the Queensway.

The talk in the early 1990s was the Quebec Nordiques and the Winnipeg Jets found the economic environment so grim they were looking to sell to American cities. Phoenix was interested in the Jets.

John Owens, the Senators' vice president of corporate communications, remembered being in a conference call about the deal: "Phoenix wanted us, not Winnipeg. The first round of the Palladium financing had collapsed. We've got young players and young contracts and Winnipeg was more established," Owens recalled. They offered Rod $80 million U.S., and he gets to keep 10 percent of the team. There's a pause, and Rod goes, 'No, hockey is going to make it in Ottawa,' and that was the end of the conversation. Holy shit! I love you, Rod. That's just balls. That's the kind of guy he was."

the frozen food folks, to the east. Firestone mortgaged his house. Bryden got Ogden to throw in $30 million for the Palladium and guarantee the loans. "He was the smartest man I've ever met, and it's not even close," said Cyril Leeder—who was in charge of the Palladium project and worked with Bryden for close to 15 years.

And Bryden was a hopeless promoter of the Senators, using his brains and his seductive patter to bring people on board. "What I always loved about Rod was his Ottawa fealty. He loves Ottawa," Owens said.

Said Leeder:

> Rod was all for the community, and we had to do more to generate business in the community. If he was going to speak, he wanted to speak to people who could buy tickets. He wasn't going to go to a government conference. He'd get these speaking engagements, and he never prepared for them. If I [was] going to one, I'd probably spend an hour preparing my notes, an hour practicing, probably a couple hours of prep before I [went]. He wouldn't do anything. He would just wing it.
>
> A lot of times he would call me the day of and say, "Cy, I'm running on a tight schedule today. I'll meet you at the chamber of commerce, out front of the room, five minutes before the thing starts." We'd be in there socializing just before it's supposed to start, and I'd go out in the hall and start pacing. I'd call Rod. "Yeah, I'm just pulling up. Don't worry, I'll be there." Rod would come up and say, "Who are we meeting today?"
>
> "Rod, we sent you the notes."
>
> "I know, I haven't had a chance to review them. Who are we meeting? Who's in the room?"
>
> "It's 175 people. It's the chamber of commerce, and they're all from downtown Ottawa. You've got small

businesses mainly, but two big businesses…, Bell and Mitel, are here."

He would just say, "I need a minute." He'd think about it, organize it all in his head, and he'd say, "Okay."

[He'd ask,] "What are we selling right now? What's a main package we're selling a lot?"

"Well, these 10-game plans…" He'd get up there and have those guys mesmerized, talk for half an hour—no notes—make a sales pitch, and he'd say, "See Cy or one of those guys afterward," and people would be running up and saying, "That was amazing. Where do we get one of these 10-packs?" He was just so good, and it happened all the time.

"He was a magnet every place he spoke," said Roy Mlakar, the Senators president from 1996 to 2009. "I remember one time he was speaking to a big group at the Kiwanis Holiday Inn downtown. When he spoke he created an audience of people who listened. He was so good and so popular. Everywhere he went, they bought stock in Rod Bryden."

Bryden wanted the Senators to work. Twenty-five years later, the Senators would have a slogan: "Here. Now. Ottawa." That was Bryden's credo in 1992. "He was the type of owner in a small market that everybody really, really respected," Mlakar said. "I don't think Rod got the accolades for keeping it going on a shoestring. All the tax money he was screwed on. The change in government from one party to the next. He never got the accolades."

6 The House That Rod Built

When Bruce Firestone and Terrace Investments were bidding for an NHL franchise for Ottawa in 1988, they managed to take a negative—the fact that Ottawa didn't have an NHL-caliber rink—and turned it into a positive.

Since they didn't have a rink, they could make the new facility state-of-the-art and make it the centerpiece of a real estate play that has since become the model for many such projects, including TD Place in Ottawa, a mix of retail and residential projects around the refurbished football stadium.

After Firestone told Terrace executives Randy Sexton and Cyril Leeder of his plan to bring an NHL expansion franchise to Ottawa, they quietly began assembling 600 acres of land in Ottawa's West End. The rink would be called the Palladium and it would be the centerpiece of a new community, West Terrace, that Firestone envisioned.

Terrace's Jim Steel was put in charge of assembling the land near the intersection of the Queensway and Huntmar Rd. The area had what they needed: a relatively flat area with access to a major arterial route at a relatively cheap (by standards then) price.

Steel's first deal was with farmer Lawrence Semple, who agreed to sell his land for $500,000. Steel said:

> Then he wanted to have have a drink to seal the deal. He's an old farmer, and a handshake was all he needed. We had a rum. Then another rum. This is the morning, and now I'm half in the bag. Now I'm worried I'm going to get in trouble when I get back there because I'm reeking of booze.

I bought a pack of cigars [and was] sitting in my car. Should I go in now or wait a couple of hours? I've got this signed agreement, and that's got to overrule everything. I went right in. They could tell I was drinking. They could smell it on me, and I told the story. Bruce loved that story.

Leeder made an important observation after Terrace built the Mallorn Centre on Moodie Dr., in the West End, one of Terrace's bigger projects to that point. The land had been purchased for about $100,000 an acre. After the Mallorn Centre went up, it immediately made that area seem more attractive. The land in the area went up in value: a car dealer paid $400,000 an acre within three years. "That planted the seed that if you build something of significance, then you'll drive up the value in the area," Leeder said.

"Cyril had pointed out that wherever Terrace did a project, land value tended to go up around us and that in our next project (which he did not know would be a National League building) we should benefit from our own hard work," Firestone wrote in his story of the Senators, *Don't Back Down*. "As you already know, when Cyril Leeder speaks, people should listen. He's quiet, but he knows stuff. You can trust his judgment."

Along with their ambitious plan to enhance the value of the land, Terrace wanted to change the conversation when it came to the rink. From Firestone's introductory letter in Terrace's leather-bound bid book:

In order for an arena to generate significant new revenues, I believed that a new generation of design was needed. The multi-purpose facility that I had in mind when I first considered initiating a bid for an NHL expansion franchise in 1987, involved a sports and entertainment complex unlike anything that had yet been seen in Canada. I believed the facility had to incorporate office space, hotel space, retail space and lots of parking because this had to be a 365 day a year development.

It had to be a private sector initiative, owned and controlled by Terrace Investments Limited. Owning and controlling the arena complex was important to us because it would ensure that we, and the Ottawa Senators, would receive full benefit from the facility's many revenue sources. As well, if we owned the land, and we were going to finance the arena, we controlled the timing and could react quickly to any NHL expansion plans or requirements.

When they pitched their idea of building the Palladium, which would increase the value of the land around it (Firestone figured the land would increase in value by about $50 million, which

Rod Bryden announces his bid to buy the Senators in 2003.

just happened to be the cost of the franchise fee), the idea of the rink generating a boost in the value of the land around it was a new concept. It became a critical reason why the rink was built where it is and not downtown. Terrace needed control of the land upon which the rink was built and the surrounding real estate to make the project work. (LeBreton Flats, now being discussed as the potential home of a new rink, was not an option because the National Capital Commission was not interested in developing the land in 1987.)

This new idea of creating value impressed the NHL governors. "[Dallas Stars owner] Norm Green stood up and said this [was] a model we should all be thinking about. It's a way to finance our teams," Leeder said.

It wasn't immediately evident at the time, but one of the biggest hurdles the Palladium project would have to overcome had its foundation in the change of Ontario government in September 1990 with Bob Rae's NDP defeating David Peterson's Liberals. Peterson's government had been friendly toward the Terrace bid, but the NDP challenged it at every opportunity. The feeling in Ottawa was that the NDP favored the Hamilton bid, backed by Tim Horton's doughnut king Ron Joyce, because that was close to the seat of its union-backed power.

The Palladium project, specifically the rezoning of the farmland to allow the construction of a hockey rink, was subject to scrutiny by the Ontario Municipal Board through the summer of 1991. It was a long and quite boring 13½ weeks of testimony, with Firestone having to take the stand for three and a half days. Advised things weren't looking good for Terrace, he offered to put a moratorium on development of 500 acres, but that was rejected.

At one point a frustrated Doug Logan, an executive with Ogden, the arena-management company that was financially immersed in the project, offered Firestone $20 million to move his franchise to the new rink in Anaheim that Ogden was running. Firestone turned that down.

The OMB ruled the project could go ahead but reduced the capacity of the building from 22,500 to 18,500 (the Senators later further reduced it themselves, to 17,000, by tarping 1,500 seats for the 2017–18 season) and the number of luxury suites from 176 to 104. The OMB also ruled the Senators had to pay for the interchange off the Queensway, at a cost of about $24 million. That was outrageous when you think about it: a private company being told it had to build public infrastructure. But Terrace did it.

Leeder was appointed the president of the Palladium Corporation in January 1992 and was responsible for all aspects of the project. Firestone, Leeder, and Terrace management visited more than 30 stadiums around North America to grab ideas.

The Senators were impressed with the work of Gino Rossetti, who had revolutionized arena configuration with the Palace of Auburn Hills in Michigan, the home of the Detroit Pistons. Inspired by the Vienna Opera House, Rossetti's biggest contribution was moving the first ring of luxury suites from the top of the building to a dozen rows from the playing surface.

After Firestone sold his half of the team to partner Rod Bryden after the first season, much of Bryden's focus was on coming up with the $240 million needed to construct the rink. It was originally scheduled to open in December 1993, but numerous financing plans fell through and delayed the process. On July 7, 1994, construction finally started on the project. John Owens, the Senators' vice president of corporate communications then, later remembered the scene when the construction activity started to swing into high gear. "They needed to sink 1,200 pilings down into solid clay to hold the Palladium up," he said. "I'm watching it. They're putting in 100-foot pilings to get down to the bedrock, and the first trucks started coming out. The Ottawa ceramics society was there collecting the clay drippings from the trucks to make ashtrays," he said with a laugh. "The truck drivers were laying on the horns. These guys were so thrilled to be working again. There were like 50 trucks with the horns blaring."

On January 15, 1996, the Palladium opened with a concert by Canadian star Bryan Adams. Two nights later, the Senators played their first game in the House That Rod Built. A month later, the naming rights to the building were sold and it became the Corel Centre.

"He's done the best he could with the hand that he was dealt. Nobody else could have done it better," Tom McDougall, Bryden's lawyer, told the *Globe and Mail* in March 2003, when Bryden was working on a deal to buy the Senators out of bankruptcy. "The Corel Centre would never have been built but for the tenacity and brainpower of Rod Bryden."

7-for-11

In the lead-up to the 2008 All-Star Game, as the Ottawa Senators hit the 50-game mark of the schedule, they were struggling. They were still riding high in the standings, thanks to a 15–2 start under new coach John Paddock, who had replaced Bryan Murray after Murray was kicked upstairs after leading them to the 2007 Stanley Cup Final. But for the past couple months, cracks had been showing. They lost 17 of their next 32 games, but they were still in first place in the Eastern Conference with a 30–15–4 record, though the pack had closed on them.

Led by captain Daniel Alfredsson, they were still capable of showing flashes of the offensive juggernaut they'd been when they went to the Final the previous spring, and they were second in the league in goals scored with 166 in 49 games. But Alfredsson had missed the past two games, both losses, with a hip flexor injury sustained against the Carolina Hurricanes on January 17. He returned for a 5–3 loss to the Florida Panthers on January 22, and heading into a game against the Tampa Bay Lightning on January 24, the Senators camp was in turmoil.

Senators owner Eugene Melnyk had Murray and Paddock remain behind in Sunrise, Florida, to answer questions about the team's performance. Murray met with the players before the game against the Lightning and told them to "play the right way"— the first time I had heard him use the expression, which has since become a staple in NHL-speak.

The Lightning, their expansion cousins, were last in the Southeast Division—then the "Southleast Division"—where the Carolina Hurricanes were in first place with a 24–24–4 record.

Alfredsson, sporting a shaved head, was 35 years old and coming to the end of what would be one of the most productive seasons in his 18-year career. On this night, he showed he could still bring it, much to the chagrin of Tampa goaltenders Karri Ramo and Johan Holmqvist.

Alfredsson scored his 30th goal of the season at 13:43 of the first period in classic Alfredsson style, cutting in on his off wing, using the defenseman as a screen, and ripping off a wrist shot (it was reminiscent of the goal he scored against the Buffalo Sabres the previous spring to send the Senators to the Stanley Cup Final).

He assisted on a goal by Jason Spezza 29 seconds later and added a power-play goal during a two-man advantage with a huge slap shot from the point before the first period was out.

Alfredsson earned his sixth of eight hat tricks he would have with the Senators with a shorthanded goal set up by Mike Fisher at 4:38 of the second period, taking a pass and going straight down the slot, from where he flicked in his 32nd goal of the season. Alfredsson added an assist on a goal by Antoine Vermette to close out the second period, and he already had a good night in the books. It would become great.

Ramo was replaced by Holmqvist for the third period. Alfredsson had assists on goals by Randy Robitaille and another by Spezza to polish it off with three goals and four assists. Seven points in a game still stands as the team record as of 2018. It is only one away from the record for most points in a road game, set by Peter and Anton Stastny of the Quebec Nordiques, who each had four goals and four assists in an 11–7 win against the Washington Capitals on February 22, 1981.

Alfredsson is the last of 15 players to have seven points in a road game. With those seven points, Alfredsson vaulted past the Lightning's Vincent Lecavalier to take over the NHL scoring lead with 67 points (32 goals, 35 assists). Alfredsson would wind up ninth with 89 points; Alex Ovechkin won the Art Ross Trophy that season with 112 points (65 goals, 47 assists).

"The way I look at it, you add them up at the end of your career...maybe it will be 'Remember that night in Tampa?'" Alfredsson said. "When they come, you take them. It doesn't happen that often."

Paddock used that night to push for Alfredsson's candidacy for the Hart Trophy as the NHL's most valuable player. "Are the rest of you going to get on the campaign trail? I certainly have a lot of respect for Lecavalier and [Sidney] Crosby, but Alfredsson has been as good as any player in the league from the playoffs last year until now," Paddock said. "I don't think anybody can argue that."

That night turned out to be a highlight of a tumultuous season. The Senators' mediocre play continued under Paddock, and he was fired with 18 games left in the season. Murray went back behind the bench, and the Senators finished the season 7–9–2 for a 43–31–8 record. They were swept by the Pittsburgh Penguins in the first round of the Stanley Cup Playoffs.

The Best Goal in Senators History

A tape-to-tape saucer pass that traveled at a height of 10 feet and a distance of 116 feet in the air and resulted in a goal? In a playoff game? C'mon. There might be more significant goals or bigger goals in Senators history, but for sheer demonstration of skill and execution on an important stage, there is none better.

Mike Hoffman's goal to open the scoring in Game 3 of the Senators' opening-round playoff series against the Boston Bruins in 2017 comprised the best seven seconds of skill in the Senators' 25-year history. Hoffman's finish, dekeing Bruins goaltender Tuukka Rask with a classic one-handed Peter Forsberg move, was enough to make the goal memorable. What put it over the top and into the realm of legend was its beginning.

"Oh, yeah, yeah, that was nice," Rask said in an interview on Sportsnet a couple months later. "No way he meant to do that." The "he" to which he referred was Senators defenseman Erik Karlsson.

With a flat *smack*, Karlsson hefted a saucer pass from his own goal line to the Bruins' blue line and onto Hoffman's stick. What was remarkable was that it was close to a perfect Frisbee throw: the puck remained flat and spinning for its entire flight. If you've ever tried a saucer pass, you know how hard it is just to saucer it over the blade of a stick, never mind above 6'9" Zdeno Chara, one of the Bruins defenders over whom the puck flew.

With the puck on his stick below the goal line to the right of Senators goaltender Craig Anderson and with Bruins forwards Brad Marchand and David Pastrnak closing in on him, Karlsson imagined the play in an instant and hefted the puck up the ice. "As soon as I saw he had control, I just took off," Hoffman said. "He's a smart enough player that, if he sees me out there, he'll be able to put the puck near me. "I didn't want to get too far ahead of the play. If the pass would have been a little softer, it probably would have been offside, but our timing was great."

Hoffman read the play at the Senators' blue line by the boards on the opposite side of the ice. One of the fastest players in the game, he accelerated diagonally in the neutral zone, bursting behind the Bruins defense.

"That was a genius pass, not just a saucer," Senators coach Guy Boucher said. "You've got to look at Hoff on that, too, his timing on that. He's got terrific speed. When you have Hoffman on the ice and Karlsson on the ice, you know it's going to be dangerous for the opponent."

The puck flew over the defenders and up into the dark background of the crowd. That made it even more incredible that Hoffman could track it. "You do lose it once it gets to a certain height," Hoffman said. "The puck is in the air and you can't even see it. Once it got below the glass line, I was able to pick it up. And then, fortunately, I was able to handle it on my tape. If I would have missed it, it would have been right on Tuukka's tape. I was kind of fortunate I was able to pick it up at the last second."

With the puck on his stick, Hoffman opted to go with a move that was fresh in his mind: he had watched Alexander Radulov, then with the Montreal Canadiens, score on New York Rangers goaltender Henrik Lundqvist with the so-called "Forsberg move" (the player extends his stick to his top-hand side and tucks the puck in on the far side of the goaltender) a night earlier. "Luckily he was there," said Karlsson, slyly. "It was a little bit of a fluke play, and he made a good read. He saw I had time, and I pulled something out of my back pocket and it worked out."

Yes, yes it did.

And yes, he did mean to do it.

Opening Night Part II

On January 17, 1996, the final piece of the vision Bruce Firestone had to bring NHL hockey back to Ottawa fell into place when the doors to the Palladium opened to welcome its first hockey crowd. It was about three years, at least four financing plans, and 20,000 legal documents later than originally planned, but the Senators finally had a home.

For years the site had been marked by a small billboard by a rusted fence in tall grass that showed an artist's rendering of the building, the Senators' original logo, and the words PALLADIUM FUTURE HOME OF THE OTTAWA SENATORS. With each delay and financing false start, it was starting to look like that sign might ultimately become a tombstone. But Senators owner Rod Bryden had once again performed his monetary magic, and now the sign was gone and spotlights lit up the glass lobby at the spectacular new rink.

Compared to the glitzy opening at the Civic Centre four years earlier, the opening of the Palladium—again, featuring a game between the Senators and the Montreal Canadiens—was much more understated. The Roman columns from the opening night at the Civic Centre made a reappearance, but the ceremony was pretty stripped down.

There were a lot of hiccups along the way to the opening of the Palladium, so of course the opening itself couldn't go off without a hitch. It was actually a winch. As part of the move from the Civic Centre, the Senators raised the Stanley Cup banners commemorating the championships won by the original Senators and No. 8 for Frank Finnigan, a member of the 1927 Stanley Cup champions and the last from Ottawa, and No. 18 for former NHL player–turned–CJOH broadcaster Brian Smith, who was slain by Jeffrey Arenburg, a schizophrenic viewer, in 1995.

The banners got stuck before they made it to their spot in the rafters, blocking the view of fans who were seated on the north side of the building. "We can't see! We can't see!" they chanted. As it turned out that night, they might have been the lucky ones. (They wound up being offered tickets for another game. In the first intermission, the banners were lowered to the ice and dragged off.)

Firestone and Bryden dropped the puck between Senators captain Randy Cunneyworth and Canadiens captain Pierre Turgeon. The Canadiens were determined they would not lose this opening game as they had in the Senators' first game back in the NHL at the Civic Centre on October 8, 1992, a 5–3 upset by the expansion Senators over the team that would go on to win the Stanley Cup that season. Canadiens goaltender Patrick Roy was in goal on that night in 1992, and he went on to win the Conn Smythe Trophy as the playoffs MVP.

But Roy was not in goal on opening night at the Palladium. No, he was in Detroit with the Colorado Avalanche and losing 3–2 to the Red Wings. Opening night at the Palladium came about six weeks after one of the most memorable nights in Canadiens history, when Roy up and quit the team after being left in the net by new coach Mario Tremblay, an old adversary of Roy's, in an 11–1 humiliation at the Forum at the hands of the Wings. He was traded four days later, on December 6.

Tremblay and the Habs were determined to prove to everybody they were bigger than Roy (boy, were they wrong). And they certainly weren't going to lose to the Senators, who—once again—were on their way to a last-place finish.

The Palladium opening came just before the All-Star Game in Boston, and this was the Canadiens' final game before the break. Several of the Canadiens had made flight reservations to get out of

Dodge first thing the next morning (7:00 AM) and get an early start on the All-Star break in Florida. Tremblay got wind of it. "The reservations are made, but if you lose this game tonight, they'll be canceled," Tremblay told Canadiens forward Martin Rucinsky who was planning on heading south with Brian Savage and Vincent Damphousse.

There was no scoring in the first period. Andrei Kovalenko became the first player to score in the Palladium at 11:12 of the second period. Rucinsky scored with 1.4 seconds left in the second period to make it 2–0, and Damphousse added an empty-net goal with four seconds left to give the Canadiens a 3–0 win and an early trip to Florida. When asked after the game if the Sunshine State was on his mind when he scored, Rucinsky replied, "I wasn't thinking about Florida then, but I am now."

The Senators would have to wait until their next game to get their first goal. Steve Duchesne scored to give the Senators a 1–0 lead against the Chicago Blackhawks on January 22, but the Blackhawks scored the final five goals of the game for a 7–3 victory.

By the next game, the Senators had gone through their own upheaval. New general manager Pierre Gauthier traded for goaltender Damian Rhodes and defenseman Wade Redden and fired coach Dave Allison, replacing him with Jacques Martin.

In the midst of a nine-game homestand to open the Palladium, the Senators lost Martin's first game 4–3 to the Pittsburgh Penguins. They lost 4–2 to Detroit and tied the Toronto Maple Leafs 2–2. The Senators would have to wait until January 29 to get their first win at the Palladium, 4–2 against the St. Louis Blues.

About a month later, the naming rights for the building were sold, and it became the Corel Centre. Since then, the Senators have done pretty well at what is now known as Canadian Tire Centre. As of June 2018, they had a 457–284–48–78 all-time record in that barn.

10 A Star-Studded Weekend

The NHL All-Star Game is a weekend that often lacks much in the way of gravitas. It's 48 hours of corporate schmoozing, stargazing, and players playing a game that doesn't come close to resembling NHL hockey. As is often the case with events such as All-Star Games and outdoor game, the events don't move the needle much on the broader stage but are big in the market in which they are held.

The 59th All-Star Game in Ottawa in 2012 resonated with Senators fans beyond the chance to see the NHL's top players in their city. The game represented a passing of the torch, a chance to celebrate the long career of an established star and to contemplate the rise of another.

Senators captain Daniel Alfredsson, 39, was coming to the end of his time in Ottawa, during which he had established himself as the defining personality of the franchise. The All-Star Game would be a celebration of his career and an opportunity for Senators fans to salute their greatest player on a big stage. Defenseman Erik Karlsson was 21 and in the middle of a season that would see him win his first Norris Trophy that summer. It was a glitzy opportunity to honor the past, enjoy the present, and contemplate the future.

The All-Star Game used a draft format to set the teams at that time, and Alfredsson was selected as a captain along with former Senators defenseman Zdeno Chara of the Boston Bruins. Alfredsson, as promised, used his first pick to take Karlsson, much to the delight of the crowd at Casino du Lac-Leamy. Karlsson had led the fan voting for the game with 939,951, followed by Alfredsson (897,055) and Senators forwards Jason Spezza (817,483) and Milan Michalek (743,977). Toronto Maple Leafs defenseman Dion Phaneuf (614,933) and Boston Bruins goaltender Tim Thomas (626,540) rounded out the starters.

Karlsson had told reporters he "would be pissed" if Alfredsson, with whom he had lived when he came to the Senators as a rookie, didn't take him with the first pick. Karlsson was beaming when he walked onto the stage to be welcomed by Alfredsson and assistant captain Henrik Lundqvist of the New York Rangers. "I worked his kids pretty hard," Karlsson said of Alfredsson's four sons—Hugo, William, Fenix, and Loui—whom he had babysat while living with the Alfredssons. "I'm really happy I could join my fellow Swedes."

"The kids will be happy," said Alfredsson. "Erik is a great babysitter, and the kids really enjoy being with him."

Alfredsson also added Senators teammates Spezza and Michalek and the Swedish twins from the Vancouver Canucks, Henrik and Daniel Sedin. "Erik's part of Alfie's family. You've got to pick family first," Spezza said. "We're just happy that we're all together. This is for the fans, and the people here are so passionate about hockey."

Playing with the Sedins, Alfredsson had a couple goals and his teammates spent the rest of the afternoon trying to get Alfredsson the hat trick. It didn't happen, but that didn't diminish the love-in with fans. "It was an honor for both of us to play with him," Henrik said. "He was a guy we looked up to growing up."

His fellow Swedes were impressed with the outpouring of emotion for Alfredsson in his adopted city. "It was cool to watch the reception," Lundqvist said.

Team Chara wound up winning 12–9 on 10 points from the line of former Senator Marian Hossa with Detroit Red Wing Pavel Datsyuk and New York Ranger Marian Gaborik. Alfredsson finished things off in dramatic fashion. With retirement surely being pondered, *Hockey Night in Canada*'s Elliotte Friedman told him he could really make the weekend complete by telling fans there was a good chance he would be back for another season.

"I can give 50 percent yes," Alfredsson replied, adding the other 50 percent belonged to his wife, Bibbi. Alfredsson would indeed return for a final season with the Senators.

Cheers rained down in Scotiabank Place. It was the end of a dream weekend.

"The only thing that would have made it better," NHL commissioner Gary Bettman said, "is if the Rideau Canal was frozen this morning. This has been great. Everything has been just terrific."

11 Alfie's Night

They chanted his name on a night in late December, the first sellout crowd of the 2016–17 season. "Alfie! Alfie! Alfie!" Whenever something good had happened to the Senators in their first 25 years, Daniel Alfredsson was usually somehow involved. Now, in a season that had been marked by waning interest and expanses of empty seats at Canadian Tire Centre, the seats were filled with Ottawa hockey fans turning out to see Daniel Alfredsson's No. 11 retired, the first number in the modern era to be cranked up into the rafters.

Like the return of the Senators franchise itself, his was a story of overcoming long odds, and maybe that's why a late-round draft pick who became the face (and haircut), voice, and conscience of a young franchise enjoyed such a special connection to a team and its fans.

Alfie is all smiles at team practice in 2013.

He was a sixth-round draft pick who became Rookie of the Year. He scored perhaps the biggest goal in franchise history, the overtime goal in the Eastern Conference Final in 2007 that sent the Senators to their first Stanley Cup Final. He scored it on a one-on-three situation against the Buffalo Sabres, beating the odds.

The night of December 29, 2016, was a chance to honor Alfredsson's legacy and relive a time when the Senators were a high-scoring, glamorous team in the NHL, blessed with some of the great individual talents in the game. That was far different from the current cautious squad, built around the generational talent of captain Erik Karlsson but relying on new coach Guy Boucher's crowded neutral zone defense for its modest success to date.

Whether it was the decidedly tepid feelings of much of the Ottawa fan base toward owner Eugene Melnyk and his sometimes overly optimistic proclamations or the club's mediocre showings since its only appearance in the Stanley Cup Final in 2007, there was a malaise around the Senators going into the 2016–17 season. But Alfredsson's big night was a chance to celebrate a time when the Senators really mattered, when ubiquitous red Senators car flags had people arriving at work and telling their coworkers how many they had counted during the commute.

Alfredsson was a big reason why. From his first earliest moments with the Senators, Alfredsson enjoyed a connection with hockey fans in Ottawa. Stuck between cosmopolitan Montreal and Toronto, the self-styled Centre of the Universe, there always seemed to be a bit of an inferiority complex among Ottawa's citizens, at least those who lived and worked outside the bubble of self-entitlement on Parliament Hill.

If you called yourself a sports fan in the Velvet Rut, you knew true suffering. The annual success of the Ottawa 67's in junior hockey under Hall of Famer Brian Kilrea was celebrated, but pretty much only within the 613 area code. In the rest of the country, Ottawa was more closely identified with the Ottawa Rough Riders, a pathetically inept franchise (they drafted a dead guy) from the 1980s (they went 2–16 in Super Season '88) until their demise in 1996, and the short-lived and almost as embarrassing existence of the Ottawa Renegades from 2002 to 2005. Alfredsson came along when the Rough Riders were mercifully administered their last rites.

Up against established rivals in Montreal and Toronto, Alfredsson and the Senators were underdogs. Maybe that helped Ottawa hockey fans fans identify with him. Ottawa had been an underdog when it came to winning an NHL expansion franchise, but here they were.

If Alfredsson didn't quite spit in the eye of the hated Maple Leafs, he mocked their captain (and his friend), Mats Sundin, by fake tossing a broken stick into the stands at the Air Canada Centre. Sundin had been suspended for throwing his broken stick into the crowd. Alfredsson knocked down Toronto agitator Darcy Tucker with what was likely an illegal check into the boards in a playoff game, stole the puck, and scored the winning goal. The Senators didn't get the better of the Leafs in a playoff series at the height of the Battle of Ontario in the early 2000s, but Alfredsson was at the heart of whatever small victories were mined and polished over the years.

He saved some of his best games for on the road in Montreal (his 107 points against the Canadiens was his most against any team).

When his name rolled down the stands in waves on that December night, the passion in the people's voices was as much for what Alfredsson had done for the city as he had the hockey team. His contribution made the Senators a contender and gave a city a sporting pride it had not felt in decades. His contributions and leadership in removing the stigma from mental health issues—one of the first such initiatives—made him a community leader. But perhaps what those fans were celebrating, finally, was that there's always a chance the prodigal son can come home, even for a little while.

It hadn't happened before. The players who were—or who were at least built up to be—stars with the Senators almost all left under clouds of bitterness and disappointment. Alexei Yashin, shipped out after years of incessant contract disputes. Alexandre Daigle, the dashing bilingual first pick overall who never lived up to the unfair hype and was traded away. Dany Heatley, the club's first 50-goal scorer, and Jason Spezza, who succeeded Alfredsson as captain, both forcing the hand of general manager Bryan Murray by asking to be traded.

It looked for a bit like the same fate might await Alfredsson. But after a messy split that saw him leave the Senators as a free agent in the summer of 2013 for one season with the Detroit Red Wings, Alfredsson returned to retire as a Senator in December 2014. In 2015, he joined the front office as senior advisor of hockey operations.

12 Senators and Habs Take It Outside

Erik Karlsson danced the night away in the frigid air, and that became one of the enduring images of the 2017 Scotiabank NHL100 Classic at Lansdowne Park on December 16, 2017.

The first outdoor game hosted by the Senators, to commemorate the centennial of the first game in NHL history between the Senators and Canadiens, became an instant highlight of the Senators' first 25 years back in the NHL. Cameras caught the Senators' captain dancing and mugging to Fitz and the Tantrums' "HandClap" on the bench and gesturing to the sellout crowd of

39,959 during a commercial break in the Senators 3–0 win against the Canadiens.

Despite a bone-chilling temperature of 12.5 degrees Fahrenheit at game time, the crowd arrived early and stayed late. They danced and clapped along with the captain, their breath hanging in clouds in the frosty night air.

A Good *Habit*

Jean-Gabriel Pageau has a knack for coming up big on the big stage. The Scotiabank NHL100 Classic was no exception. Pageau scored the winning goal in the Senators' 3–0 win against the Montreal Canadiens, and once again he saved his best for the Habs.

That brought his total to eight goals in 18 regular-season games against the Canadiens. He also had a hat trick in a 6–1 win against Montreal in Game 3 of the Eastern Conference First Round of the 2013 Stanley Cup Playoffs.

Senators fans delighted in singing "Pageau, Pageau, Pageau" to the tune of "Ole, Ole, Ole," a favorite of Canadiens fans when their team was having a good night.

Speaking of big performances, Pageau also scored four goals in Game 2 of the Senators' second-round series against the New York Rangers in the 2017 Stanley Cup Playoffs, helping the Senators to a 6–5 win in a game during which they trailed by two goals three times. His third and fourth goals tied the game 5–5 and scored the winner in overtime.

"He's a big-time player and he likes to play in important games, and this was an important game," Senators captain Erik Karlsson said. "Whether it's against Montreal or someone else, he always shows up. He's a character guy. He doesn't get the most publicity all the time and he doesn't score all the goals all the time, but when it comes down to it, he always does the right thing, and that shows in games like this and the playoffs. When we need someone to step up, he's usually one of the guys."

Pageau, an Ottawa native, said the crowd of 33,959 contributed to making the experience of playing in 12-degree conditions memorable. "It was fun for the whole game. The atmosphere from warmup to the last second, it was unbelievable," he said.

"How could you not enjoy yourself?" Karlsson asked. "It was great. The turnout was better than we expected, the fans stayed from before warmup to the end of the game, and we appreciate that a lot. I think that made us more excited. During commercial breaks, you just wanted to absorb the experience. We love playing in the city. Why wouldn't you? You'd look up in the stands and the fans were dancing and having a great time."

While players were doing whatever they could to stay warm, Karlsson said that wasn't why he was dancing in his seat on the bench. "I saw him doing that," said Senators forward Jean-Gabriel Pageau, who tipped a Karlsson shot for the game-winning goal. "I thought maybe he was just bopping around to keep warm."

Erik Karlsson moves past the Canadiens at the NHL 100 Hockey Classic.

"No, nothing like that. I was just having fun, man," Karlsson told NHL.com. "I was just going along with the music and making the most of the moment. The entire experience was awesome."

It was actually a bit of a rare moment that cameras were able to catch Karlsson on the bench. He played 32:55, an NHL regular-season outdoor game record. He also blocked a record eight shots.

"When our captain has his swagger going like that, we feed off of it," Senators coach Guy Boucher said. "He was just so in tune with everything that was going on, both on and off the ice."

It was a significant performance for Karlsson, who had been battling to come back from surgery on June 14 to repair torn tendons in his ankle. In describing the procedure, Karlsson said, "They took out half my ankle bone" and inserted an "artificial tendon." Karlsson missed five games to start the season and was off to a good start with a goal and 16 assists in his first 11 games, but he had just two assists in the 14 games before the NHL100 Classic, including 10 games without a point from November 16 to December 6, the longest pointless streak of his nine-year career. The Senators were 2–10–2 in those 14 games.

But Boucher proved to be a bit of a prophet when he said he sensed a positive turn in Karlsson's game going into the NHL100 Classic. "This guy, I think he's the best defenseman in the world, but he doesn't have a red cape on his back," Boucher said. "He's a human being and needs some time. To be honest with you, I didn't think he would be himself until Christmas. We're right on pace for that. He's getting better every game. I really like his last games. He's getting his mobility back. He's getting his stamina back. He's getting his timing back."

13 Stop and Gaze upon the Mighty Carp River

In what was an often surreal journey from dream to plan to reality for the Senators, it shouldn't be a surprise that Coast Guard officers in hip waders wielding poles—looking like misplaced gondoliers—occupied a treasured place in Senators history.

The Carp River had meandered for thousands of years almost unnoticed until it was suddenly just east of the site for the Palladium, the proposed 20,500-seat home of the Senators. It was a shallow stream, really, quite this side of being called a river, and depending on how much rain had fallen, it was sometimes barely deep enough for a bullfrog to make it across with water completely covering its back.

If you were to walk west from Terry Fox Drive along Palladium Drive toward what is now the Canadian Tire Centre, you might not even really notice the Carp River unless you were looking for it. Driving from the east along Palladium Drive? Forget it. If not for a low concrete wall topped by a metal railing, you probably wouldn't even know you were crossing it.

You might be able to jump across the Carp in spots and forge it by barely rolling up your pants, but there was a time when the Carp looked like a barrier as wide as the Atlantic Ocean between the Senators and the new home necessary for their future success. Plans for the roadways that would have provided access to the Palladium site from the east would have rendered the Carp River unnavigable, if it wasn't already, and the Navigation Protection Act deemed navigable waters stay that way. The answer to whether or not the Carp River was navigable would impact the suitability of the proposed Palladium site and, at the very least, potentially delay its construction by up to a year.

So it came to be that on a Monday afternoon in early May 1994, Coast Guard official Allan Robertson and assistant Ted Cater spent an hour wading in the Carp, poking, prodding, and measuring. Their discovery that day: the Carp was about 2.3 feet deep at Maple Grove, one road south of Canadian Tire Centre, and just 4.3 inches deep at the Queensway.

By the end of the week, on Friday the 13th, the news leaked: the mighty Carp was not navigable in the Coast Guard's estimation, and another hurdle to the building of the Palladium had been removed. The mighty Carp could be diverted to make room for the Palladium site. "I'm happy at the ruling," Senators spokesman John Owens said, adding sarcastically, "We'd been planning on having tall ships sail to the opening."

14 A Valley Boy Comes Home

In February 2005, on a cold winter's day when the brilliant sun glinted on the snow, I rode shotgun as Bryan Murray guided his Cadillac station wagon westward toward his hometown of Shawville, Quebec. The English enclave across the Ottawa River in western Quebec is about an hour west of Ottawa. Murray, the Senators' coach at the time, grew up in a small house on King St., built by Murray's father, Clarence, where he shared a bedroom with four brothers. Five sisters shared bunkbeds in another room.

Murray had left the Anaheim Ducks, where he was the general manager, to come back here to coach the Ottawa Senators. The NHL was in the midst of a lockout that would wipe out the 2004–05 season, and Murray was using the time to do something he hadn't done in 25 years: spend some of the winter in Shawville.

He had to deliver some banana bread and hamburger soup to his mom, Rhoda, that day. She still lived on King St. in the old house; Clarence had passed away about a month earlier, in his 97th year.

Hats from each of the teams Bryan and his brother Terry had coached in the NHL (seven of them at that time) still hung on the wall of the small bedroom off the kitchen. It would have been easy for Murray to wind up his distinguished NHL career in Anaheim, but a phone call a few months earlier had changed his path and put him on this road. Senators general manager John Muckler fired coach Jacques Martin after another Ottawa spring ended early with the fourth loss in five years to the Toronto Maple Leafs.

While Murray was scouting in Prague at the world championships, the Senators asked the Disney Company, owners of the Ducks, to talk to Murray about their vacant coaching position. "It had never crossed my mind," Murray said of returning to coaching, and certainly of it being so close to home.

His mind suddenly churning with the possibilities, he told the Disney execs to sit tight until he got home. "But as I thought about it, you get excited about things like that," he said. "For the balance of the week, I started thinking a great deal about it. Making notes, the pros and cons. Another Disney executive called me. 'If you want to talk to them, don't feel you're slighting us. If you want to talk, we know it's your home area. Why not talk to Ottawa and see where it goes?'" Murray became the fifth coach of the Ottawa Senators, the only team, he says, for which he would have left Anaheim.

Murray's pride in his hometown was evident on that cold February day. "As you get older, those memories are what draw you back to where you are from. The things you did as a kid, the baseball and hockey teams.... Shawville is different now, I understand. But that's what kind of created an attachment that brings you back. You were part of something that was real important to the town," he said. "There's a sense of pride. I'm coach of the local NHL team. And there's lots of Ottawa fans up here. I know there will be days when you don't win a hockey game when you will be analyzed and criticized. That's part of our game. There's a chance here for a real sense of pride for the whole area if this team could ever be a champion."

Murray had initially left Shawville to go to Macdonald College (part of McGill University in Montreal) and returned to his hometown to teach. He took the opportunity to return to Macdonald College as athletic director but was unfulfilled. Back in Shawville, he taught and dabbled as an entrepreneur: a sporting goods store, the local hotel, and some coaching on the side in the Central Junior Hockey League. He thought that would be his life.

But he got the coaching bug, and he was good at it. He won the Centennial Cup, Canada's Junior A championship, with the Rockland Nationals in 1976, and that led to an opportunity to coach the Regina Pats of the Western Hockey League in 1979–80. He told his wife, Geri, he'd try it for one year. The Pats won the WHL championship. After a year in the American Hockey League with the Hershey Bears, he started his NHL coaching career on November 11, 1981, with the Washington Capitals. "One year," he had said. Twenty-six years and 14 moves later, they were back home.

A quick story that sums up Murray's pride and competitiveness as a coach: On November 27, the Capitals played the Montreal Canadiens at the Cap Center in Landover, Maryland. The Caps were 4–1–2 since Murray had taken over from Gary Green. On their way to a 5–2 win over the Canadiens, Murray called a timeout late in the game. The referee skated over to the bench and asked the rookie coach if he knew what he was doing. "You referee the game, and I'll coach the game," Murray said. Murray felt a perceived slight, like the Canadiens—not far removed from their Cup dynasty—had been laughing at the sad-sack Caps. He called the timeout late in the game to rub it in. Across the ice (the benches were on opposite sides of the ice then) Canadiens tough guy Chris Nilan took a water bottle and threw it across the ice at Murray.

I got to hear both sides of the story when Nilan wandered into Hurley's Irish Pub in Montreal and spotted Murray in the corner, where we were having a beer.

"I hit you right in the head," crowed Nilan at the end of the table.

"No, you didn't," Murray said indignantly. "It bounced off my shoulder."

Then they both had a good laugh.

Murray went on to coaching and managing roles with the Detroit Red Wings, Florida Panthers, Ducks, and Senators. The fifth head coach in Senators history, Murray had a 107–55–20 record and helped the Senators to their first Stanley Cup Final in 2007.

Former Senators captain Daniel Alfredsson said Murray empowered his teams with belief in themselves. "He just gave you a feeling no matter how good or bad the team was playing, you could win every game. You just had that feeling," Alfredsson said. "You go back to Bryan yelling at the referees all the time; I think there was a bigger plan behind that. He always had the players' backs. Looking back, that's probably the biggest thing why our team did so well was because he was like the big father figure, and no matter what happened during the game, no matter what was happening, he was backing you up, and that was very powerful."

Murray ranks 15th in all-time games coached (1,239) and is 13th in wins (620) through 2017–18.

While winning the Stanley Cup eluded Murray, his greatest accomplishments have been that he has left all the franchises for which he worked in better shape than when he arrived. The Capitals averaged 95 points a season in his eight and a half seasons there, and he won the Jack Adams Award in 1983–84 as Coach of the Year. He put down the foundation for future Stanley Cup champions in Detroit and Anaheim—he assembled the core of the Anaheim team that defeated Murray and the Senators for the Stanley Cup in 2007—and built the Florida team that went to the Final in 1996.

In his 36 years in the league, Murray developed a reputation for being a great communicator and a coach who had the respect of his players. "I still mention his name to guys when coaching comes up, different guys you've played for," former Senators forward Mike Fisher said. "He's one of my favorites for sure. He was a players' coach who made it fun. A lot of humor too. I loved playing for him.... You always knew where you stood. He knew exactly what he wanted out of each guy, and he knew how to communicate that. He's awesome."

You can argue who has been the best coach in the Senators' first 25 years: Martin, who took the team from a bumbling expansion team to a league power, or Murray, who stands as the only coach to get the Senators to the Stanley Cup Final. I'll take the guy who propelled them to the Final.

15 A Sour Note: Paul Anka and the Senators

It seemed like a Hollywood story because, well, it was a Hollywood story: the Ottawa-born superstar singer with connections to big money in the show-business world coming to the rescue of his hometown NHL expansion team. But it wouldn't have a Hollywood ending, unless your idea of a Hollywood ending is the last reel of *Titanic*.

The *Ottawa Sun* broke the story in February 1991: entertainer Paul Anka, who had hit it big when he was 16 years old with his 1957 hit "Diana," was in negotiations to become a part owner of the cash-strapped Ottawa Senators. Terrace Investments was struggling behind the scenes to come up with the money to pay what remained of the $50 million expansion fee after winning the franchise in December 1990 (they had put down a nonrefundable $5 million at the outset of the process). It was music to the ears of people at Terrace and Senators fans: Anka was poised to come to the rescue.

Sun colleague Drew McAnulty and I got an exclusive interview with Anka from his Beverly Hills home when we broke the news. "This is very exciting for me," Anka, 49 at the time, said. "Without being jaded or blasé, this is an exciting project. Hockey is a part of my culture. A big part of it is it involves my hometown. If somebody had come to me from Tampa, this deal would not have been struck. I can do something for the team and for Ottawa. He continued, "I love this sport. A lot of the guys I know own teams. At this stage in life, I'm ready for something like this. It's exciting for me. This has a different sizzle."

Anka brought the Senators instant credibility. "We wouldn't waste time looking at it if we didn't think we would succeed in it," Anka's financial advisor, Donald Abraham—Anka's cousin and also an Ottawa native—told the *Sun* when the story of Anka's interest in the Senators broke. "We think they will make money from Day 1."

After hitting it big with "Diana," Anka had become one of the most successful songwriters of the 1960s and '70s. By the time he was 18, he had four other top five hits to his credit: "Put Your Head on My Shoulder," "You Are My Destiny," "Puppy Love," and "Lonely Boy." His 1969 song "My Way" became a signature song for both Frank Sinatra and Elvis Presley. And he wrote the theme for NBC's *The Tonight Show* when Johnny Carson took over in

1962, and after sharing a songwriting credit with Carson (for lyrics that were never used), they each reportedly earned $200,000 a year from royalties. The theme was played 1.4 million times during Carson's 30-year run as host.

Negotiations between Abraham and Senators president Jim Durrell began in earnest a couple weeks after Terrace executives met with Anka in Atlantic City (where he was performing at the Trump casino) on April 7, and on May 9 I wrote a piece for the *Sun* that a deal had been struck. It all became official on May 14. Anka would put $1 million into the franchise and act as a salesman to bring another $10 million in from his contacts in Hollywood. He had an option to buy half of the new rink project, the Palladium, for $4 million, a $450,000 deal for three concerts, and a $50,000-a-year salary.

The Senators looked like they were on their way. "I think it's wonderful for him and the city," said Diana Ayoub, the subject of Anka's 1957 hit, who still lived in Ottawa.

A year later, the Senators and Anka were squaring off in court, and both sides were singing the blues. The Senators had managed to come up with their two payments of $22.5 million (one in June 1991 and the other in December) with little thanks to Anka, they contended. On February 12, 1992, Terrace Investments went to court for a declaration that Anka no longer had an option to purchase half of the Palladium site for $4 million. Terrace claimed the option had expired on December 16, according to a letter of intent signed in May. If they didn't need Anka to make it happen, why share the spoils, right?

Anka's lawyers contended his option on the Palladium was still in force because Anka had been misled about the franchise's financial health. Anka wanted $7 million and a 10 percent interest in the Palladium to walk away. "We have never let ourselves be blackmailed, and we are not going to start now," Terrace's Rod Bryden told the *Ottawa Citizen*.

On November 19, 1992, with the Senators off to a miserable 1–17–1 start on the ice in their first season, a judge ruled the dispute would go to trial. There was a feeling the lawsuit was hanging like a cloud over the Palladium project and scaring off potential investors and financing. Anka countersued for $41 million—$26 million in damages for breach of contract and another $15 million in punitive damages related to loss of reputation. Both sides were accusing the other of breaching the agreement. Anka said, "[I] made every effort to live up to my end of the bargain.... I have been forced to turn to the courts to have the agreement honored." Bryden dismissed the suit as "a completely unfounded nuisance claim."

The lawsuits were settled out of court in September 1993. Anka got $375,000 as compensation for the concerts and $150,000 as an option to buy his shares. "I wish Terrace and the Senators well and look forward to enjoying a hockey game in 1995 at the new Palladium," Anka said in a statement. He was off by a year.

That story just seemed to sum up the Senators' early days. Every time there seemed to be some positive news, something would happen to turn it into a crisis.

16 The Ghost

Frequent topics among self-absorbed media types are pregame meals at sports events and press box food. The hot dogs in the Jacques Beauchamp Lounge at the old Montreal Forum were legendary. In 2016 the Ottawa Senators introduced hot dogs as a first intermission snack in the Brian "Smitty" Smith Press Box at Canadian Tire Centre.

Early in the 2017 season, former Senators general manager Pierre "the Ghost" Gauthier, now the director of player personnel for the Chicago Blackhawks, was standing off to the side as the press box occupants queued up for their tube steak (a vegan, you wouldn't have caught the Ghost chowing down).

"Hey, Ghost," I said, "did you see the sign?" In front of the hot dogs doing their slow dance on the rollers was a sign: Hot Dogs in First Intermission. One Per Person. A micromanager, part of the urban legend of the Ghost in Ottawa was him policing the cookie platter at the pregame meal for the media and scouts. One per person. He looked at the hot dog sign and laughed.

Gauthier was one of the most influential figures in Senators history. He arrived in December 1995 and made a flurry of moves that put the team on the path that would see them go from being the worst expansion team in NHL (and maybe professional sports) history to making the Stanley Cup Playoffs 11 years in a row.

With the Ghost managing everything from cookies to coaches, the Senators finally had a recipe for success. During his time in Ottawa, he kept a low profile, suddenly materializing in a hallway after weeks of not being seen, which led to him being nicknamed the Ghost.

He was a guy with a reputation for being aloof. "He had terrible people skills," former Senators president Roy Mlakar, then a consultant to the Senators—and who helped hire Gauthier—said with a chuckle. "I used to talk to him about it. We hired [media consultant] Andrea Kirby to work with him. He was awful dealing with the media."

Gauthier grew up in the Montreal suburb of Outremont, played hockey at CEGEP (Quebec's version of junior college), and coached some Tier II junior hockey in Joliette, a town north of Montreal. He left Montreal to pursue his postsecondary studies at Syracuse University and went to the University of Minnesota for graduate school.

While in Minnesota, he was hired by the Quebec Nordiques (he had gotten to know some of their staff during his days around junior hockey) to do some part-time scouting and wound up making a career of it with the Nordiques in various scouting roles from 1981 to 1993. When the Mighty Ducks of Anaheim joined the NHL as an expansion team, Gauthier was hired away from the Noridques as assistant general manager.

In the fall of 1995, the Senators were lurching toward a critical moment in early franchise history. A move to the new Palladium in Kanata would be made in January, and in their fourth season, the Senators were once again in the basement of the NHL. They had started the season 6–5 but then lost eight in a row.

Rick Bowness, the first coach in Senators history, was fired on November 20 and replaced with Dave Allison, who was promoted from the club's American Hockey League team in Prince Edward Island. Things didn't change. The losing continued under Allison, and Senators general manager Randy Sexton was the next to fall, fired on December 5.

Behind the scenes, Mlakar, had been a presence in Ottawa to help prepare for the move to the Palladium. He was a consultant to Ogden Corp., the arena-management company, which had a financial stake in the Palladium. They had been involved with the Ducks and their rink, the Pond, and Mlakar had connections with the Ducks organization.

Looking for a guy with a track record of building through the draft (the Nordiques were now a Stanley Cup contender and would win that season), Gauthier was hired away from the Ducks. He was handed a mess of monumental proportions. Star center Alexei Yashin was holding out in the first of what would turn out to be a series of controversial contract disputes. Bryan Berard, the first pick overall in the 1995 NHL Draft, took a look at what was going on and demanded a trade. The team had won one game in the previous month.

"[*Sports Illustrated* reporter] Kostya Kennedy called me the first week I was there," Gauthier said. "[He said,] 'I'm writing an article about the worst teams in the history of professional sports and your team is No. 1.' I said, 'Thank you, Kostya, for the nice welcome note.' Worse than the [New York] Mets. They were second."

The Ghost started doing his ghostlike things, disappearing to plot his next moves. "There were some pieces to keep and some others that were assets you could play with, you know? I made a list," he said.

Gauthier resolved the Yashin holdout situation. Yashin played the rest of the season (47 games) for $720,000 and had a deal that would pay him $12.3 million for the following four seasons (he would infamously sit out the last year of the deal in 1999–2000).

Next, he dealt with the Berard situation. "I said, 'Okay, I'm going to say I'm not trading him until I trade him,'" Gauthier said. "I told his agent, Tom Laidlaw, 'I guess you're going to miss a full year when you should be playing in the NHL, because if that's what you're going to do, go back in the draft because I'm not going to trade him, so I hope you change your mind.'"

Gauthier started scouting potential trading partners. He heard the New York Islanders weren't happy with their first pick in 1995, defenseman Wade Redden, who had been taken second behind Berard. "I went to see Wade Redden and he played 50 minutes that night, a Sunday in Brandon," Gauthier said. "Him and Justin Kurtz. Fifty. What was going on was those two guys would go off and on the ice at their leisure. Nobody was telling them. When they came to the bench, as soon as they were ready, they would stand up and you could tell the other guys knew, 'I [have] to get off. These guys are going on.' They were on the ice the whole time, sometimes stretches of four or five minutes." Gauthier had heard Islanders GM Mike Milbury didn't like Redden's lack of intensity.

Gauthier wanted a goaltender and looked down Highway 401 at Damian Rhodes of the Toronto Maple Leafs. He made two critical moves on January 23, 1996, that would set the Senators' course for the next decade.

First, Gauthier traded veteran goaltender Don Beaupre, forward Martin Straka, and Berard in a three-way deal with the Leafs and the Islanders. Rhodes would play 181 games for the Senators and help them to their first win in the playoffs a year later. Redden became one of the greatest players in Senators history, playing 838 games with Ottawa and 1,023 in the NHL.

Next, Gauthier fired Allison, who was clearly in over his head and had a 2–22–1 record. "It's one of those things I've been thinking about, but I didn't want to do it until I knew that it was right in my heart," Gauthier said. "I felt that the change had to be made. Dave was just in the wrong place at the wrong time. It was a change I felt that was important. I just felt that we needed an experienced person."

Gauthier snuck out of Ottawa and met with a coach he had come to know in their days with the Nordiques. Gauthier always liked Jacques Martin's consistent demeanor and his ability to teach. A call was made to the Colorado Avalanche where Martin was an assistant coach to Marc Crawford (the Nordiques had moved to Denver for the 1995–96 season). "There was a press conference [in Ottawa] around 6:00. We had just made the trade and we had let go of the coaches. The group of media there had a lot of questions, and I had to interrupt and say, 'I'm sorry, I've got a flight out. I've got to leave you,'" Gauthier remembered.

He continued:

> Jacques was flying in from Denver. He was supposed to get in at 10. He got in at 1:00. We sat down all night, never slept. We made a deal in the morning and got on a flight. Wrote down the deal, shook hands, and he had to get ready for the game that night.

If you're going to build, there are going to be a lot of young players, and that's where Jacques came in. Because I thought Jacques would be the right guy to work with young players, make them work as a team and make us competitive while we [were] developing young players.

It's also the person. Jacques is the classiest guy you'll meet. He's very consistent in what he does. If you've got young players, you better be consistent. If you're going right and left, they are going to be even more confused. He's very, very consistent in his formula to build a team, make it play a certain way, and get it done. I thought for those reasons he was a good guy for that.

The events of January 23, 1996, represented a turnaround for the Senators franchise. Gauthier left the Senators after the 1997–98 season to return to the Ducks as president and general manager, but his moves of January 23 reverberated for years. "There are turning points, but when you act, you don't know how it's going to turn out," Gauthier said. "Both the deal and bringing in Jacques. He's such a stable person, you knew you would at least get stability going, and that gives you a chance to build.... That day was dramatic for the franchise because Damian Rhodes helped us in net and Wade Redden was a very good player for a long time. That was the day. Those were good years. I have good memories of everything here."

That day ended a tumultuous four months in which the Senators went through three coaches, two general managers, a president, and two buildings.

Gauthier confirmed the cookie story, by the way. He showed up for dinner one night to find all the cookies were gone. Next game there was a sign at the cookie tray: One Cookie Per Customer. There might have even been a security person standing there to enforce the rule. All true, it turns out. "That was typical.

My biggest challenge was getting Pierre not to worry about the minutiae," Mlakar said.

"It was right off the bat. I asked 'What's the matter?'" Gauthier remembered asking the staff taking care of the buffet when he found the cookie tray empty. "[The staff said,] 'The guys, they put some in their pockets.' I said, 'Okay, that's it.'" Gauthier said with another laugh, "I ruffled some feathers along the way."

He looked at the line for the hot dogs and quipped, "I'm going to stand here and make sure nobody takes more than one."

17 Bloody Domi

It seemed, finally, it would happen: the Ottawa Senators would win the Battle of Ontario. In the second round of the Stanley Cup Playoffs in May 2002, the Senators led their best-of-seven series against the Toronto Maple Leafs 3–2 and were on home ice with a chance to avenge their second-straight elimination at the hands of the Maple Leafs (the Senators fell to the Maple Leafs in the first round, 4–2, in 2000 and were swept in 2001).

The Senators were up 2–0 less than five minutes into Game 6 on goals by Marian Hossa and Daniel Alfredsson. Senators fans had waited for this. The Senators had entered the playoffs as the seventh seed in the East and drew the Philadelphia Flyers. Senators goaltender Patrick Lalime had a series for the ages with three shutouts and only two goals allowed as the Senators won the series 4–1. (Incredible to think it wasn't a sweep. In fact, the Senators trailed in the series after the Flyers won Game 1 1–0 in overtime on a goal by Ruslan Fedotenko.)

The fourth-seeded Maple Leafs played the Islanders, seeded fifth, and it was a homer series. Both teams won all their games on home ice, with the Leafs winning Game 7 4–2 without captain Mats Sundin, who was injured after getting hit in the wrist with the puck. Bring on the Battle of Ontario III.

The Senators won Game 1 5–0 on the strength of goaltender Lalime's fourth shutout of the playoffs in six games. The Leafs had taken a 2–0 lead in Game 2 only to see Sami Salo and Mike Fisher tie it up and send it into overtime. Senators killer Gary Roberts finally ended it at 4:30 of the third overtime.

Back in Ottawa, Magnus Arvedson had a pair of goals and the Senators won Game 3 3–2, but the Leafs, carried by a pair of goals by Alyn McCauley, bounced back to tie the series 2–2 with a 2–1 victory in Game 4. Back to Toronto.

In Game 5, Alfredsson slammed Toronto forward Darcy Tucker into the boards, turning the puck over, and scored the winning goal with 2:01 left in regulation time to put the Senators up in the series 3–2. The Leafs were on the brink and Alfredsson had stuck it to Tucker to do it.

Now, with the Leafs missing Sundin and Tucker, the Senators were up 2–0 early in Game 6. Just past the 13-minute mark of the first period, play was along the right-wing boards in the Ottawa zone. Toronto winger Tie Domi took a slash at Ottawa's Jody Hull and the puck came back along the boards to Domi, who was facing the boards.

Senators defenseman Ricard Persson, a third-pair journeyman, raised his arms and shoved Domi from behind. Domi's face struck the top of the boards and he went down, throwing off his gloves and rolling on the ice, his hands covering his face. When he got up, blood streamed from a cut over his left eye that would require 15 stitches to close. Persson received a five-minute major for boarding and a game misconduct.

"So as I went down, I controlled my fall and turned my head into the boards, head-butting myself off the corner of them," Domi wrote in his autobiography, *Shift Work*. "I knew full well that I would get cut wide open. As crazy as it sounds, I collided with the top of the dashboards to give myself a better chance of getting cut. And it worked. I drew blood—a lot of blood, in fact—on the play and refs had an easy call to make on Persson."

It made me think of a piece I had written about Domi when he was the heavyweight champion of the Ontario Hockey League with the Peterborough Petes (he was a good player too—an above-average skater with a decent shot). Players in the OHL talked about how big and hard Domi's head was. One player said, "His skin is like leather. You can't cut him."

You can watch the replay of the hit on YouTube. Does Domi turn his head? It doesn't look like it. It doesn't matter. Turned head or not, it was the turning point of the series. Toronto's Bryan McCabe scored 22 seconds into Persson's penalty to make it 2–1. The Senators got a bit of a reprieve when Maple Leaf Alexander Mogilny was penalized for holding Curtis Leschyshyn's stick at 13:43 and Toronto only had a one-man advantage.

But with the five-on-three restored when Mogilny returned, and with 19 seconds left in Persson's major, Roberts scored to tie the game. He scored again at 13:09 of the second period to give the Maple Leafs the lead, but Ottawa's Todd White scored with 25 seconds left in the period to tie it 3–3.

Facing elimination, it was a cautious third period. The Leafs had six shots and the Senators managed just four on Toronto goaltender Curtis Joseph. The only goal went to Mogilny at 4:28 for the win.

The Leafs forced a Game 7, which, of course, they won 3–0, backed by another couple of goals scored by Mogilny. That was a formality, of course. Just about every Senators fan knew it was over when Domi's skin split open in Game 6.

Leave it to Alfredsson to sum it up, as he often did: "If Tie Domi had better balance, we would have won the series."

18 The Bald Wayne Gretzky

The National Hockey League is a big business, but it's a small world. First, the big business part: In the fall of 1995, the management at Ogden Corp., which had sunk more than $100 million into the Palladium project in Ottawa, was getting antsy. After years of false starts and financing plans falling through, Ogden had guaranteed the loans to get the project into the ground and signed a $30 million deal to manage the building.

As the Palladium moved closer to its January 1996 opening, the Ottawa Senators were a mess. In their fourth season, they were as much of a gong show as ever and were headed for their fourth-straight last-place finish. Original coach Rick Bowness was fired in November by general manager and president Randy Sexton and replaced by Dave Allison, promoted from their farm club in Prince Edward Island. Things got even worse.

Faced with having twice as many seats to sell after the move from the 10,500-seat Ottawa Civic Centre to the 20,500-seat Palladium, Ogden wanted something done to improve the product. Loris Smith, an Ogden executive, turned to a man he had hired to work for the New Haven Nighthawks years earlier. Roy Mlakar was a young, aggressive go-getter from Parma, Ohio, who had worked selling tickets for the Cleveland Barons of the AHL and merchandise for baseball's Cleveland Indians and the NBA's Cleveland Cavaliers, before Smith hired him in 1978.

After 11 years with the Nighthawks, which were owned by the Los Angeles Kings, Mlakar moved up to become an executive with the Los Angeles Kings, his last two seasons as president, when Kings owner Bruce McNall was becoming one of the biggest players in the NHL.

Mlakar played a big role in the trade that brought Wayne Gretzky to Southern California in 1988. The Kings went to the Stanley Cup Final in 1993 and played in front of a record 282 consecutive sellout crowds.

McNall's empire spectacularly fell apart in December 1994 when he was convicted of five counts of conspiracy and fraud after he bilked half a dozen banks of $236 million. Mlakar moved on to the Pittsburgh Penguins. After two years, owner Howard Baldwin had the Penguins in bankruptcy, and Mlakar, whose final two years of his contract were lost in the Penguins' financial disaster, became a consultant with Ogden. Armed with a deal that paid him $5,000 a week, a setup at the Minto Suites, and a car, Mlakar set about figuring out what was going on in Ottawa.

Now we get to the small-world part: When Mlakar showed up in Ottawa, he was given the office that once belonged to John Ferguson, the Senators' former director of player personnel. Ferguson had left the team over disagreements about how things were being handled, including the contract battles with star center Alexei Yashin.

Mlakar had an incredibly personal connection to Ferguson. "He was the person responsible for taking me to my first hockey game when I was 11 years old," Mlakar said. "I babysat for his children in Parma, Ohio. He saw me playing in the street and asked me if I babysat. I said 'I do everything. I shovel snow. I cut lawns.' He said, 'We just rented a house on James St. Can you babysit? I play for the Cleveland Barons.' At [the] end of [the] year, he asked me if I had ever been to a hockey game. No, I hadn't. I got a stick and I met all the players. That's how I started life in hockey." Now, here he was sitting in Ferguson's office.

I ran into Mlakar at the Civic Centre at a game in the fall of 1995. I had been told he was going to be an influential man in the next few months. "Think of me as the bald Wayne Gretzky," he joked. "I'm here to assist people in whatever way I can."

Over the next three tumultuous months, Mlakar, while not really having any kind of official capacity with the club, played a critical role in just about every decision that was made. When owner Rod Bryden, facing heat from Ogden leadership and his financial backers, decided to fire Sexton in December, it was Mlakar who accompanied him to New York to meet with the big players to decide the next course of action.

Bryden, according to Mlakar, wanted to make a bold play and hire former Montreal Canadiens Hall of Fame defenseman and general manager Serge Savard, who had been let go by the Habs, who had turned—disastrously, as it turned out—to the tandem of GM Rejean Houle and coach Mario Tremblay.

Mlakar didn't think Savard was a good fit at that point in his career, the sting of being fired by the Canadiens still too fresh. He told Bryden and his partners:

> He's not the kind of guy you want. He's never had a budget in Montreal. He's been able to do exactly what he wants to do there. He's going to look at Ottawa as a step down after working in Montreal. I don't think you're going to get the guy you want. My recommendation to you: get the very best No. 2 guy. If you're doing this, you're doing it in December. You're eliminating the top 25 guys. They're already working.
>
> With a budget team in a small market, the only way you are going to win is with the draft and kids [who] grow in a system. There's a guy who did it in Quebec and

is implementing it in Anaheim. There's this guy Pierre Gauthier.

They came up with a list of three candidates: Savard; Larry Pleau, who was assistant general manager for the New York Rangers, fresh off a Stanley Cup win in 1994; and Gauthier.

Mlakar said the interview with Savard went exactly the way he thought it would: "What do you mean you only have $38 million to spend on players?" Then Pleau didn't have a great interview.

Gauthier won the day in an interview at the Ritz-Carlton, Marina del Rey. "Everybody is blown away by his knowledge, and he's a gentleman with Canadian ties," Mlakar said. "Very systematic. Very thorough. Extremely focused. He always knew a step ahead the next step he was going to take. I was really impressed with the way he went about his business. He was a tireless worker, scout, and evaluator. So thorough. He was just a very diligent operator."

Gauthier fired Allison, hired Jacques Martin as coach, and swung a series of trades that set the team on a path that would see them make the playoffs for 11 seasons in a row beginning in 1997.

Having brought some stability to the franchise on the ice, and with the move to the Palladium completed, Mlakar didn't know what his new move would be. Then Bryden offered the vacant job of team president to him. Bryden offered him a decent deal with a $50,000 escalator built in for each year of his first three-year deal. "Rod was very, very fair to me," Mlakar said. "I hit it off with him."

Mlakar was one of the first hockey men I heard say: "Owners own, managers manage, coaches coach, and players play." He stuck to that philosophy with the Senators. Gauthier said:

> To turn that corner takes a long time, and you've got to be lucky. Those were four tough years, and a tough way to start a franchise. It took a lot of support from Mr.

Bryden. He put himself out there unbelievably, financially and everything. Roy Mlakar, he did a hell of a job too. He worked so hard. He had no life outside of this. He was there all the time. He knew: "Take care of the hockey and I'll take care of this." We [helped] help each other with a lot of things, but there was no crossover or interference or anything.

Mlakar, recently single, lived with assistant coach Perry Pearn and pretty much spent all his waking hours building the fan base. He spoke to whatever group or organization or business would listen to him, often bringing Bryden, a mesmerizing speaker, along. "I don't think they had any clue how to go about marketing this team once they left the other building," Mlakar said. "They only had 9,000 seats. You thought you were going to go out there and there were going to be 9,000 people waiting to come in? Nine thousand more people? Their marketing was attack the negative. Attack the people who think it's too far away. Attack the people who think it's too expensive. Attack this, attack that, rather than have a plan."

Mlakar hired Steve Violetta as his marketing man, and together they assembled a 500-page marketing manual. "We implemented a lot of plans that got people in the door without the dramatic discounting, giveaways," Mlakar said. "All the time we were there, we were never in the top 10 in either of those categories [in the league]. It's not been the case lately." Corporate sales doubled.

Under Bryden and then Eugene Melnyk, who bought the team out of bankruptcy in 2003, Mlakar drove attendance from an average of 15,371 in the first full year in the Corel Centre to an all-time peak of 19,821 in the 2007–08 season. But there was friction with the new ownership. "It took one meeting for me to realize life as I knew it had changed," Mlakar said.

Despite what he had done to turn the Senators around and put them on a solid foundation, the team's strong performance at the gate and on the ice, and the strong reputation he had created for the Senators as a solid corporate citizen in Ottawa, Mlakar's contract as president was not renewed at the end of the 2008–09 season. A hockey lifer, he became the president and alternate governor of the Erie Otters of the Ontario Hockey League in 2015, stepping down due to health reasons in April 2018. It's probably just a coincidence, but in the last couple seasons, the Otters have achieved record numbers in attendance and corporate support.

19 Wing It in Buffalo

A good road trip for Senators fans will take you to Buffalo for a game against the Sabres at KeyBank Center. The Sabres have become one of the Senators' biggest rivals because of their meetings in the Stanley Cup Playoffs. The Senators have played the Sabres four times in the postseason (1997, 1999, 2006, and 2007), with a 1–3 record. The only team they've played more often is the Pittsburgh Penguins (five times).

One of the biggest games in Senators history took place at KeyBank Center in 2007 when Daniel Alfredsson scored in overtime to defeat the Sabres in five games in the Eastern Conference Final to advance to send the Senators to their first Stanley Cup Final.

Getting to Buffalo is relatively easy. It's about a five-hour drive from Ottawa if you take Hwy 416 to Hwy 401 West and then the Hill Island exit to Interstate 81 South. You get on Interstate 90 at Syracuse heading East for Buffalo (be warned, it's a toll road—$7.50 U.S.).

If you want some cross-border shopping in the mix, there are some good stops along the way. Watertown's Salmon River Mall is a good first stop with a few of the big chain stores (JCPenney, Burlington Coat Factory, and Dick's Sporting Goods) as anchor tenants. And if you're into craft beer, check out Skewed Brewing, a local craft brewer (try the Tropic Thunder IPA).

A little farther down I-81, Destiny USA (formerly the Carousel Mall) is just south of the I-90 at Syracuse. It's a six-story shopping and entertainment center that has been undergoing considerable expansion over the last few years. It's now the sixth-largest mall in the U.S., according to atlas.com, and even has its own ZIP Code.

If outlet malls are your thing, the Waterloo Premium Outlets are located about a 50-minute drive west of Syracuse on I-90.

If you haven't been to downtown Buffalo in a few years, this isn't your dad's Buffalo anymore. It used to be on a Saturday morning it looked like it was the setting for one of those postapocalyptic movies in which the entire population has been wiped out. Thanks to the investment of Sabres owner Terry Pegula, the area around the rink has undergone a massive facelift. Where once there was a parking lot, there are now a couple hotels—the Marriott HarborCenter and the Courtyard Downtown/Canalside. They are right across the street from the arena.

There's a lot to do in the area now too. The Seneca Buffalo Creek Casino is just a short walk away, east of the arena. Canalside, just west of the arena, is a historic park district that was once the western terminus of the Erie Canal (great for a walk if you go to a game in the spring or fall). There are food and shopping options there too.

My favorite spots: As you may already know, I prefer good, gritty local places to have a pint, and the Swannie House—not far from the casino, east of the rink (if you need a landmark)—fits the bill perfectly before or after a Sabres game. It's located at 170 Ohio

St., near the General Mills plant. The kitchen is open late and has a solid wing game.

If craft beer is your thing, the Pearl Street Grill & Brewery (76 Pearl St.) has a good selection of western New York beers, including a Don Cherry Cherry Wheat. Their signature beer is Trainwreck, an amber ale.

In 2015 the National Geographic Society ranked Buffalo third on its list of the world's top 10 food cities. Yes, Buffalo. Buffalo is, of course, the home of the chicken wing, and if you're a first-time visitor, you should hit the Anchor Bar (1047 Main St.), the home of the chicken wing. The staple of every bar got its start there in 1964. Teressa Bellissimo, asked to make a late-night snack for her son and his friends, took the leftover chicken wings, usually used to make soup, and flavored them with a mystery sauce—and wings became a thing! Gabriel's Gate (145 Allen St.) might be my favorite wing spot. It's got an old-school tavern vibe.

If you want a fancier meal, my go-to (thanks to a recommendation years ago from Hockey Hall of Famer Mike Farber) is Hutch's (1375 Delaware Ave.). It's first-class dining without being stuffy or pretentious.

If you're looking to get your drink on (please, do so responsibly), the Chip Strip on Chippewa St. is Buffalo's club scene. Elmwood Village and Allen St., are also worth a look. You have to finish up a night on the Chip Strip with a stop at Jim's Steakout (92 W. Chippewa St.) for a submarine sandwich.

A final note: If you're an architecture fan, one of the things people might not appreciate about Buffalo is it is home to some of the greatest American architecture from the 1800s and early 1900s. A lot of it is a short walk from the arena area. My favorites: the Guaranty/Prudential building (28 Church St.), a terra-cotta high-rise that was one of the first skyscrapers, and Buffalo City Hall (65 Niagara Sq., but you don't need the address; it dominates the skyline). The art deco style has a tower almost 400 feet high.

20 Ottawa Apologizes

It became the buzz phrase that summed up the Ottawa Senators' return to the NHL and a foreshadowing of their first four seasons: "Ottawa apologizes." The phrase was uttered by general manager Mel Bridgman after the Senators made a series of gaffes during their first real moment on the NHL stage.

The setting was a ballroom in the Gouverneur Hotel in Montreal on June 18, 1992, where the Senators and the Tampa Bay Lightning were participating in the expansion draft to stock their teams.

It was an awful start to what would turn out to be an awful first year for the Senators. "Snow in winter," was the way one executive summed up the quality of players that would be made available to the Senators and the Lightning, who had each paid $50 million to pick up 42 (21 each) journeymen, castoffs, aging veterans, and draft busts.

In typical fashion, the other teams scrambled to cover their assets. There was a flurry of deals and roster manipulations so teams wouldn't lose somebody who was actually good. Teams could protect 14 skaters and two goaltenders, and players with fewer than three years of professional experience were exempt. There was also another twist: there had been an expansion draft in 1991 to stock the San Jose Sharks, so any team that had lost a goaltender or defenseman to the Sharks couldn't lose one to the Senators or the Lightning.

Teams needed to expose a goaltender who had to have played at least a game to make him eligible for the expansion draft. The Chicago Blackhawks, for example, called up minor leaguer Ray LeBlanc and played him one game and exposed him. They

Snow in Winter

Here are the players selected in the 1992 Expansion Draft:

Ottawa Senators

Goaltenders
Peter Sidorkiewicz, Hartford Whalers
Mark Laforest, New York Rangers

Defensemen
Brad Shaw, New Jersey Devils
Darren Rumble, Philadelphia Flyers
Dominic Lavoie, St. Louis Blues
Brad Miller, Buffalo Sabres
Ken Hammond, Vancouver Canucks
Kent Paynter, Winnipeg Jets
John Van Kessel, Los Angeles Kings

Forwards
Sylvain Turgeon, Montreal Canadiens
Mike Peluso, Chicago Blackhawks
Rob Murphy, Vancouver Canucks
Mark Lamb, Edmonton Oilers
Laurie Boschman, New Jersey Devils
Jim Thomson, Los Angeles Kings
Lonnie Loach, Detroit Red Wings
Mark Freer, Philadelphia Flyers
Chris Lindberg, Calgary Flames
Jeff Lazaro, Boston Bruins
Darcy Loewen, Buffalo Sabres
Blair Atcheynum, Hartford Whalers

also engaged in some pre–expansion draft shenanigans with the Winnipeg Jets and the Buffalo Sabres to protect other players.

The Jets acquired goaltender Daniel Berthiaume from the Boston Bruins for the purposes of exposing him in the draft. Then they traded goaltender Stephane Beauregard to the Sabres for Christian Ruuttu. Both were protected by their new teams. After

Tampa Bay Lightning

Goaltenders
Wendell Young, Pittsburgh Penguins
Frederic Chabot, Montreal Canadiens

Defensemen
Joe Reekie, New York Islanders
Shawn Chambers, Washington Capitals
Peter Taglianetti, Pittsburgh Penguins
Bob McGill, Detroit Red Wings
Jeff Bloemberg, New York Rangers
Doug Crossman, Quebec Nordiques
Rob Ramage, Minnesota North Stars

Forwards
Michel Mongeau, St. Louis Blues
Anatoli Semenov, Edmonton Oilers
Mike Hartman, Winnipeg Jets
Basil McRae, Minnesota North Stars
Rob DiMaio, New York Islanders
Steve Maltais, Quebec Nordiques
Dan Vincelette, Chicago Blackhawks
Tim Bergland, Washington Capitals
Brian Bradley, Toronto Maple Leafs
Keith Osborne, Toronto Maple Leafs
Shayne Stevenson, Boston Bruins
Tim Hunter, Calgary Flames

the draft, the Sabres traded Beauregard and a fourth-round draft pick to the Blackhawks for a young goaltender named Dominik Hasek. Then the Blackhawks traded Beauregard back to the Jets for Ruuttu. The Jets got to keep Beauregard, and the Blackhawks basically turned Hasek into Ruuttu and the fourth-round pick (Eric Daze).

The Washington Capitals tried something even shadier: they signed former goaltender Bernie Wolfe, 40, who hadn't played in 13 years, and tried to use him as the goalie they could expose (the rules didn't say *when* he had to have played at least one game). The NHL would look the other way on a lot of things back then, but not that one.

On June 18, the Senators and Lightning went about picking through the remainder bin for bargains. Things were going along as well as could be expected until Bridgman rose to make the 33rd selection. The Senators went for Montreal Canadiens tough guy Todd Ewen. Not so fast, said NHL executive vice president Brian O'Neill. The Canadiens had already lost their maximum two players: goaltender Frederic Chabot to Tampa and Sylvain Turgeon to the Senators. "Ottawa apologizes," Bridgman said, clearly embarrassed and perhaps a little angry.

The Senators had brought a laptop computer with them, but there was no electrical outlet near their table, and it had died. They were having to wing it with paper and pen. Nobody had crossed Chabot off the list. Bridgman regrouped and took forward Mark Freer from the Philadelphia Flyers.

Six picks later, Bridgman selected forward Tood Hawkins of the Toronto Maple Leafs. The Lightning had taken forwards Brian Bradley and Keith Osborne from the Maple Leafs a few picks earlier, so the Maple Leafs also had lost their quota. Wrong again.

Bridgman regrouped and selected forward C.J. Young, which was followed by an uncomfortable silence. Young, who had played at Harvard University, in the 1992 Olympics in Albertville, and was signed by the Calgary Flames, wasn't eligible. He was on an original list of eligible players, but he had been removed from an updated list that had been handed to the Senators on the way into the draft. It got lost in the shuffle and was never consulted. "The list we had included Young's name," an embarrassed Bridgman told reporters afterward. "Late this afternoon we were handed an envelope which contained a list on which his name did not appear. I never saw that list."

There was a big meeting on the stage between NHL executives and the Senators contingent. There was some animated discussion. Bridgman then selected forward Darcy Loewen from the Buffalo Sabres.

After a slick campaign to win the franchise, the expansion draft performance created the impression that the Senators were bumblers who didn't know what they were doing.

"Ottawa apologizes" pretty much summed it up.

The Brawl on Broad Street

On March 5, 2004, the Ottawa Senators and the Philadelphia Flyers combined for 419 minutes of penalties at the Wells Fargo Center in the City of Brotherly Love. That's an NHL record for most penalty minutes in one game. Given the way fighting in the NHL has declined over the 2000s, that is likely going to stand as a single-game record forever.

According to hockeyfights.com, 42.2 percent of NHL games in 2001–02 had at least one fight. In 2017–18, that number had declined to 17.9 percent. There were 803 fights in the 2001–02 season. In 2017–18 there were 280.

It seemed like there were at least that many between just between the Senators and the Flyers on that March 5 night. The table had been set a week earlier when Senators forward Martin Havlat had slashed Flyers forward Mark Recchi in the face and was kicked out of the game for intent to injure. Afterward, Flyers coach Ken Hitchcock, with one of his more memorable quotes, said of

Havlat: "Someday someone's going to make him eat his lunch." He also said, "This is something in my opinion that the players should take care of."

Recchi agreed with his coach. "He two-handed me across the face," Recchi said. "He's known for it.… It might not come from our team, but he better protect himself." Oh, boy.

Havlat apologized and said he didn't mean to hit Recchi in the face. "I don't feel good about what I did," he said. "I was getting frustrated with all the hooking going on before that. I wanted to hit him but not in the face. It was a bad decision."

Halvat was suspended two games for the incident, his second suspension of the season (he had already been suspended two games for kicking New York Islanders forward Eric Cairns). So you can imagine the anticipation when the teams met back in Philadelphia eight days later.

Most of the game went by with the two teams sticking to hockey (there were only five minor penalties in the first 40 minutes). In the third period, with the Flyers up 5–2 and 1:45 left in the game, things veered off the rails and into classic YouTube territory.

Tough guys Donald Brashear of the Flyers (2,634 career penalty minutes) and Rob Ray of the Senators (3,207 career penalty minutes) came together in front of the Philadelphia goal, and it was on. They had a true heavyweight bout, and Ray skated off bloodied. As Brashear was being escorted off the ice, Ottawa's Brian Pothier and tough guy Todd Simpson got involved with Brashear, and it went sideways from there.

Ottawa's Shaun Van Allen squared off with Philly's Branko Radivojevic. Senators goaltender Patrick Lalime skated the length of the ice and took on Flyers goaltender Robert Esche. Simpson then tangled with Daniil Markov. "Old-time hockey is back in Philadelphia!" commentator Greg Millen said on the Senators television broadcast.

Senators forward Chris Neil said the players took things into their own hands at that point. Senators coach Jacques Martin wasn't a guy know for liking the rough stuff. "We didn't like what happened when Brashear went after Razor and then [defenseman] Brian Pothier after," Neil said. "They were upset at Jacques at the time, but it wasn't even Jacques that initiated the second part of it. It was the players, sticking up for one another. We weren't going to let that go on undefended."

Lalime got tossed and was replaced by Martin Prusek, a native of the Czech Republic, whose next fight would be his first. "I remember after Lalime fought, after the first line brawl, I went down to Prusek and said, 'Be ready to go, because as soon as the puck drops, there's going to be another line brawl,'" Neil said. "That's what I told him, and he said, 'Okay.' After it was all said and done, I look down and he's got his arm resting on the crossbar. It was funny."

On the next faceoff, Neil took on Radovan Somik, and Senators defenseman Zdeno Chara fought with Mattias Timander. Neither of the Flyers was a fighter, and Philadelphia general manager Bob Clarke, a veteran of the Broad Street Bullies era, didn't like the infraction of "the Code."

After Chara got thrown out of the game, Martin sent Havlat, playing his first game after serving his suspension, to serve Chara's instigator penalty in the safety of the penalty box. There's some irony for you. The guy who was responsible for the whole thing got to kick back and watch it all.

After the next faceoff, Ottawa's Mike Fisher and Philly's Michal Handzus tangled. That's seven fights, if you're keeping track.

After Recchi took a run at Senators defenseman Wade Redden, Redden fought Flyers forward John LeClair and Ottawa's Bryan Smolinski battled with Recchi.

After the next restart, the final bout of the night took place. It was hardly a heavyweight tilt, with Ottawa's Jason Spezza going with Patrick Sharp of the Flyers, two guys who knew each other and shared the same agent. "He knew it was coming," Sharp said. "Thankfully, it was a harmless fight. Two guys who didn't really know what they were doing too much. We got through it and added to the NHL record penalty minutes."

Sharp continued, "I got a call from my agent the day after the fight. He said, 'What are you doing fighting Spezza?' Because he was the golden boy back then. He was the second overall pick. I didn't have much choice. That's what makes you nervous, too. It's one thing to fight in a game. I've had lots of fights when it's just heat of the moment and you're angry. But when you're sitting there

Most Penalty Minutes

The Flyers and the Senators put themselves in the record books for most penalty minutes with their marathon brawl on March 5, 2004. Here are the records they set, along with the previous records:

Most Penalty Minutes, Game
419, Senators (206) at Flyers (213), March 5, 2004
406, Minnesota North Stars (211) at Boston Bruins (195), February 26, 1981

Most Penalty Minutes, Both Teams, Period
409, Senators (200) at Flyers (209), March 5, 2004, third period
372, Los Angeles Kings (184) at Philadelphia Flyers (188), March 11, 1979, first period

Most Penalty Minutes, One Team, Game
213, Flyers, March 5, 2004
211, Minnesota North Stars, February 26, 1981

Most Penalty Minutes, One Team, Period
209, Flyers, March 5, 2004, third period
190, Calgary Flames vs. Anaheim Mighty Ducks, December 8, 2001, third period

thinking about it and they're sorting out the penalty minutes over there and I know I got to go out there and fight somebody, the nerves were going pretty good."

Spezza was assessed a fighting major misconduct and a double game misconduct, and his 35 minutes in penalties stands as the Senators franchise record for most penalty minutes in a game. The Senators finished the game with two players on the bench to the Flyers' four.

"When it was all said and done, they had six guys get stitched up and we had five," Neil said. "It was awesome. That was the thing. You had guys out of their element doing stuff they aren't normally used to doing, sticking up for teammates. It brought us closer together as a group, and...we were on the airplane after and we were watching it, everyone was gathered around the back on the plane. It was awesome, it really was. It was a night I'll never forget."

Clarke, upset because he felt some of his European players had been taken advantage of, tried to get into the Senators' dressing room area to get at Martin, whom he called "a gutless puke," according to the *Ottawa Citizen*.

Brashear, who started it all, wasn't making any apologies. "Why wouldn't I start it? Did you see the last game?" Brashear was quoted by the Associated Press. "I fought a tough guy. They went after guys who don't fight. I could've fought one of their good players and hurt them, but I didn't."

How did it go over in Philadelphia? Comcast Sportsnet, the Flyers' broadcaster, replayed the game on March 10. The replay got a Nielsen rating of 1.0, higher than most Flyers regular-season games.

22 The First Star

In the fall of 1992, Norm Maciver was sitting at home in Duluth, Minnesota, three weeks into a contract dispute with the Edmonton Oilers. Maciver, 28 years old and in the middle of a solid NHL career, was coming off a season in which he teamed with Dave "Charlie" Manson to form one of the best defensive pairings in the league. Maciver, a little shorter than six feet tall and weighing 180 pounds, was a fine puck handler and smooth skater gifted with hockey sense. Undrafted, he signed with the New York Rangers after a college career at the University of Minnesota–Duluth Bulldogs (he had 152 assists in 165 games, a school record) and was a finalist for the 1985–86 Hobey Baker Memorial Award.

Manson was 6'2" and 200 pounds and a first-round pick (No. 11) of the Chicago Black Hawks in 1985. He was big and mean (2,792 career penalty minutes, 13th on the career list). His rough-and-tumble persona was enhanced by a raspy voice caused by a punch to the throat in a fight with Sergio Momesso that damaged his vocal cords.

Maciver and Manson were a strong duo. Manson had 47 points in 1991–92 (15 goals and 32 assists) and Maciver had 40 points on six goals and 34 assists. Maciver was looking to get paid, but contract talks with the Oilers were going nowhere.

As the NHL season approached, so did the waiver draft. Maciver's agent told him not to worry, that the Oilers would protect him. "I wasn't expecting to be put on waivers," Maciver recalled. "My wife and I were out, and we came home and there was a message on our voice mail. This was prior to the Internet [and] iPhones. We got home at maybe 6:00 Central time, so it was a little later. All the message said was, 'This is John Ferguson's secretary. Can you please give John a call?'"

Maciver's days with the Oilers were over. (After having won a big NHL players Pro-Am, Maciver got a note from Oilers GM Glen Sather: "Good luck with your golf career.")

Like Maciver said, this was pre-Internet. No Google. Maciver knew Ferguson had been the general manager of the Winnipeg Jets. He had no idea he was now the director of player personnel for the expansion Ottawa Senators. "At the time I didn't know who John was working for. I remember I was racking my brain. I remember I went to a bookstore, like a Barnes and Noble, to see if I could find a book to see who he was working for. I never found out," Maciver said.

He continued, "The next morning, I called and I had to ask the secretary, 'Sorry, but can you tell me which team this is?' She told me, and that's how I found out it was the Senators."

Maciver got on the line with Ferguson:

I get John on the phone, and he said to me, "Welcome. We selected you for the Senators. I hear you were in a contract dispute with the Oilers. What were you asking for?" It totally caught me off guard, so I said the number, the final number we were at—which I think was like $300,000— and he said, "Okay, good, we'll have that drawn up and you can sign it when you get here."

I remember getting off the phone and saying to my wife…"I don't know what I could have said, some crazy number, but he caught me so off guard and I just said the number and he said okay, good, and that was that."

I can't believe I said that. That was some good contract negotiating right there. That's how I ended up with the Senators.

Maciver was claimed on October 4 and four nights later dressed for the Senators on opening night of their inaugural season. He hadn't skated for about three weeks, since all the other NHLers who worked out together in Duluth had left to go to their training camps. "One of the defensemen [Brad Shaw] got hurt about five minutes into the game and we were down to five defensemen," Maciver said. "I just remember I couldn't believe how tired I was. I hadn't had any preseason games. I had hardly been on the ice for three weeks. I just remember being exhausted."

Maciver had two assists in the Senators' 5–3 win against the Montreal Canadiens. He had two more assists in their second game in Quebec against the Nordiques. He had 11 points in the Senators' first nine games, in which they scored 20 goals.

On a team that had a 10–70–4 record and flirted with being the worst team of all time, Maciver was the star of the show. Remarkably, he didn't go more than three games without a point that season. The player the Senators picked up on waivers right before the season started wound up leading them in scoring that first season with 63 points (17 goals, 46 assists).

"He was our best puck-moving defenseman and our best defenseman, period. I remember him telling me a couple times, because back then we did spend a lot of time in our zone, yeah, we weren't very good; he said he spent a lot of energy defending," Alain Vigneault, an assistant coach on that first team, said. "If we had been able to get the puck and move, he would have been even better. He was without a doubt our best player. He was a hardworking and skilled defenseman, just smaller for that era."

Maciver later said, "When I first got there I didn't know what to expect. I was totally caught off guard by the whole situation. I didn't know anything about the team, and then we won the first game and it was like, 'Well, okay, that's pretty cool,' and then the next two weeks, reality hit. Whoa. From that point on it was, 'How are we going to make the best of this situation?' I was having some individual success, so that was the easiest way to cope with it." After that opening night win, the Senators went 21 games without a win (0–20–1).

Maciver had a scary incident after that first season while playing for Canada at the world championships. He took a big hit and sustained a bruised heart. He recovered and played another season with the Senators (23 points in 53 games) and was traded to the Pittsburgh Penguins along with Troy Murray for Martin Straka during the 1994–95 season. He went on to the Winnipeg Jets and moved with them to Phoenix, where he finished his NHL career.

Maciver has had a successful post-playing career in management, winning three Stanley Cups with the Chicago Blackhawks. He said there were some tough lessons learned in those early years of the Senators franchise. "You never take anything for granted, never take winning for granted. It was a very humbling experience," he said. "I had just spent two years with the Oilers and we had made it to the semifinal the previous two years, and prior to that they had won five Cups in seven years. That organization was really the top of the mountain. It was a pretty humbling experience. Don't ever take anything for granted, and be thankful for what you have."

Lace 'Em Up on the Rideau Canal

If a Senators fan or visitor to Ottawa wanted to get at least a little bit of a sense of how far a National Hockey League player skates in a game, they could lace up their blades and skate the length of the Rideau Canal Skateway, which bills itself as the world's largest skating rink.

With the development of GPS tracking technology and some experiments with NHL players, it's estimated the average NHL player skates about five miles in a game (about eight kilometers), and that just happens to be the length of the Rideau Canal Skateway.

The Skateway is on a stretch of the Rideau Canal—Ontario's only UNESCO World Heritage Site—from the Hartwells Locks near Carleton University on Dow's Lake, winding through Ottawa's downtown to the National Arts Centre and close to the doorstep of Parliament Hill.

While the Skateway is the largest rink in the world, it is just a small part of the Rideau Canal, a 126-mile (202-kilometer) network of lakes, rivers, and canals that links Ottawa with Kingston, Ontario, at the head of Lake Ontario.

The Rideau Canal was built after the War of 1812 between Great Britain and the United States as a safe route for goods away from the Saint Lawrence River, which was shared with America. Work on the canal began in 1827 under Colonel John By and was opened in 1932. Many of the original locks are still in use today by recreational boaters.

Hockey isn't allowed on the Skateway except during special occasions, so skaters don't have to worry about some Zdeno Chara–sized yeti of a defenseman blocking their path to their goal.

While NHL players' best bet for some midskate refreshment might be some sports drink from a bottle who knows how many guys have handled, skaters on the Skateway can skate up to booths along the way and snack on a BeaverTail, a unique fried dough pastry that is stretched out to resemble a beaver tail and complemented with a variety of toppings, such as cinnamon, bananas, and chocolate. You'll see skaters go after a BeaverTail like Sidney Crosby after a loose puck in the crease.

The 2018 skating season is the 48th for the Rideau Canal. The skating season is typically from early January to the end of

February, about 60 days, though the 2016 skating season was the shortest on record: 18 days.

Ice crews roam the frigid night, plowing snow off the canal, drilling holes in the ice, and pumping water to flood the surface. The National Capital Commission (NCC), which oversees the Skateway, even has a special Zamboni that scrapes the surface to give skaters the smoothest surface possible.

According to the NCC, about 900,000 take to the Skateway each year, many of them during Ottawa's winter festival, Winterlude, which runs for the first three weekends of February. The Skateway is opened to skaters for free, though the NCC welcomes visitors' donations, which can be deposited in boxes at various entry points.

24 The View from the Alfredsson Deck

It was a cool and cloudy early October day in Partille, a suburb of Gothenburg in Sweden, but the view from the deck on the front of the Alfredsson family home was too good to pass up. It looked out over the low hills of a leafy neighborhood. We were led there in a convoy of a few cars from downtown Gothenburg to take advantage of the Alfredssons' generous invitation to visit the home of the Senators' captain, Daniel Alfredsson.

Daniel's father, Hasse Alfredsson, wobbled onto the deck and tucked his crutches under a table as we took our seats. He had recently had hip-replacement surgery, but accommodating host that he was, he didn't let that stop him from welcoming a couple members of the Ottawa media to his home. Hasse, once a carpenter by trade—among other things—built the deck that expanded the size of the modest bungalow, which had a garage to its left and an interlocking brick driveway connecting it to the street.

He settled into his chair by the table and under the flat light began to pick through the usual parents' collection of paper and photos and touchstones marking their children's journey through life.

Close by on the planks put in place by Hasse, Daniel's mother, Margareta—confined to a wheelchair by a neuromuscular disorder—enjoyed the buzz around the house with the nosy reporters visiting and the excitement of the Senators in town to start the season with a pair of games against the Pittsburgh Penguins.

Daniel sat just inside the door of the house with his brother, Henrik, a pretty good player in his own right and a member of the 1999 Memorial Cup champion Ottawa 67's. Sister Cecila was close by, a little deeper into the house.

Hasse was a sturdily built man with a thick wave of hair and a mustache that if allowed free rein could wrestle Lanny McDonald's to the ground and make it cry. He was a good soccer player ("I could keep the ball in the air for 20 minutes," he said) and played some hockey, but life got in the way. "I had two kids and I couldn't live on it," he said.

When asked to recount Daniel's childhood and hockey, Hasse recalled, "Even the teacher believed him when he wrote that essay [when he was seven] about wanting to be a hockey player, because he was so determined."

Hasse continued, "When we were going to the practice, he would ask, 'Dad, do you think I have a chance to play for this team?' He would ask if he could take another step, and I told him, 'It's up to you.' I know so many people in hockey here in Sweden, but I never told anybody they had to take him. He's done it all by himself. Sometimes you can get it easy because somebody is helping you. He's always been struggling, always fighting for his position…always."

When Daniel Alfredsson was 17, he almost quit hockey. He was to play for Molndal, and Hasse was asked to be an assistant coach. "Daniel said, 'If he's going to coach me, I'll put my skates in the closet.'" Margareta said. Daniel didn't want anybody to think he got anything because his dad was the coach.

Daniel started out in school to become a carpenter like his father but opted for economics at Burgardens High School. Ask Senators fans about Alfredsson's career, and they should say his was the collision of talent and a fearless embracing of a good day's work. It started when Hasse would drop Daniel at 7:00 AM every day at the rink, where Daniel had a set of keys to let himself in. A daily hockey school was part of his curriculum, and he would sleep on a bench in the dressing room until the coach showed up.

The family moved into their bungalow in Partille around the time Alfredsson left to take a wild stab at playing in the NHL. The bungalow was best to accommodate Margareta's wheelchair, with a cozy kitchen and a sauna off the bathroom ("More common than a pool here," Hasse said of the sauna, "and I'm not one for fancy things.").

It was clear Daniel learned a lot from his parents. It went both ways. The Alfredssons were so accommodating on the day of our visit, but for years Hasse declined requests to be interviewed. "I didn't want to make my kids embarrassed, but Daniel said, 'Do just what you like.' He's very good at that. Even with his own kids. He always gives them a chance to try. If they ask, 'Can I take a picture with his camera?' he says, 'Just do it.'"

Sitting on the deck as the Swedish night slowly crept in around us, it was evident why Daniel Alfredsson was the person he was. When Daniel was nine, he was selected to be a flag bearer on the ice at the world hockey championships, which had come to Gothenburg. Hasse said, "One day he said to me, 'Dad, can I take my autograph book with me?' and I said yes. He asked [Vladimir] Petrov of the Russian team for an autograph, and he pushed

Daniel aside. This is something we talked about. I said, 'If you're ever a player, don't be like that.'" That explained why Alfredsson had stood at the rink the day before and accommodated every kid who asked for a moment of his time, until every request had been fulfilled.

25 The Joker

On the day Senators forward Chris Neil retired—December 14, 2017—skate lace manufacturers surely shed a tear. The gritty forward played 1,026 games for the Senators before he called it quits, and they were some of the hardest minutes anyone played in the NHL. Neil kept himself going with an underdog's mentality, a prankster's sense of humor, and a hockey player's love of routine.

Before every one of this 1,026 games, Neil would sit in his stall in the dressing room and go through one of his most noticeable superstitions: he would put new laces in his skates. Not one pair was needed for this operation but two. He would string a lace through the bottom two eyelets on each skate and tie a knot exactly in the middle and cut off the surplus lace. Then he would use another pair of laces to tie up each skate. Many an unsuspecting visitor to the dressing room would get hit with the end of a lace as Neil held one end and flicked the other out into the room from his stall to unfurl it.

It was a superstition that started in junior hockey, he said. "Fresh laces felt good, especially when you were banged up some nights," he said. And there were nights when Neil was banged up.

He had 212 fights during the preseason, regular season, and postseason for the Senators in the NHL, according to hockeyfights .com. He played most of his career at 6'1" and 210 pounds or so, so he gave up some size in just about every scrap, but he still won most of them, exorting the crowd with his "Let's hear it" gesture on the way to the penalty box. (Senators fans loved it; it drove opponents nuts. They thought he was showboating.)

He fought for everything he got in his 15-year career. Neil was selected in the sixth round (No. 161) in the 1998 NHL Draft and worked his way up from the United Hockey League and the East Coast Hockey League to carve out a career with the Senators.

Only defenseman Chris Phillips (1,179) and former captain Daniel Alfredsson (1,178) played more games for the Senators than Neil. He had 250 points (112 goals, 138 assists) and is the Senators' all-time penalty minutes leader with 2,522, 20th in NHL history. Neil and longtime New Jersey Devils defenseman Ken Daneyko are the only NHL players to have played 1,000 games and had more than 2,500 penalty minutes while spending their entire career with one franchise.

"One of the things I'm most proud of is I've always been an underdog," Neil said. "I was a late-round draft pick to the OHL, a late round pick to the NHL. I always had something to prove. I never took it for granted that I was on a team."

"I think it's amazing, to be honest. He's had a fabulous career," Alfredsson said. "Coming in and having to adapt and find a role that would fit in the NHL. His determination is second to none. His work ethic is second to none. He's a real pro's pro. He would come and show up every day—practices, games—and give it everything he had. His parents did a good job bringing him up, because he had a will that was there all the way to the end."

Neil inspired Senators defenseman Mark Borowiecki, who grew up in Ottawa as a Senators fan and then got a chance to be a teammate. "He was always one of my favorite players growing up,

Chris Neil displays his signature grit during a game against the San Jose Sharks in 2016.

him and [former forward] Andre Roy together—the Bash Brothers. I used to love those guys," Borowiecki said. "Most kids growing in Ottawa in my situation would probably echo that same thing. He meant a lot to this community. He always brought energy to the games. For a town that is not thought of as being the most blue-collar city in Canada, having a blue-collar guy like him really resonated with people."

Neil was among the last of two diminishing breeds in the NHL: a tough guy and a practical joker. Borowiecki said the perception he had of Neil as a fan wasn't much different than what he came to know as a teammate. "The exact same way you would think in addition to all the jokes he tried to play on everyone," said Borowiecki. "You had to have eyes in the back of your head around him."

"He really liked to laugh at his own jokes," Senators assistant general manager Randy Lee, who started out as a strength coach working with Neil, said. "He loved to be a prankster, but most of all, he lived by the [philosophy that] it's a privilege to play the greatest game in the world and you have to appreciate each and every day. Chris's dedication to the game and commitment to the uniform will be used as a measuring stick by which future players can be judged."

Two of Neil's favorite practical jokes:

"One of the best ones was when I hid in the dryer on [equipment assistant] Doug Moffatt under the warm towels. He came in to fold them all up for us, and I grabbed his arm. He didn't know what was going on. I scared the crap right out of him. I was in the big tumbler, just sitting in there," Neil said. Neil then struggled to get out of the industrial machine while Moffatt grabbed a hose in the laundry room and started spraying Neil.

"One of the best was when I hid the back of [goaltender] Patrick Lalime's car. It was running and waiting for him," Neil said with a laugh. "He's sitting there and starts pulling ahead, and I jumped over the seat. I thought he was going to have a heart attack."

Chris Phillips remembered another one: "I think it was [Neil] who took someone's jeans out of their locker and sewed the pockets shut with their wallet and keys in the pockets. It may have been the same pair of jeans that got cut short, and the guy that it happened to lost his mind. He lost his mind."

Practical joking, of course, is a two-way street. "We cut his stick two-thirds of the way through, so it looked like it was okay," Alfredsson said. "When he went out and it broke on his first shot, he almost fell on his face. He had to get the guy back, but he didn't know who it was. So he cut 15 sticks to get everybody back. He usually had a good idea of who [did] what in the dressing room."

Neil said the best joke played on him was by forward Magnus Arvedson, who took Neil's false front teeth from his locker and colored them black with a permanent marker. "He thought I cut his favorite socks, but it wasn't me; it was Stevie Martins. [That marker] was tough to get off," Neil said.

Neil lamented the passing of the practical joke. "The game has changed," he said. "There's not as many pranks. Guys are too sensitive. Those teams we had, everyone would be involved in it. It didn't matter if it was the Czech Mafia, everybody would be involved with it. It was fun."

Neil was a significant figure throughout the 2000s, when the Senators were an NHL power, winning the Presidents' Trophy in 2003 and going to the Stanley Cup Final in 2007. Neil's role expanded when Bryan Murray took over as coach for the 2005–06 season. "He saw potential in me and gave me an opportunity," Neil said of Murray.

Neil said his favorite memory is the Senators playing in the 2007 Stanley Cup Final under Murray. "That was a remarkable year," he said. "We had a group of guys that…came together. We played for one another and we played for our coach. He had everyone going on all cylinders. It didn't matter if you played 2 minutes or 22 minutes. He had everyone on the same page. That's just the way Bryan was. All those guys in that locker room would go through the wall for him."

The Senators didn't offer Neil a contract after the 2016–17 season, though he added to his legend in the playoffs. Cast aside by Coach Guy Boucher, he dressed for the first time since February for Game 5 of the second round against the New York Rangers and neutralized Rangers tough guy Tanner Glass. He had taken advantage of some Senators in the Rangers Game 4 victory to tie the series, including fighting Kyle Turris. "I didn't like what he did to Kyle, and if you guys had the camera on me up in the press box, you would have seen that," Neil said. "For me, I don't like guys taking liberties with my guys and the way the play [happened]. If I was in his boat, I'd probably do the same thing. I've got to go out and let him know. It is what it is. For me, I just wanted to let him know his fun [was] done."

"I've never known a guy so passionate about the game," center Derick Brassard said when he found out Neil was dressing for Game 5.

Neil grabbed Glass at 3:13 of the second period when the Rangers were up 2–1. Neil got a minor penalty for roughing and a misconduct, but the Senators were up 3–2 by the time he returned to the bench to a stick-tapping salute from his teammates. Neil played just 2:26, but in his teammates' minds, he made the most of the time. "That's the best penalty I've seen anybody take in a long time," Turris said. "He didn't play much, but maybe he has been our most important player."

With no contract offer from the Senators, Neil contemplated an offer from the Montreal Canadiens to attend their camp on a professional tryout, but at 38 years old, he wanted more security than that. "I felt like Benjamin Button. I thought I could play forever," Neil said. "If I could just show up and play games, that's different. To play in the NHL nowadays, you've got to have the mental capacity to really partake and really be involved in the gym. I miss playing the games. Those were the fun times. I don't miss the grind of the day-to-day that goes on behind the scenes."

Being at home with his wife, Caitlin; daughter, Hailey; and sons Cole and Finn, he realized "it just wasn't the right fit" when he looked at other playing opportunities for the 2017–18 season. "I had been so spoiled playing here in Ottawa as a Senator my whole entire career," he said. "It just didn't feel right. Once the season got going, just being able to be a part of my kids' lives, go to their practices, figure skating, take them to school, be a part of their life. It's a lot of stuff that people don't realize you miss out on."

The Neils will continue their charity work, particularly with Roger's House, for which Chris and Caitlin are honorary co-chairs, having taken over the role from former Senator Mike Fisher.

Senators general manager Pierre Dorion pretty much summed up Neil's impact on the franchise. "It's an honor and privilege to be here to recognize one of the greatest Senators of all time in Chris Neil," Dorion said the day Neil retired. "Chris was a leader, a warrior, and one of the toughest men to ever wear the jersey. He was a player that was always there for his teammates and a player feared by the opposition. He made defensemen and forwards keep their heads up for many years." And he kept Senators fans on their feet.

26 A Beautiful Night

A journey that started with a phone call from North America and got off to a poor start with some forgotten skates ended 17 years later with a tearful night and a banner in the rafters of the Canadian Tire Centre.

Daniel Alfredsson, the sixth-round draft pick who became the heart of a hockey team and a city, had his No. 11 retired by the Senators in a ceremony on December 29, 2016. It became one of the signature nights in Senators and Ottawa sports history.

Alfredsson was joined at center ice by his parents, emotional father Hasse and mom Margareta; his wife, Bibbi, and their sons, Hugo, William, Fenix, and Loui; his brother, Henrik, and sister, Cecilia; and former teammate Wade Redden.

In his speech that night, Alfredsson said:

Tonight it's not only the number 11 that goes up into the rafters; it's also the Alfredsson family name, our family name. And I want to thank the two people who made this possible: Mom and Dad.

Mom you have the biggest heart of anybody on this earth. Mom, you have the biggest heart in the world. I cherish the memories of coming home late after a game or practice knowing there would be hot chocolate and sandwiches waiting regardless if we won or lost; it didn't matter. I love you.

Dad, you are a true mentor and role model. Thank you for all your advice through all the years, even though I did not like some of it, especially for always reminding me that hockey was a game meant to be played and enjoyed at all times [and] at [all] levels.

Henrik and Redden warmed up the crowd before Alfredsson took over the proceedings. "Daniel was probably not the most talented player to come [into] the NHL," Henric said, drawing some hoots from the crowd. "But…there's always a but. He has an incredible determination and will to win, a will to try and do the best at everything he does every single day. This will to win meant no one would outwork him at practices or games or even card and board games at the Christmas table at home. This will to win helped to make him the great competitor that he is."

In 2008, inspired by his sister Cecilia's battle with generalized anxiety disorder, Alfredsson became the face of the Royal Ottawa Foundation for Mental Health's You Know Who I Am campaign to end the stigma attached to mental illness. "Without a doubt, as a family, we are most proud of the voice he gave to many people touched by mental illness," Henrik said.

Redden talked about the legacy his former teammate left for future Senators. "We were a group of selfless, hardworking kids who grew up together, became men together, and won lots of hockey games together," Redden said. "From day one, back in '96, I could see the special player Alfie was. Your legacy will be a benchmark for current and future Ottawa Senators."

Alfredsson's introduction on his big night started with a video of him working at a desk and then walking through the Senators offices and into the dressing room, where former Senators GM Randy Sexton presented him with his No. 11 sweater. He strode onto the ice to the chants of "Alfie, Alfie, Alfie!"

After thanking his parents, Alfredsson turned to his wife, Bibbi, and his sons. "I think today's ceremony says I've done a few good things to get to this point, but the best thing I've ever done was marrying my high school sweetheart. Thank you, Bibbi," he said. And to his sons, he said, "I see myself as the luckiest father in the world."

Senators captain Erik Karlsson presented Alfredsson with a painting done by Ottawa artist Tony Harris, and then Alfredsson paid tribute to his hockey family, Senators owner Eugene Melnyk and former Senators director of player personnel John Ferguson, who really pushed for a Swedish kid who wasn't on anybody's radar.

He told this story about Rick Bowness, the Senators' first coach, after he turned the puck over to a Boston Bruins Hall of Fame winger: "I think it was in Boston maybe 10 games into the season. I was still on the edge. *Have I really made the team? Am I going to stick?* I get on the right side and I throw a cross-ice pass, and Cam Neely picks it off, goes in, and scores. Instead of giving me shit, [Bowness] came over and patted me on the back and said, 'Kid, that's Cam Neely. You aren't the first one to do that, and you won't be the last.' I remember that night."

After Dave Allison replaced Bowness as coach for a couple months in 1995–96, the Senators finally made progress when new general manager Pierre Gauthier started making changes after the move from the Ottawa Civic Centre into the new Palladium. "Jacques Martin came in and was my third coach four months into my NHL career. He brought structure and team play. He pushed his team. He was into team play. He was awesome. One of the first to really put a lot of emphasis on fitness. I know a lot of people used to make fun of us because we did the interviews after the games on the bikes. He was really ahead of his time and a good teacher," Alfredsson said.

Alfredsson had particularly kind words for former Senators coach and general manager Bryan Murray. "He came in and gave us swagger. He brought us a new way to attack, to be more aggressive and succeed. But Bryan also showed us what true character is and what it meant to be a good person," Alfredsson said.

He also recognized his former veteran teammates who helped show him the way: "In my first years with the Senators, guys like [former captain] Randy Cunneyworth, Kerry Huffman, Chris Dahlquist, Steve Duchesne helped to teach me how to be a professional and how to try to win in the NHL," Alfredsson said. "I was taught how to play the right way, the Senator way, and I hope that over the years some other young players I played with…will continue to do the same…to play with the passion and will to win that can electrify this city."

Alfredsson saved some particularly passionate words for his adopted hometown (he became a Canadian citizen in September 2016 in a ceremony at the World Cup of Hockey in Toronto). "Ottawa, you have shaped my entire adult life, and for that I am eternally grateful to the city, the Senators, and the NHL for allowing me the opportunity to take this incredible journey," said Alfredsson. "Ottawa is my home. I learned hockey here. I became a father here. I cried here. I won here. I lost here. I became a captain here. I helped bring awareness to mental illness here. I became a

Canadian here. I have shared almost all of the greatest moments of my life with you in this city. Thank you so much."

Former Alfredsson teammates Chris Neil and Chris Phillips came onto the ice with the red banner featuring Alfredsson's name and number, and, helped by Karlsson, it was cranked up into the banners while U2's "Beautiful Day" played (that was the song that would play after Alfredsson scored a goal at Canadian Tire Centre). "For me, today really is a beautiful day," Alfredsson said. "This is the most incredible honor of my life, and I'm so proud to have my number retired here in Ottawa. I will forever be a Senator."

When it was over, he summed it up this way: "It's a huge honor. I think we talked about it—I did and Wade—what we accomplished here as a young group under Jacques and bringing a franchise that was young into respectability and [making it] a contender in the league…all the work we put in, a lot of us, coaches and players and staff. I think I'm part of that success, and I think it reflects that period of time. That's what I'm going to think of when I see my jersey up there."

27 Worst Senators Trade Ever

At the 1993 NHL Draft in Quebec City, Alexandre Daigle, taken first by the Ottawa Senators, famously said "I'm glad I got drafted first because no one remembers No. 2." In this case No. 2 was Chris Pronger, who was taken by the Hartford Whalers and went on to win the Norris Trophy, Hart Trophy, Stanley Cup, and two Olympic gold medals, and went into the Hockey Hall of Fame in 2015. Okay, so maybe people do remember the identity of No. 2.

Certainly few would remember No. 227. Senators general manager Randy Sexton and director of player personnel John Ferguson used that pick, which had been acquired from the Toronto Maple Leafs for defenseman Brad Miller in February 1993, to take a slight forward from Slovakia.

There are lots of stories of heartbroken kids who showed up at the draft expecting to be drafted and weren't, so it wasn't a surprise when after the Senators made their ninth-round selection (there were 11 rounds then), there wasn't that little pocket of cheering family, friends, and maybe an agent or two when the name was announced in the Quebec Colisee.

Hours later, the Senators were celebrating their good fortune of having the first pick, and Daigle was the star of the show. Former Senators president Cyril Leeder remembered:

> We go back to a reception at Le Club Sportif and everybody wants to meet Daigle. Daigle shows up. Maybe 45 minutes later this [other] guy shows up in the ugliest suit I've ever seen. Purple. Looked like he got it at a Halloween store. Big, thick tie.
>
> He sticks out his hand and says, "Hey, Randy, it's me, Pavol Demitra. Nice to meet you." He was there. He found out the Senators were meeting at Le Club Sportif, showed up, and introduced himself.

Demitra would go on to a great NHL career, but his legacy with the Senators was that he was part of the worst trade in the team's history before the salary cap and trades being evaluated as much on what a player was paid as how he played.

Demitra showed up unannounced for training camp that fall with nothing but "a bowling bag" for luggage, as former Senators vice president of corporate communications John Owens remembered. The team put him up at a downtown hotel until they could arrange accommodations, and the teenager—loving life in the NHL—racked up a nice bill for room service and movies.

Demitra was a training camp sensation even if he wasn't quite up to speed on NHL traditions. After being named a star in a 3–3 exhibition game against the Washington Capitals, he skated out to center ice and stood with teammate Alexei Yashin, not quite sure what to do. They stood there and shook hands. They stayed there until Capitals forward Peter Bondra came out as the third star and shooed them off the ice.

Demitra scored in his first NHL game against goaltender Curtis Joseph of the St. Louis Blues. A broken ankle derailed his season, and he spent most of the rest of the season with the Prince Edward Island Senators of the American Hockey League recovering from the injury.

He spent the bulk of the next two seasons going back and forth between Ottawa and PEI. After he had 28 goals and 81 points in 48 games in PEI, he earned another shot in the NHL and did well: he had 7 goals and 10 assists in 31 games.

Feeling like he had done enough to earn a shot in the NHL, Demitra was a contract holdout to start the 1996–97 season. He played with his old team in Slovakia, Dukla Trencin, and for the Las Vegas Thunder of the International Hockey League. Pierre Gauthier had taken over as Senators general manager then, and he solved the problem by getting rid of it.

The St. Louis Blues had had their eye on Demitra. Bob Plager was scouting for the Blues and told Coach Mike Keenan that Demitra had been the best player in the American Hockey League.

Keenan had a relationship with Senators coach Jacques Martin going back to their days with the Peterborough Petes of the Ontario Hockey League. They spoke, and the wheels for a deal were put in motion. Recounted Plager to Jeremy Rutherford in *100 Things Blues Fans Should Know & Do Before They Die*: "I get a phone call and it's Mike. He says, 'Bob, I got your guy. We got Pavol.'"

In the midst of the contract battle, the Senators traded Demitra, two days before his 22nd birthday, to the St. Louis Blues for defenseman Christer Olsson, who had been taken with the 275th pick in that 1993 draft. "It was the discussion, and then the circumstances were such that it got public and it became a little bit bad blood on the players' part, not on our part, so we just did it," Gauthier said. "There comes a time when you just move forward."

Cyril Leeder said, "I remember Randy Sexton telling me, the day we made it, 'That might be the worst trade you ever made.' I said, 'C'mon, Randy. A ninth-round pick.' He said, 'Cy, this kid can play.' Fergie loved him, Randy loved him. They knew that he could play. He came to camp and he was embarrassing everybody."

Olsson played 56 games in the NHL, 25 of them with the Senators, before returning to Europe to play out his career. He is now a coach. Demitra went on to score 304 goals, 464 assists and 768 points in 847 games over 16 seasons in the NHL with the Senators, Blues, Los Angeles Kings, Minnesota Wild, and Vancouver Canucks. His last season in the NHL was 2009–10 with the Canucks, and he led the 2010 Olympic tournament in scoring.

He went to the Kontinental Hockey League and died when the plane carrying Lokomotiv Yaroslavl crashed on September 7, 2011. He was 36. His death left a hole in every NHL team for which he had played, and a rift in the hearts of those who had known him. His best friend with the Blues was Keith Tkachuk. They were an unlikely duo. The big, brash American and the slight Slovak.

Recounted Rutherford: One day Tkachuk bragged to Demitra about his $11 million salary. "In U.S., $11 million is $6 million after taxes. In Slovakia, $7 million is $7 million," shot back Demitra.

Said Tkachuk: "I like it better when he just sat there and took it."

Tkachuk summed up Demitra's passing this way: "Pav was like a brother to me, and I cannot believe that he is no longer with us."

There were, no doubt, a lot of players around the NHL who felt the same way.

28 We Have a Trade to Announce

There aren't many public situations in which NHL commissioner Gary Bettman doesn't take his share of abuse from the fans. It has become a tradition for fans to boo him mercilessly when he walks onto the ice to award the Stanley Cup at the conclusion of the Final. Three work stoppages and one canceled season under his watch justify fans' wrath, but he has also worked to save bankrupt teams (yes, we're looking at you Pittsburgh, Ottawa, and Buffalo), and maintains a steadfast position that relocation is a last resort has kept teams in other markets (hi, Carolina, Florida, and Arizona). The Jets were repatriated to Winnipeg, and there's still hope in Quebec City that one day their Nordiques will return.

If the fans boo him because he's viewed as the "owners' commissioner," well, that's kind of the job description in a nutshell. But there are circumstances when the commissioner can quell the boos and actually create an air of positive anticipation. It's usually at the NHL Draft, and it's usually when he says, "We have a trade to announce." It happened in 2008 at Scotiabank Place when, as the draft approached the middle pick of the first round, he stepped to the mic and said: "We have a trade to announce…and you're going to like this one."

The minutes before the announcement had seen Senators general manager Bryan Murray, at the prodding of his scouts, make a deal to move up three spots in the draft. The Senators were sitting at No. 18. The word on the floor was that the Anaheim Ducks, sitting one spot ahead of the Senators, had their eye on a defenseman, and it just might be the same guy the Senators wanted.

Defensemen were flying off the shelves in that draft (Drew Doughty to the Los Angeles Kings, Zach Bogosian to the Atlanta Thrashers, Alex Pietrangelo to the St. Louis Blues, Luke Schenn to the Toronto Maple Leafs, Tyler Myers to the Buffalo Sabres, and Colten Teubert to the Los Angeles Kings—all gone within the first 13 picks). With the intel that the Ducks might be looking at a defenseman, and the inventory clearly diminishing, Murray looked to make a deal to move up. An obvious target was the Predators, run by his old friend and first boss, David Poile. The theory around the NHL is a general manager has a circle of about a half dozen GMs with whom he is particularly close. Given their history, Poile and Murray were both within each other's orbit, so it's logical they would talk.

Murray asked Poile about his plans for his pick. The Predators, rich in defensemen, were looking at taking a goaltender. The offer of a third-round pick in 2009 was enough to get Poile to swap picks (he wound up taking goaltender Chet Pickard). Bettman, with the crowd abandoning their abuse and expectantly hanging on his every word, announced the Predators had traded their first-round pick, No. 15, to the Ottawa Senators for the No. 18 pick and a third-round pick in 2009.

The Senators contingent organized itself at its table, grabbed a sweater, and headed for the stage. Senators captain Daniel Alfredsson stepped up while the crowd chanted his name. Alfredsson announced the Senators were taking Swedish defenseman Erik Karlsson. When the 5'10", 157-pound Karlsson walked up to the podium, he could have been mistaken for one of the kids who assist at teams' draft tables. You couldn't blame some fans were thinking, *Who's that?* That's *who they traded up for?*

Karlsson's size was the topic when Murray and Pierre Dorion—then the Senators' director of player personnel—discussed what they were going to do with their pick. Murray was skeptical about Karlsson's size. Dorion remembered Murray saying, "You know I like big bodies." Dorion pleaded his case, saying this would be the best pick for the long-term benefit of the club.

Murray finished off by asking Dorion, "How long do you want to work for me?"

Dorion answered, "A long time, but I know this is the right pick."

In his post-draft interview, Karlsson showed that while he might have been small in stature, he was big in confidence. "As first choice, it's always a lot of pressure, but I can handle pressure," he said. Asked to compare himself to a player fans might know, he replied, "I have my own game, I think."

Karlsson said the Senators' willingness to spend a draft pick to move up to select him made him feel a little in debt to the team. "That they made a trade, it says they believe in me and they want me, so I'm going to make them happy someday," he predicted.

I think he's done that.

29 Bryan's Battle

In April 2017 Bryan Murray went to Irving Greenberg Family Cancer Centre at the Queensway Carleton Hospital for the first treatment of his second wave of chemotherapy to battle his terminal colon cancer. It was his second kind of chemotherapy to treat the cancer that had been diagnosed in June 2014. In November of that year, Murray, then the Senators' general manager, had gone public with the news that he had stage 4 colon cancer and it was terminal. A feature with TSN's Michael Farber, himself a cancer survivor, helped Murray get the word out to people to go for colonoscopies.

He hadn't had a colonoscopy himself. "Like a lot of men do, I put it off," Bryan told Farber. "A simple colonoscopy, in my case, probably would have solved this problem I have." That was Murray: he chose to take the worst circumstances imaginable for himself and turn them into a positive for others.

On that rainy day in April, he was at the cancer center for a treatment with brutal side effects that would hopefully prolong his life—he was already beating the odds by making it this far—but the thing that stood out that day was the life he gave to others around him at the cancer center. He hadn't been there for a few weeks. A scan had revealed his first type of chemotherapy treatment was no longer effective, and tumors in his colon, lungs, and liver had begun to grow again. He took time to consider other options: a radical new treatment in Toronto, this different chemotherapy, or just do nothing and let the cancer proceed unabated.

The side effects of the experimental treatment were quite unpleasant, plus he didn't want to spend any number of his remaining days commuting to Toronto. He opted for the new chemotherapy treatment.

As we made our way to Pod 4 for his treatment, faces lit up as Murray, in a gray dress shirt, jeans, and black loafers, made his way through the ward. "Hi, Bryan. We haven't seen you for a while," beamed one of the nurses. "I was going to quit, but I'd miss you," Murray said, to the nurse's delight. "I was looking at other options, and one of them was death, so I just decided to come back." That summed up Murray's sarcastic sense of humor. It was one of the best parts of his personality.

As we made our way to the check-in where Murray would be weighed and answer some questions, a woman popped out from around the corner. She recognized Murray immediately. "Oh, I'm going to faint," she said, her eyes immediately filling with tears.

Her brother had colon cancer and was undergoing treatment. Since Murray had been so public with his battle, she took a chance and contacted the Senators to see if maybe Murray could send back an email with some advice about her brother's treatment. She was shocked when Murray called her back and spent a long time on the telephone explaining what had and hadn't worked for him, including the wonderful things they were doing at the Ottawa Integrative Cancer Centre. When she said she was unsure if they could afford the supplementary treatments, Murray told her he would put in a good word for them at the OICC to see if they could work out a deal. (He later told me that if they hadn't been able to work that out, he would have paid for the brother's treatment himself. That was the kind of man Bryan was.)

Murray became the honorary chairman of the OICC's first fund-raising campaign in April 2016. The $5 million goal was to make the center's services available to people who couldn't afford them. Murray said yoga, mistletoe injections, and acupuncture had all helped him. That was the message he had passed on to this woman and her brother.

"I'm just going to get [my brother] a coffee," the woman said, swiping the back of her hand across her cheeks. "Thank you again, Bryan, thank you," she said.

As we walked away, Murray said, "This is not a good place to meet people."

He settled into his reclining chair, and the nurse attached the IV and pump contraption to his portacath. "This is going to give you cold hands and cold feet," she said. "You don't want to touch anything cold. I'm not kidding. If you have to go into the fridge, put gloves on. When you go outside, wrap your face in a scarf."

"At least it's springtime," Bryan said of the promise of warmer temperatures.

Coach Bryan Murray yells at an official during a 2008 game.

One after another, workers on the ward came over to say hello. It was clear how happy they were to see him. The man created a positive buzz in the ward. That was Bryan and his cancer battle. As grim and dark as it was for him, he managed to inspire others and put smiles on their faces.

30 The Hamburglar

It became a picture that summed up Andrew "the Hamburglar" Hammond's historic run in 2015: Ottawa Senators forward Curtis Lazar holding aloft and eating a hamburger that had been thrown onto the ice at Canadian Tire Centre.

It was moments after a 6–4 win by the Senators over the Boston Bruins on March 19, 2015, that drew them within two points of the Bruins in the Eastern Conference playoff race and continued Hammond's transformation into legend. People took to throwing hamburgers onto the ice during the run. A few days earlier, Hammond had held aloft an unwrapped hamburger that had been tossed onto the ice. This night, Lazar unwrapped one and ate it as he left the ice. "That burger really could have used some ketchup," tweeted Lazar (@CurtisLazar95) afterward. "C'mon people!!!"

It was an unimaginable scene just five weeks earlier. On February 10 the Senators were 14 points behind the Bruins in the battle for the second wild-card spot in the Eastern Conference, and the season appeared lost. On February 16 things apparently got even worse. No. 1 goaltender Craig Anderson was already out with a hand injury when Ottawa forward Clarke MacArthur, trying to break up a breakaway by Carolina Hurricanes forward Jay McClement late in the second period, collided with Senators goaltender Robin Lehner. Both sustained concussions that would profoundly affect their careers with the Senators and alter hockey history.

MacArthur would play just eight regular-season games over two seasons; have a brief, spectacular return to the playoffs in 2017; and then be forced to retire. It would be Lehner's last game as a Senator.

Hammond, signed as a free agent in March 2013, was a 27-year-old with a 7–13–2 record and an .898 save percentage with Binghamton of the American Hockey League that season. He was pulled 36 seconds into a game against the Lehigh Valley Phantoms on December 17 when he gave up three goals on three shots in 21 seconds. He had 35 minutes of NHL experience. What he did over the next two months has become legendary in Ottawa and resonated across the NHL. It was a story of possibility, improbability, and just plain fun.

As he prepared for his first NHL start against the Montreal Canadiens on February 18, I stood waiting by his locker stall. Respecting the game-day routines of a lot of goaltenders, who don't speak on the day of games, I asked, "Andrew, do you talk on game days?"

"I guess so," he said. "I've never really had anybody want to talk to me on a game day." Beautiful. As we came to discover over the next couple months, Hammond had a wonderful everyman quality about him, never taking what was happening around him or to him for granted.

"He's the most normal goaltender I've ever met," defenseman Mark Borowiecki said. "He's an easy guy to talk to. He's not weird on game days. He's just a normal guy, and I think that's what is so cool about him. You get some goalies, where they're either so intense on game days you can't even look at them, or some of them that have so many weird superstitions."

But what was the Hamburglar origin story? Hammond got the nickname from a teammate at Bowling Green University; it was bestowed upon him because of his name and his ability to steal games (instead of hamburgers). He had a Hamburglar likeness on his mask but with a twist: the face was that of Alfred E. Neuman of *Mad* magazine fame.

Hammond reeled off five straight wins, giving up five goals, before the Senators lost in a shootout at the Minnesota Wild on March 3. He then had another nine wins to go 14–0–1 in his first 15 NHL starts. He equaled the record set by Boston Bruins goaltender Frank Brimsek in 1938–39 by allowing two goals or less in his first 12 games as an NHL starter.

With a chance to match the record set by former Senator Patrick Lalime of a point in his first 16 NHL starts (Lalime went 14–0–2 in 1996–97), Hammond suffered his first loss on March 26 against the New York Rangers, giving up five goals on 22 shots while nursing a lower-body injury he sustained in the previous game.

"I'm very, very impressed with the way he's handling himself," Lalime said. "It's a great story. The way he came in, a little bit like I did at the beginning, like someone who's not supposed to be there, someone who's been waiting to get a chance to play and prove he can do the job, and that's what he's doing."

As Hammond racked up the wins, the hype around him grew. TSN 1200, the Senators' radio rights holder, had a Hamburglar tribute song that used a riff from Billy Idol's "White Wedding." McDonald's gifted him with a card good for hamburgers for life after Senators fan John Bergeron—who owned six McDonald's franchises in the Ottawa Valley and was the father of Hammond's college coach, Chris Bergeron—worked out a deal with the head office in Toronto. "I guess at the end of the day I know I'll never end up starving," Hammond said. "If hockey doesn't work out, I'll have a meal plan."

Hammond just went with the flow. "It's something, you know...if it ended today and I looked back on it and I wasn't having fun, it wouldn't be worth it," he said. "It's something I've worked hard for, and there's a fine line between having fun and doing your job still, and I think I'm able to manage that right now. I'm really enjoying it, though. It's a lot of fun. The city is kind of rallying around the team right now, and it's been a blast."

He finished it off with six more wins, vaulting the Senators into an unlikely playoff spot. The total: 20–1–2, with a 1.79 goals-against average and a .941 save percentage.

The Senators met the Montreal Canadiens in the playoffs. They didn't play well in front of Hammond and lost Game 1 4–3 in Montreal. The team lost Game 2 3–2 in overtime. Hammond gave up seven goals on 81 shots (.914 save percentage) in the two games and gave up the net to Craig Anderson for Game 3 in Ottawa. The Senators lost Game 3 by a 2–1 score in overtime (and, ultimately, the series 4–2).

Hammond was rewarded with a three-year, $4.05 million contract in the off-season, but he would play only 30 more games for the Senators. In 2016–17, Nicholle Anderson, the wife of Senators goaltender Craig Anderson, was diagnosed with cancer, requiring Anderson to be away. It looked like another opportunity for Hammond, but he sustained a hip injury, which would require surgery. The Senators acquired Mike Condon in Hammond's absence. Condon started 27 games straight and helped the Senators make the playoffs. The bottom line: Hammond was placed on waivers almost two years to the day after his historic run had begun.

Back in the American Hockey League to start the 2017–18 season, he was part of a trade with the Colorado Avalanche on November 5 that brought Matt Duchene to Ottawa. "You look all around the league and it happens very quick," Hammond said of the way things unfolded. "I was happy for Mike, and people might not necessarily believe that, but look how quick things change. Last year he was basically in the same position as me, and it worked out very well for him. Things change quick."

His brief, spectacular run is now held up as hope for any team that finds itself on the outside looking in come February.

"Hey," they can say, "remember the Hamburglar run?"

31 A Game Puck for Nicholle

No doubt, 2016–17 was one of the most complicated, unexpected, compelling, and inexplicable seasons in the Ottawa Senators' first 25 years. There was a lot going on, on and off the ice, and it all coalesced into a remarkable season that left the Senators one goal short of going to the second Stanley Cup Final in their modern history.

The Senators had Guy Boucher behind the bench in his first season as coach, defenseman Erik Karlsson had a regular season that made him a contender for his third Norris Trophy, and the team bought into Boucher's plan and played its best hockey when it mattered most. But what made the season particularly special was the way the team coped with the situation that engulfed No. 1 goaltender Craig Anderson and his wife, Nicholle, as the season got under way.

On October 29, after Anderson had taken a couple personal leaves—including one beginning on October 27—an emotional Senators general manager Pierre Dorion announced that Nicholle had been diagnosed with stage 4 nasopharyngeal carcinoma—a rare form of cancer in the nose and throat.

Anderson left the team to be with her as she underwent treatment. But in the first game after Anderson's latest departure, backup Andrew Hammond injured his groin against the Calgary Flames, leaving the Senators with inexperienced Chris Driedger as their last line of defense. In what became one of the remarkable story lines in a season full of them, Nicholle told her husband to return to his shorthanded team.

In one of the most epic performances of recent memory in the NHL, Anderson returned to the team and had an emotional 37-save shutout in the Senators' 2–0 win against the Edmonton Oilers. Anderson was named the game's first star, and the reaction of the classy Oilers fans—and Edmonton goaltender Cam Talbot, who remained in the tunnel by the ice to applaud Anderson's performance—put an exclamation point on one of the most memorable nights in Senators history. It was Anderson's second shutout in a row, coming off a 22-save shutout in a 3–0 win against the Vancouver Canucks the night before he left the team.

In a touching scene in their dressing room at Rogers Arena, as recounted by those who were there, the Senators awarded the game puck to Nicholle. "Words can't describe it. It was Game 8 of a season, but…it's something I know I won't forget in my hockey career," Senators veteran forward Chris Kelly said of the atmosphere in the Senators' dressing room after the Edmonton game.

"We gave him the puck to give to his wife, because definitely she was the one that [had] the biggest battle and she was the one who told her husband, 'You've got to go [t]here,' and it freed him to be able to come and get as free of a mind as you can get to focus on a game," Boucher said.

Senators captain Erik Karlsson said the players had done a good job of focusing on the game, but when it was over and they gathered in the dressing room, the impact of the situation hit home. "Very emotional. Very emotional. That's when everything kind of all let down," Karlsson said. "We all knew what was going on. Craig came in a day early and we didn't really touch on it before the game. Once the game finished, with the result we had and the performance we had from Andy…everybody let their guard down and it was very tough. It was very emotional, but I think it was something that was necessary to do, and you could really see how much everybody in here cares for each other and especially for Andy."

Anderson played 13 more games before taking what would turn out to be a two-month leave of absence beginning on December 6. He returned February 11.

Mike Condon, who was acquired from the Pittsburgh Penguins for a fifth-round draft pick on November 2, 2017, wound up appearing in 27 straight games for the Senators and saved their season. He had a record of 13–8–5 and helped the Senators keep their head above water until Anderson's return. Anderson, 35, was brilliant down the stretch with a 13–5–3 record. The Senators finished in second place in the Atlantic Division with 98 points. They defeated the Boston Bruins 4–2 in the first round and the New York Rangers 4–2 in the second round.

They fell to the Pittsburgh Penguins—who would go on to win their second Stanley Cup in a row—in double overtime of Game 7 of the Eastern Conference Final. Anderson's 2017 playoff stats: 11–8, with a 2.34 goals-against average and .922 save percentage with one shutout.

On May 27, as the Senators lamented their exit from the playoffs and the end to their remarkable season, there was good news. Anderson said Nicholle told him on the morning of Game 7 of the Eastern Conference Final that tests had shown she was cancer-free. Her message, as paraphrased by Anderson: "Things are going in the right direction. Her message was go out there and have fun."

Anderson described the season as a "roller coaster," saying, "Ups and downs. Emotionally. Physically. I think a lot of life lessons learned this year not only by myself but staff and players all together. He said, "Hockey is a job for us, and it put it in perspective this year. I think we played better because we realized life happens and you make the most of your opportunity when you have a group that we all cared about so much together in this room. It makes you play a little bit better and care about each other a little bit more."

Anderson said the experience of the 2016–17 season made him a changed player. "One hundred percent. We always grow as players," he said. "When you go through adversity, it's not what happens to you, it's how you react. I think we all responded in the right way. I was able to use hockey and use my teammates as a source to get away from personal life and have a three-hour moment of peace. When you're on the ice, there's nothing in the world but that puck, and you're competing, you're at peace. You have nothing to worry about. That was the three hours that I had, and then you go back to life right after."

Nicholle took her experience and turned it into a way to help others facing the same fight.

She became the NHL's Hockey Fights Cancer ambassador in November 2017. "I said yes right away, because it's something I feel passionate about, and the NHL has been great," she told the *Ottawa Sun.* "Every minute counts now," she continued. "I look at life totally different. I look at things now and things that used to stress me out.… I think, *Is this important?* I say, 'Nope, I'd rather just go to the park and swim with my kids and do other things.' It makes you really value your life, and each moment counts."

32 The Franchise Kid

At 42 years old, Alexandre Daigle still has that charisma, the star quality that contributed to him becoming the first pick in the 1993 NHL Draft and that still turns heads when he walks into a room.

On one cold February 2017 night in Victoriaville, Quebec, Daigle—handsome in a sharp suit, wearing an easy smile—strode into a room upstairs at the Colisée Desjardins, the home of the Victoriaville Tigres, where Daigle was a junior hockey star and where his No. 91 would be retired on this night.

The heads turned and watched him walk across the room, now with a wife and three kids in his wake. He didn't look a lot different from the 18-year-old kid who had walked up onto the stage at Le Colisée in Quebec City in 1993 and was the Ottawa Senators' first pick in the draft. He was built up to be the most exciting prospect to come out of Quebec since Mario Lemieux. TSN did a big feature on him: *The Franchise Kid.*

The Quebec Nordiques, led by Marcel Aubut, were hungry to own the next Quebecois superstar. They offered prospect Peter Forsberg, whom they had acquired from the Philadelphia Flyers as part of their massive deal for Eric Lindros, for the Senators' pick in the draft, according to one member of the Senators staff at the time. The Senators said no thanks. "We're aware of what's available in this year's draft, and I don't know whether we'd be willing to part with somebody we believe can be an outstanding player down the road," Senators president Randy Sexton said.

Fast-forward to 2013; a story by the Canadian Press to set up the 2013 NHL Draft branded Daigle the biggest bust of the past 20 years. Fair? Probably not. His 327 points in 616 NHL games (301 of those games with Ottawa, in which he accrued 172 points on 74 goals and 98 assists) rank him 26th in the 1993 draft (Paul Kariya was first, with 989 points). His results are solidly in the middle of the pack in the first round. There are other first picks in the history of the draft that fared much worse for various reasons, such as Greg Joly in 1974, Brian Lawton in 1983, Patrik Stefan in 1999, and more recently, Nail Yakupov in 2012, who's on his third team and still trying to find his stride.

But the hype around Daigle coming out of junior meant that anything short of a Hall of Fame career wouldn't have been enough to match the expectations when you consider he made a run at Lemieux's single-season scoring record before a couple of suspensions derailed him. He was drafted first overall and then awarded a ridiculously large five-year, $12.25 million first contract.

When things had started to sour for Daigle in Ottawa, I remember one member of the staff saying, "Alex is a great kid and he loves everything about being a hockey player except playing the games." Daigle always strove for balance in his life, and when he wasn't at the rink, he wasn't consumed by hockey. His friends were from other walks of life. He loved movies—*The Natural*, for one.

His wit was something uncommon among players known for gushing cliches. Before his rookie season, he dressed up in nine different costumes to promote Score hockey cards. One of the costumes was that of a nurse. The theme of the campaign was that if you wanted to see Daigle in uniform, you had to buy Score hockey cards. It was…well…outside the box.

John Owens, then the Senators' vice president of corporate communications, remembered:

"Johnny." One of the few people who ever called me Johnny. "They want me to wear a nurse's outfit." I said, "Tell me about it." "They've got all these uniforms." They already had the pitch line. They had the contract before he played a game. If you want Alex in a uniform, you have to buy from Score. That was the deal. I asked him, "How do you feel about it?" He goes, "I'm okay."

I was sitting there, and…"Ugggghh, if you're okay with it, I'm okay with it." I thought it was a great idea, and I still do. The week after the furor started I've got—on the same day—a producer from [Jay] Leno and a producer from [David] Letterman wanting him on the show.

The Senators, mortified by the backlash, did not allow Daigle to do the late-night circuit. Owens barely hung on to this job. It didn't make things easier for Daigle, whose quick and clever wit was something conservative NHL types didn't appreciate. They liked their kids seen and not heard. Daigle was gifted with a sense of humor rooted in sarcasm. "He was funnier in his second language than most people are in their first," Owens said.

When asked what separated him from Eric Lindros, the enfant terrible of the NHL at the time who was the first pick in 1991 of the Nordiques, Daigle replied, "I drink my beer." It was a wicked shot at Lindros, who had been accused—and found innocent—of spitting beer on a woman in a Whitby, Ontario, bar. "By commenting on [Daigle] or talking about him, I'd be making nurses look bad," Lindros later said before the Senators and Flyers met in October 1993.

After being selected first by the Senators, Daigle summed up the honor: "I'm glad I got drafted first because no one remembers No. 2." That would be Chris Pronger, who would go on to win a Stanley Cup, a Hart Trophy, and a Norris Trophy and be inducted into the Hall of Fame in 2015.

Daigle got pulled off a commercial flight by police in Pittsburgh early in the 1996–97 season for making a joke about a bomb. "I was just playing around, and [the flight attendant] took it seriously. I said to Trevor [Timmins, team scouting director], 'Watch out for your bomb there,' and pointed to his computer. She wasn't very happy I said it." The fact that Air Force One and President Bill Clinton were on the flight line at the same time might have made people a tad more skittish too.

Senators forward Tom Chorske, Daigle's teammate from 1995 to 1997, said:

> I really liked him. He kind of had a persona about him and a reputation, a public image which was somewhat created by him and the media and maybe even by the Sens. They were doing all this promotional stuff. He perpetuated the good-looking, cool guy, which was fine, and he was, but he was a good guy.
>
> He wasn't negative. For a guy under a lot of pressure, there wasn't "Woe is me" or "This is BS." He was funny. He had a really good sense of humor, always trying to make light of things and crack jokes. He was labeled as a bust, and he really wasn't. The perception was he was built up to be the next Mario Lemieux coming out of the Q, and he wasn't....He rolled with the punches, knew it was part of the territory.

On that night in Victoriaville, at his first big public event since retiring from hockey in 2010, he wasn't making any apologies for the way things had turned out with the Senators. "I had a great time," he said. "People tend to tell stories, and it's not your story. I'm not going to start correcting everybody. I had a great time. I was 18 years old. Yeah, in retrospect, would I [have liked] to go to Colorado or a big team, [a good team]? Yeah, for sure. Would that have helped me? Yeah. That was not the hand I was dealt. What are you going to do? [Ottawa is] a great city. Tough to beat."

Daigle had a good year his first season as an 18-year-old: 20 goals and 31 assists for 51 points. He finished tied for fifth in rookie scoring (Mikael Renberg of the Philadelphia Flyers led with

82 points; Daigle's teammate Alexei Yashin was second with 79 points). "On the ice it was not perfect. If you look my first year, I had 20 goals. If you look now, in the last 25 years, how many rookies at 18 had 20 goals? Do that math," Daigle said. "After that it was a half year [a lockout wiped out the first half of the 1994–95 season] and I scored 16. I was on track for 30, but it was still not good enough, because the standard was 50 goals, with nobody around."

Daigle was referring to the lack of talent on the Senators in those early seasons. "I don't want to put anybody down, but I think we had 11 rookies and the rookies were 27, 28, 29 years old. They were minor leaguers. It was a different game," he said. "At the end of the day, it was five years of my life [in Ottawa] and I had 12, 13 years of pro hockey. It was a great run, man. If you look at it, I was telling my friends yesterday, people don't realize something. We're really hard on Canadian players and Quebecois. There's only 700 jobs [in the NHL]. It's still the same amount of jobs, but now we're competing against the rest of the world."

Daigle was traded to the Philadelphia Flyers in the 1998–99 season and then to the Tampa Bay Lightning. At 25, he retired and moved to Los Angeles. He was linked to former Playmate of the Year and *Baywatch* star Pamela Anderson and got involved on the fringes of Hollywood. He came back to hockey for the 2002–03 season, signing with the Pittsburgh Penguins, and earned another shot in the NHL after playing in the minors. In a rich turnabout for a player touted as an offensive power, Daigle's second life in the NHL saw him as a defensive player.

He wound up having perhaps his best season in 2003–04 with the Minnesota Wild under defensive genius Jacques Lemaire, who wouldn't play a player unless he could take care of his own end of the ice. Daigle led the Wild in scoring and played a solid two-way game. He played one more season after the lockout year in 2004–05 and then moved to Europe to finish his playing career.

Now he was being celebrated in Victoriaville, and on that night, he was comfortable in his own skin. He was working with a partner in the television industry, running MTL Grande Studios. He was spending about six weeks a year in Los Angeles, leaning on contacts he made during his two-year sabbatical there.

"Nobody knows it, but I'm kind of shy, but I love being around those guys, and I've [known] those guys for a lot of years. I've been in L.A. since I was 21," he said. "I think it's a perfect fit as far as starting in the business, trying to know the studio business, the rental business, equipment, everything from equipment to technicians. If I can do that for two, three, four, five years, we'll see where that will lead me. I love it.… I'm in charge of bringing people in. It's not a bad job. Tough to beat, man. Living the dream."

One last question: when was he happiest playing hockey? "Happiest?" he replied. "When you play midget. That's when you have the most fun."

33 Pucks, Poutine, and Party

There are few things in hockey that can give you goose bumps like the atmosphere in the Bell Centre the moment when the Montreal Canadiens players skate onto the ice for the start of a game. They stream through the gate at the end of their bench, looking like a red power cord injecting electricity right to the rafters of the eight-story building. For Senators fans, there's nothing like the anticipation of seeing their team shut those fans up, which the Senators have done often. The Senators had a 24–26–4–4 record at the Bell Centre through the 2017–18 season.

If you're a Senators fan, a road trip to Montreal is a must. There's something about playing in Montreal that has brought out the best in the Senators. Maybe it's the food. Over the years, I've been in the visitors' dressing room after a game and seen the table in the middle of the room—usually covered with sports energy drinks, packages of gum, and tape—stacked high with boxes of the famous Montreal hot dogs.

It's such an easy trip from Ottawa to Montreal. Senators fans owe it to themselves to make the two-hour journey by car down Highway 417, or better yet—especially once the snow starts to fly—take the train, which will drop you a couple blocks away from the Bell Centre.

When the inevitable end to the long and spectacular life of the Montreal Forum finally loomed in the early '90s, the Canadiens got it right when it came to a new house. The Molson Centre, as the Bell Centre was known for the first six years of its existence, continued the Canadiens' presence in downtown, moving east and south from the Forum's location at St. Catherine St. and Atwater Ave., to their new digs at Avenue des Canadiens-de-Montréal and De La Montagne St.

The Bell Centre is part museum, and hockey fans can amuse themselves with a walk around its halls before a game and seeing pictures of the great Canadiens teams of the past. There are also guided tours on nonevent days that will take you through the Canadiens' dressing room and to the press lounge, alumni lounge, the press box, and the postgame interview room. The tour costs $20 for adults and $15 for kids and seniors.

There's also the plaza on the east side of the rink, where there are statues of Canadiens greats Howie Morenz, Maurice Richard, Jean Beliveau, and Guy Lafleur, and tributes to the 100 greatest moments in Habs history.

There's no shortage of bars and restaurants within easy walking distance of the Bell Centre for pre- and postgame food and drinks. One of my favorite spots over my 30 years of covering hockey in Montreal is Hurley's Irish Pub at 1225 Crescent St., about a 10-minute walk from the Bell Centre. It's a pub in the real tradition, with live music every night of the week. The main floor isn't a sports bar; there's one dusty television there, a holdover from the 1980s.

The crowd is a cross-section of Montreal: French, English, college kids, businessmen, tourists, hockey fans, young, old. Hurley's has also been a popular spot among media guys (stay away from them; they'll want you to buy beer), players, executives, and officials.

There's a sports bar upstairs with lots of HD screens if you're still looking for a hockey fix or can't find a seat on the main floor. Across the hall from the "rec room" is the music room, where there is more live music.

Other spots worth visiting: the Sir Winston Churchill Pub (1459 Crescent); the Irish Embassy at 1234 Bishop St., a block over from Crescent; and McLean's at 1210 Peel St.

If you're looking for a top-of-the-line meal, I have two recommendations: Da Vinci (located at 1180 Bishop St.) is where you'll get some of the best Italian cooking in the city and maybe catch a glimpse of some players or hockey executives. Steak? Go to Gibby's in Old Montreal (298 Place D'Youville), which is located in a magnificent old stone stable.

Oh yes, if you want that poutine, the decadent mix of french fries, gravy, and cheese curds, head over to La Belle Province, a fast-food place native to Quebec, at 1216 Peel St. You won't have a tastier meal in a Styrofoam bowl with a plastic fork in your life.

Hockey and food in Montreal—you can't go wrong.

34 Tanks for Nothing

It is the question that begs to be answered: if the 1992–93 Ottawa Senators were throwing a game, how would you know?

The expansion Senators were one of the worst teams of all time, losing 70 of the 84 games they played that first season. But the rumor of a plan being in place for the Senators to lose their final game of the 1992–93 season to guarantee they would get the first pick in the 1993 NHL Draft—the consensus pick was Quebec Major Junior Hockey League star Alexandre Daigle—started to circulate on the very day the Senators made Daigle the first pick of that draft. Defenseman Chris Pronger went second to the Hartford Whalers.

Two months later, on August 19, 1993, *Ottawa Sun* columnist Earl McRae first reported rumors of off-the-record comments made by Senators owner Bruce Firestone to a group of reporters and broadcasters at Le Club Sportive in Quebec City on the night of the draft. Over celebratory drinks, Firestone is alleged to have said there was a plan in place to make sure the Senators finished last.

In the *Ottawa Citizen* and in his book *Road Games: A Year in the Life of the NHL*, Roy MacGregor—one of the group of reporters who talked to Firestone in Quebec City—quoted Firestone as saying there was a plan to pull the goalie, a move usually used to try for a win, to ensure a loss. He also reported four players had been offered guaranteed spots on the team the following season in exchange for making sure the Senators finished last.

Two days before McRae's first report, Firestone sold his half of the Senators to Rod Bryden and resigned from the club in a tearful meeting with Senators staff. As the headlines said, the rumors of tanking created a "firestorm" around Firestone.

While they might have been arguably the worst team of all time, that didn't mean the players on that Senators team didn't have pride, and the allegations stung. "If Bruce Firestone talked to four players, he should name names," Senators forward Mike Peluso said at the time. "If my name was mentioned, I would challenge anybody to call me on it because that's the biggest load of bull I've ever heard. I could care less about Alexandre Daigle.... In fact, I think Chris Pronger is a better player. He continued, "I just have to worry about myself. Nobody is going to question by integrity. We had a lot of chickens on that team, but that doesn't mean we were throwing games."

Senators captain Laurie Boschman gathered his teammates after a practice in March and said it was the players against the world. Management's goal and the priority of finishing last was clear to the players: no help would be forthcoming.

"We tried our best every night," Senators director of player personnel John Ferguson told the *Ottawa Sun* after the season. "It got to the point where we knew we couldn't improve the club a great deal if we wanted that first-round draft pick. It was difficult because you have to have integrity, but we couldn't afford to improve by one or two points and blow that first pick."

"The whole thing at the end of the year, the tanking of the games story. My God, we were all playing for our jobs. We weren't good enough to tank," defenseman Norm Maciver, the team's leading scorer that season, said in an interview for this book. "That's the story. We didn't have a good enough team to tank a game. The guys were trying to extend their careers, get new contracts. That was kind of embarrassing that we were accused of that.... That was the most disappointing thing that they actually thought we really tried to do that. It was a bunch of guys that for dear life were trying to hang onto their NHL careers."

The Senators lost 17 of their last 18 games that season, including the 4–2 finale, lost to the Boston Bruins at the Ottawa Civic Centre. The Senators wound up tied with the San Jose Sharks with 24 points, but the Senators were last, and got the first pick, based on the Sharks having one more win.

The Sharks got to 24 points first with a 5–2 win against the Edmonton Oilers on April 6 and pulled two points ahead of the Senators. The Senators, who hadn't won on the road (a losing streak of 39 games), stunned everybody by defeating the New York Islanders 5–3 four days later on Long Island to get to 24 points on April 10.

The Senators couldn't afford to earn another point if they wanted to guarantee the first pick in the draft, and lost their remaining three games, 4–2 to the Bruins on April 11, 6–2 to the Quebec Nordiques on April 13, and 4–2 to the Bruins on April 14.

After Firestone's comments in Quebec City, the rumors about some kind of tanking plan were investigated internally by Senators owner Rod Bryden, who had taken over the running of the team in January. When the story broke, Bryden said:

> All I can say is that it is absolutely and categorically not true. I heard the same kind of rumors in July and I checked to see if there was any possibility it happened. I came to the conclusion there was nothing to it.
>
> I'm certain there is no such plan. All of the people who manage hockey operations from all aspects of the hockey club from early January reported to me, not to Bruce.

According to the Senators' internal investigation released to the media:

- Firestone had made it clear to the team heading into the season that the franchise goal was to earn 22 or more points to beat out the 1974–75 Washington Capitals' total of 21.

- In December 1992 Firestone reaffirmed the 22-point goal in a player-management meeting, regardless of what the Sharks did.
- In early February Bryden proposed to the Sharks that the team that finished with the most points between them get the first pick in a prearranged trade between the two teams. It would remove any speculation about tanking. Bryden's offer was rejected by the Sharks.
- The Senators admitted they were concerned that if the Nordiques or Bruins—whose places in the standings in the same division had been decided when they played the Senators—might dress a "B" team to try and prevent the top pick in the draft from arriving in their division. If the Nordiques or Bruins had dressed a less experienced lineup, the Senators would have done the same.

After the story broke, NHL commissioner Gary Bettman, on August 23, appointed lawyers Arnold Burns and Yves Fortier to assist NHL lawyer Jeff Pash with investigating whether there was any truth to the story.

Senators management, players, and media were summoned to Toronto to be interviewed. "I remember going in and just thinking, *This is ridiculous*," Maciver said. "There's no way we would have tried to tank a game. We did everything we could so statistically we wouldn't have the worst record in league history. To think we were trying to tank was the furthest thing from the truth."

"I said to them in the inquisition, 'You know, we have 60-plus losses?' We knew how to lose," Senators defenseman Brad Shaw recalled for the *Ottawa Citizen*. "We needed so many things to fall into place just to have a chance to win that it was kind of humorous they were investigating in the first place."

A good point by Maciver: as the team's best player that season, it would have made sense to have him be part of a plan to throw games, but he said he had never heard about such a plan, was never approached about, nor did he discuss, any plan to lose intentionally. "No, of course not. I was the leading scorer and probably played more minutes than anybody, and I never heard a thing," he said. "I would have figured I would have heard something. It was never uttered. I just found it very ridiculous that we had to fly to Toronto and explain it to somebody."

After the investigation, Bettman said there was no basis in fact to the comments but fined the Senators $100,000 for Firestone's "intemperate" remarks and for failing to notify the league of the remarks.

In late August 1993, Firestone was quoted in *Sports Illustrated*: "We're all human beings. To say that the importance of drafting first—the question—had not entered my mind is untrue. But you think about these things, and you reject improper behavior. What was important is that like all people of integrity, we decided not to do it."

Of the guarantee to four players of jobs in exchange for making sure the team finished last, Firestone said to sports network TSN: "I said it's no coincidence those players will be back with the team, because those players care about the team. They want to get better, they want to improve. That's a very harmless comment."

Maciver said the best evidence that the players weren't part of any tanking plan came on April 10 on Long Island when, after 39 straight road losses, the Senators finally won a game away from home. "If they had seen the celebration when we beat the Islanders and we finally won that first road game," he said, "they would have known we weren't tanking."

The legacy of this bizarre conclusion to the Senators' first season in the NHL: to lessen the temptation for teams to tank, the league adopted a draft lottery in 1995.

35 Is There Anything Better Than a Good Goaltending Fight?

Senators broadcaster Gord Wilson asked that question in a famous soundbite, and the answer is…well…no.

The Senators have had a couple dandies. What would you expect from a team that had goaltender Ray Emery, who once adorned his mask with images of boxers Jack Johnson, Marvin Hagler, and former heavyweight champion Mike Tyson? That Tyson mask didn't go over too well, by the way. Emery wore the mask for one game, a 5–0 loss to the Boston Bruins in January 2006, after which it was pointed out that it probably wasn't a good idea to have the image of a convicted rapist on his mask. "We didn't ask him not to wear the mask," Senators general manager John Muckler said. "We just had a discussion about what was right and wrong, and he said he would take it off."

Emery had perhaps the best night of goaltender fisticuffs in the history of the Senators on February 22, 2007, against the Buffalo Sabres. The game got ugly after Senators forward Chris Neil leveled Sabres star Chris Drury with a hit from the side. Emery was playing his first game after serving a three-game suspension for slashing Maxim Lapierre of the Montreal Canadiens.

At 5:07 of the second period, Neil fought Drew Stafford, and it was on. Skirmishes of varying degrees broke out among all the players on the ice, and Emery and Buffalo goaltender Martin Biron met near center ice. It did not end well for Biron as Emery pounded him down to the ice with half a dozen rights. When Biron was getting up, he took a poke at Emery and it looked like they would go again, but at that point, Sabres tough guy Andrew Peters intervened and grabbed hold of the front of Emery's sweater with his left hand.

Emery, who had shed his mask to fight with Biron, had a huge grin on his face as Peters, still wearing his helmet, threw a couple over-the-top rights. Peters threw three more rights that connected while Emery threw a couple rights that came up short before the linesmen jumped in to break it up.

At that point, Senators coach Bryan Murray was standing up on the boards at the end of the Ottawa bench gesturing and yelling at Buffalo coach Lindy Ruff. There was a lot of yelling and finger-pointing, with former Sabres tough guy Rob Ray (also a former Senator) caught in the middle in his rinkside broadcast position. The look on his face was priceless.

If you were going to list the top three goaltending fights in Senators history, the Emery scraps in Buffalo would be No. 1. And No. 2 would easily be Senators goaltender Jani Hurme against Los Angeles Kings goaltender Félix Potvin on December 20, 2001. Potvin became involved with Senators tough guy Andre Roy when their legs got tangled in the crease. Roy took a whack at Potvin's pads. They exchanged shoves, and Potvin took a wild swing with his left hand and then with his blocker before L.A.'s Ian Lapierre arrived on the scene.

The players paired off, with a linesman restraining Potvin. Adam Mair came off the bench to fight Ottawa's Chris Neil, a couple old adversaries from their junior hockey days. Potvin headed toward the Senators bench, where Hurme was lurking after Mair had come on the ice to give the Kings an advantage.

Potvin had a reputation as a good scrapper after beating Philadelphia Flyers goaltender Ron Hextall in a scrap in 1996. Both Potvin and Hurme still had their masks on, and Potvin reached over and pulled Hurme's off. Hurme had thrown off his blocker, but his trapper was strapped onto his arm. Hurme dominated, getting Potvin bent over and raining down blows with his flopping catching glove on the back of his head.

Now the best part: they were close to the Ottawa bench, and Hurme extended his left arm to get his teammates to take his trapper off. Senators Marian Hossa, backup goaltender Patrick Lalime, and Todd White worked on getting the glove off. Hossa finally flicked it off and Hurme got about another dozen left hands on Potvin before the officials broke them up.

Our final honorable mention is Lalime, turned from spectator to participant, against Robert Esche of the Philadelphia Flyers on March 5, 2004. They contributed to an NHL-record 409 minutes of penalties in one game when they fought as part of a series of line brawls.

36 That Time Darcy Tucker Could Have Been a Senator

Darcy Tucker was one of the great antagonists in the first 25 years of the Senators' return to the NHL, a central figure of the Battle of Ontario with the Toronto Maple Leafs. If Senators president Roy Mlakar had liked him a little more, he could have been on the Ottawa side for those memorable provincial battles.

Tucker, a native of Castor, Alberta, was a three-time Memorial Cup champion with the Kamloops Blazers of the Western Hockey League (1992, 1994, and 1995) and was drafted in the sixth round (No. 151) of the 1993 NHL Draft by the Montreal Canadiens.

In his third season with the Habs, in January 1998, he was traded to the Tampa Bay Lightning along with Stephane Richer and David Wilkie, for Patrick Poulin, Igor Ulanov, and Mick Vukota.

During the autumn after Tucker's arrival in Tampa, the Lightning had a front-office shakeup. Art Williams had bought the team (Williams would own the team for nine months before selling it to William Davidson, the owner of the Detroit Pistons). General manager Phil Esposito was relieved of his duties in early October 1998 after exceeding his budget. As the 1998–99 season wound down, the Lightning were looking for a new general manager.

One night in San Jose in mid-March of 1999, after a game against the Sharks, Senators general manager Rick Dudley invited Mlakar up to his room for a beer. Dudley broke the news that he had been contacted by the Lightning about becoming their general manager. (Dudley had a relationship with Davidson going back to their days with the Detroit Vipers of the International Hockey League.) "I just calmly said, "So you talked to them, huh?" remembered Mlakar. He told Dudley: "Let me go to bed and think about this."

Mlakar went to his room and called Senators owner Rod Bryden, who was dismayed by the news they would be losing their general manager after just one season. "I said, 'Rod, it's called tampering. I got 'em,'" Mlakar said. NHL rules, of course, dictate that teams must ask permission to talk to another team's personnel. Those rules hadn't been followed in Dudley's case.

Mlakar contacted the NHL to inform them of the breach and was told to try and work out a deal privately before the incident went public. Mlakar negotiated a deal with Lightning president Tom Wilson. Mlakar had a clear list in mind: a player off the Lightning roster, a draft pick, and money.

Mlakar asked for a player and was offered defenseman Cory Cross or Tucker. Mlakar turned them down and asked for and received Lightning captain Rob Zamuner. The Senators got a second-round draft pick in 2000, 2001, or 2002, and took the pick in 2002 (it was traded to the Philadelphia Flyers along with the Senators' first-round pick (the Flyers took Jeff Woywitka) and seventh-round pick (David Printz) for the Flyers' first-round pick in 2001 (Tim Gleason)). The Flyers traded the second-round pick back to Tampa, which then traded it to the Dallas Stars. The Stars used it to take goaltender Tobias Stephen (No. 34 overall).

The money came in three exhibition games, specified to be in venues east of Winnipeg by Mlakar, in which the Lightning would play for free and the Senators would keep all the gate receipts. In addition to the rights to Dudley, the Senators also sent forward Andreas Johansson to the Lightning.

"It never got ugly. It never went to [the league office in] New York," Mlakar said. "I never raised my voice, and neither did Tom Wilson. He's a gentleman. It's called 'you've got to do what you've got to do.'"

Tucker was traded by the Lightning to the Maple Leafs on February 9, 2000, just in time to become one of the most hated opponents in Senators history. It could have been different.

37 Bankrupt

If there was one inevitable constant for the first 10 years of the Senators' existence, it was the financial thin ice upon which the club's owners skated. First Bruce Firestone and then Rod Bryden skittered and slid by the cracks, managing to keep the team afloat until the weight of debts inevitably plunged the franchise into the frozen water in January 2003.

Firestone, the brash entrepreneur who had hatched the idea to "Bring Back the Senators" in 1988 and won the franchise in 1990, had the Ontario Municipal Board scale down plans for a community around a new rink. It crushed the opportunity for development to boost real estate prices around the rink and create the equity needed to pay the $50 million U.S. franchise fee.

It was a scramble from that point forward. The truth is, the Senators were never properly capitalized. Bryden was brought in to help raise the $50 million U.S. expansion fee and by the end of 1993 owned Terrace Investments, the holding company that owned the Senators.

After years of rumors about the Senators moving to Phoenix or Portland or Houston or some other greener pasture, it seemed then as if NHL hockey in Canada's capital might finally be done when Bryden was forced to declare the Senators—who owed about $160 million, and the Corel Centre, which had more than $200 million in debt—bankrupt and sought protection on January 9, 2003.

He had been working on a refinancing plan for two years that would see the club sold to a limited partnership, which would in turn sell units to investors who would get tax breaks. The deal fell apart when Covanta Energy Corp. (which used to be Ogden Corp.) went bankrupt and two banks got cold feet.

"This isn't the big, bad banks chasing us out of town," Bryden told a news conference. "Investors simply want a fair return, and are quite willing to keep the team where it is as long as they can make a profit," he said. "We need to decide whether or not we are going to have a team in the city and whether we're prepared to pay for it. There is a marvelous opportunity to have this asset here at today's values, soundly funded." That this day would come seemed inevitable. What was remarkable was that through Bryden's ingenuity it had been postponed for as long as it was.

Terrace was channeling its capital into the Senators, and by 1998, Terrace had stopped paying property taxes and mortgage payments on two Ottawa buildings. The original $14 million in loans to acquire the properties had swollen to $29 million, according to the *Globe and Mail* newspaper. There were restructurings, cash calls, and press conferences. There was an aborted plan for the federal government to establish a $20 million fund to help Canadian NHL teams, but public backlash scuttled the plan.

After yet another pregame meeting of shareholders to avert the latest crisis, Bryden met with a scrum of hockey writers who were clearly in over their heads when it came to "distressed shares," tax breaks, and financial restructuring.

As Bryden spun his corporate speak to a dozen pairs of glazed eyes, a voice asked from the back of the scrum, in my best Denis Lemieux impression, "Rod, who 'howns' the Senators?" Even Bryden, the epitome of a buttoned-down corporate guy, had a laugh at that. It was one of the few times there was some levity when it came to discussing the Senators' financial health.

Finally, as 2003 wound down, the Senators were bankrupt and in real danger of having to move to another city, a proposition of which Bryden said "there was more than a chance."

The irony was that as the Senators grew from being the worst expansion team of all time, as crowned by *Sports Illustrated*, into a regular-season powerhouse (they would win the Presidents' Trophy as the NHL's top regular-season team that season), the Senators were going the other way in the financial arena.

The Senators were fighting for first place in the NHL while wondering if they were going to get paid. Now, the players all had a few bucks in the bank, or should have, so missing a paycheck or two wouldn't have meant they'd miss a meal or two. But they did have to put up with being asked about not getting paid everywhere they went. "We've still got enough sticks around, and there's hot water coming out of the taps, and the lights are on in the dressing room," Senators defenseman Wade Redden said in his laconic Western Canada way.

"If we could control it, we'd worry about it, but since we can't control it, we don't worry about it," Senators forward Shaun Van Allen said. "We just go out and play hockey. It's a tough game. You've got to be focused every night, and when you've got something else on your mind, you're not going to play very well."

NHL commissioner Gary Bettman, who was also dealing with the bankruptcy of the Buffalo Sabres, pushed for solutions that would keep the teams in their respective cities. The Sabres and the Senators met at the Corel Centre on January 25 in what was dubbed the Creditors Cup. "Well, I'm glad to be part of NHL history," Sabres defenseman Jay McKee told the *New York Times.* "Unfortunately, it's not a good thing."

Bryden kept working on trying to maintain control of the team. He teamed up with American billionaire Nelson Peltz, who had been sniffing around the Senators for a couple years. Peltz, whose company, Triarc, owned the Arby's roast beef chain, used to have a stake in the Colorado Avalanche. He had cash on hand after Triarc sold the Snapple drink brand and Royal Crown Cola in 2001 for $1.5 billion.

But Peltz withdrew from Bryden's bid over concerns about the accounting treatment of the deal. Bryden had finally run out of time and maneuvering room. Somebody was going to own the Senators, but it would no longer be him.

38 Marshall Law

He was an All-American college player who graduated to the NHL before college guys got respect, an Olympian before it was big business, and he played for and coached the California Golden Seals before they became an answer to a trivia question. He knew the New Jersey Devils when they were the Colorado Rockies, feuded with Don Cherry when Cherry was a coach with the Rockies and far from the star of *Coach's Corner* every Saturday night, and helped make the Devils into Stanley Cup champions.

Marshall Johnston, finally settling into retirement at age 75 in 2016, has had a long-lasting impact everywhere he has worked, but there's an argument to be made that he is the man most responsible for making the Senators a contender in the 2000s.

The native of Birch Hills, Saskatchewan, was a barrel-chested man with a gravelly voice and a gap-toothed smile who always seemed to have a five-o'clock shadow. He was ruled by a pragmatism instilled in rinks off the beaten path. He played and coached at the University of Denver and played in the 1964 and 1968 Olympic Games. He was the captain of Canada's bronze medal–winning team in 1968.

After finishing up his NHL career as a player with the Seals in 1974, he started an outstanding career off the ice. After coaching the Seals and the University of Denver, he joined the Colorado Rockies and moved with them to New Jersey, where he helped them build a Stanley Cup champion in 1995.

Like he had with the Rockies/Devils, Johnston helped the Senators transition from the worst team in hockey to one of the best. He was hired by Pierre Gauthier in 1996 as the Senators' director of player personnel and contributed to the Senators transitioning from the doormats of the NHL to a Presidents' Trophy winner. His fingerprints, along with Gauthier's, were all over the Senators teams that dominated in the early 2000s.

Johnston's greatest contribution to the success of the Senators was the deal that ended years of frustration and controversy with Alexei Yashin. In exchange for Yashin, Johnston grabbed the Senators two players who became the cornerstones of those excellent Ottawa teams that culminated with a trip to the Stanley Cup Final in 2007: center Jason Spezza and defenseman Zdeno Chara.

By the summer of 2001, the patience of Senators owner Rod Bryden—and that of most Senators fans—was exhausted with yet another demand by Yashin to have his contract renegotiated. With Yashin sitting out the 1999–2000 season, an endless stream of press conferences updating the stalemate between the two sides—most of them tasking Johnston with stating the Senators' position—wore everybody out. "Rod Bryden was a very, very smart guy. I was just the mouthpiece, basically. No. 1, I knew that [Bryden] didn't have the money," Johnson said. "He wasn't going to pay him. He was good at interpreting the legal aspects of it. I didn't like doing it, but it was part of the job. I'd rather have been doing something else, but it wasn't something that was difficult, you know what I mean?"

After having won the arbitration case that ruled Yashin owed the Senators another season after sitting out 1999–2000, it was time for the Senators to move on, especially after Yashin had an unproductive playoff against the Toronto Maple Leafs (one assist in a sweep) and the Senators lost another Battle of Ontario in 2001.

"Nobody had to tell me. I knew," said Johnston. "I don't recall anybody saying, 'You have to do this, you have to do that.' To me, it was clear. The other side of it, and I often thought about this: if he had renegotiated again, I would have had a hard time staying there as the manager because that's not where I'm from.... He had signed the thing. He signed it up front and everything. Now you come back. Uh-uh. No. I wasn't there when he renegotiated the first time. When he came back the second time, I'd have had a hard time because personally it was against everything that I believe in."

So Johnston set about trading Yashin. Johnston growled:

It wasn't anything that required rocket science or anything like that. What was involved was a guy who had already had his contract renegotiated once, then wanted it renegotiated again. The owner didn't have any money to renegotiate it again. The fans were fed up with the whole situation.

He was a good player, but it wasn't a case where this guy was leading the Senators down the golden path. You know what I mean? So really, there was no way that we were going to re-sign him no matter what. That was a fact. Naturally, there was some interest. I wouldn't say a whole lot of interest, but there was some interest there. That interest slowly dissipated. When it came right down to the day before the draft, there was really only one team that was really interested, and that was the Islanders.

Incredibly, despite the market for Yashin shrinking to but one team, Johnston dealt him for the No. 2 pick in the 2001 draft, a pick Johnston used to take a true No. 1 center in Spezza, a guy who would become a point-a-game player. Johnston also got Chara, a future Norris Trophy winner. Johnston was familiar with Chara. He was working for the Islanders when they drafted the 6'9" gangly prospect based in large part on a poor-quality tape converted from a video. Oh, and they had to take forward Bill Muckalt too.

Johnston, working on a strict budget that had been set by the Senators' bankers, told Islanders general manager Mike Milbury he couldn't afford to take on Muckalt's deal, which was to pay him $1.1 million for 2001–02, according to hockeyzoneplus.com. Marshall said:

> We had a cap before the cap. The bank told Bryden, "This is how much money you've got to spend on players." It wasn't a league cap. I didn't mind that. I came up through the New Jersey system, and we didn't spend a lot of money in free agency or that stuff there, either.
>
> They wanted to get rid of Muckalt. If they had said, "No, we're not picking it up," we would have still made the deal and tried to figure it out. At that time Zdeno wasn't making a lot of money. The second pick that wasn't going to be a lot of money at the time. We ended up getting rid of a guy who was making three times as much money as those two guys put together.

"I pushed because we didn't have money. [Muckalt] was on a one-way contract. So I asked, 'Do you think you could pick up half his contract?' They wound up picking up half his NHL salary. That was another bonus, you know?" Johnston chuckled down the phone line from his home in Bemidji, Minnesota.

Milbury, meanwhile, scoffed at Yashin's contract battles in Ottawa and welcomed him with a 10-year, $87.5 million deal. "Mother Teresa would have a bad reputation in Ottawa," Milbury said. Yashin was bought out by the Islanders after the 2007 season, with $17.6 million to be paid over eight years.

Johnston finally retired in 2016, a year after the Islanders stopped paying Yashin, still loving the games, but the airports, rental cars, and hotels "finally got the best of [him]."

39 Bosch's World

It seems almost impossible to consider now, the idea of an NHL expansion team not winning a game on the road for almost an entire season. The Vegas Golden Knights, who joined the NHL for the 2017–18 season, had won three road games in the first month of the season and ended up playing in the Stanley Cup Final.

But that's how bad the 1992–93 Ottawa Senators were that first season—so inept that the idea of not winning a single game on the road was not only a possibility but was anticipated. They came close to winning their first road game late in the season on March 27, 1993, against the mighty Montreal Canadiens, who would go on to win the Stanley Cup that season and had been the victims in the Senators' opening night 5–3 victory at the Civic Centre in Ottawa. The Senators led 2–0 early and 3–2 late in the game at the historic old Forum but blew it in the waning minutes when Vincent Damphousse scored for the Canadiens with 1:19 left in the third to tie it and Oleg Petrov won it for the Habs at 1:29 of overtime.

When the Senators rolled onto Long Island on April 10, they had lost 38 road games in a row, which is still an NHL record (and probably always will be), and it seemed inevitable that they would finish the season winless on the road. (That would be a record that could only be tied; what made it even more impregnable was that the Senators played 43 games away from home that season. Teams played two "neutral site" games back then: the Senators played in Hamilton on October 20 in a 5–3 loss to the Toronto Maple Leafs and in Saskatoon on February 23, an 8–3 loss to the Winnipeg Jets.)

That the game against the Islanders would be another loss appeared inevitable after Senators coach Rick Bowness had the wrong lineup on the ice to start the game (defenseman Darren Rumble was on the ice instead of Norm Maciver) and the Senators were penalized.

It quickly became a five-on-three when rough-and-tumble forward Darcy Loewen took a roughing penalty and Derek King scored at 1:54 for the Islanders. Ottawa's Sylvain Turgeon tied it before the first period was over with his 25th goal of the season, but 2:28 into the second, King made it 2–1 with his second of the night.

But this was a night when the Senators finally wouldn't go quietly. Captain Laurie Boschman, playing the final games of his 14-year NHL career, tied it 2–2 at 8:56. New York's Pat Flatley scored what looked like a crusher, a power-play goal with 32 seconds left in the second period for a 3–2 Islanders lead.

But the Senators, led by Boschman in a late-career blaze of glory, had their best period on the road that season in the third. Bob Kudelski scored hs 24th of the season to tie it at 9:57, and Boschman delivered the win with a goal with 56 seconds left in the third, beating Islanders goaltender Glenn Healy. Boschman cemented it with a hat-trick goal into the empty net. (Boschman scored nine goals that season, a third of them that night.) Boschman was swarmed after the insurance goal. As was the custom for Super Bowl and Stanley Cup champions at that time, Boschman yelled out in the celebration scrum, "I'm going to Disneyland!"

Goaltender Peter Sidorkiewicz delivered his performance of the season—42 saves—but suffered a shoulder injury with six minutes to go and underwent surgery the next morning. His career with the Senators was over (and he would only play four more games in the NHL, with the New Jersey Devils, until a young goaltender named Martin Brodeur won the starting job), but what a way to go out.

"It felt like we won the Stanley Cup," Senators defenseman Brad Shaw told the *Ottawa Citizen* years later. "We were near the end of the season, and it was like 'Holy blank.' Put whatever expletive in there you want.... I've never seen a happier room. I've won championships and I've never seen a happier room. I think we all felt it was a huge monkey off our backs."

As the Senators entourage waited in the loading bay beside the Senators' bus to leave for the airport after the game, the happy players wandered out of the dressing room and milled about. When Boschman emerged, they lined up and began to bow, arms outstretched. "We're not worthy, we're not worthy," they chanted, mimicking the voices of Wayne and Garth from the popular *Saturday Night Live* sketch (and later movie) "Wayne's World."

In a season with so few happy moments for the players, the chants of "We're not worthy" (just ignore the irony) rank as one of the best.

40 Shake It Off

The Ottawa Senators went through a tumultuous stretch from 2007 to 2016, during which coaches had about as much job security as a White House press secretary in the Donald Trump administration. After Bryan Murray coached the Senators to the Stanley Cup Final in 2007, he was kicked upstairs as general manager to replace John Muckler. Murray, who never seemed to find a coach who could live up to the standard he set behind the bench, then went through five coaches in nine seasons. They were:

- John Paddock, 2007–08 (fired after 64 games despite a 15–2 start)
- Craig Hartsburg, 2008–09 (fired with a 17–24–7 record)
- Cory Clouston, 2008–11 (he had a 95–83–20 record when he was let go)
- Paul MacLean, 2011–14 (won the Jack Adams as Coach of the Year in 2013)
- Dave Cameron, 2014–16 (fired by Pierre Dorion when he took over as GM from Murray)

There were a lot of comings and goings under Murray, but there is no question the most colorful run was that of MacLean, who, as he self-proclaimed, was "just a fisherman from Nova Scotia." He already had a connection to the national capital region before he got to Ottawa as coach. While playing junior hockey for the Hull Olympiques of the Quebec Major Junior Hockey League, he was traded to the Quebec Remparts during a game, but the deal was called off by Hull after Murray scored five goals in the game.

Nicknamed Slap Shot because the glasses he wore made him look like one of the Hanson brothers from the movie of the same name, MacLean was a three-time 40-goal scorer in the NHL with the Winnipeg Jets (and had eight seasons of 30 goals or more).

He coached in the minors for 10 years before becoming an assistant coach to Mike Babcock with the Mighty Ducks of Anaheim (where Murray was GM). He followed Babcock to Detroit, where he won a Stanley Cup as an assistant coach in 2008.

MacLean had instant success with the Senators. After Clouston, who Murray didn't think communicated well enough with his players or management, MacLean's experience having been a player, along with his down-to-earth sensibility, got a positive response from the players. The Senators were 41–31–10 for MacLean that first year and they made the playoffs, losing to the New York Rangers in seven games. MacLean was a finalist for the Jack Adams Trophy, losing to Ken Hitchcock of the St. Louis Blues.

Things continued to track nicely for MacLean in 2012–13, which was shortened to 48 games because of a lockout. They made the playoffs again with a 25–17–6 record and won a vicious first-round series against the Montreal Canadiens.

MacLean was a star, winning the battle of words with Canadiens coach Michel Therrien, who accused MacLean of a lack of respect for a series of real or perceived slights. Canadiens forward Lars Eller was left bloody after a devastating check by Senators defenseman Eric Gryba in Game 1. MacLean said rather than blame Gryba, Eller should look at "Player 61" (Montreal defenseman Raphael Diaz) for giving him a suicide pass. That didn't sit well with Therrien or Canadiens forward Brandon Prust. "I don't care what that bug-eyed, fat walrus has to say," Prust said of MacLean.

The Senators won Game 3, famous for a line brawl in the third period, and with Canadiens goaltender Carey Price out with an injury, closed out the series in five games.

The Senators were overmatched against the Pittsburgh Penguins in the second round and lost in five games. This time MacLean won the Jack Adams, beating out Bruce Boudreau of the Washington Capitals and Joel Quenneville of the Chicago Blackhawks.

It looked like the Senators were moving forward under MacLean despite some unflattering defensive numbers that continued the trend of the Senators ranking near the bottom of the league in shots allowed.

A different Paul MacLean showed up for the 2013–14 season. It was a tougher, more demanding coach, according to players, and there was less give and take. MacLean's intention was to squeeze more out of his players and to improve defensively. The relationship between MacLean and Jason Spezza, who had been named captain after Daniel Alfredsson left as a free agent to sign with the Detroit Red Wings, became particularly strained and led, in part, to Spezza requesting a trade after the season. "Your best players have to be your best players," MacLean said. "I pushed them to be."

"There was an uneasiness in our room, without a doubt, that some of the better players felt they were singled out a little too often maybe, and that's today's athlete," Murray said. "They want to be corrected, coached, given a chance to play without being the center point of discussion in a room." He added, "Our players have to have fun. It's a game."

In MacLean's final game behind the Ottawa bench, a win against the Vancouver Canucks, he and star defenseman Erik Karlsson got involved in an animated discussion. "You don't always share the same opinion, and you might sometimes look like you're in a disagreement, but I don't think I've ever had an issue with him," Karlsson said. "He's helped me tremendously in my career and he's been really good for me personally. I think he's a great guy."

The defensive numbers didn't improve under the "new" Paul MacLean, and the Senators missed the playoffs with a 37–31–14 record. "The players liked the old Paul. They liked the Paul who sat and talked to them, who treated them in a more easygoing fashion.

Who taught, not confronted," Murray said in evaluating how the relationship between the players and MacLean had changed. "There were some mistakes made, obviously. You don't go to some of your better players early in the year and expect change. The change is usually in the negative form."

The Senators got off to a decent start in 2014–15, going 4–1 in their first five games, but then they hit a slump, winning only five of their next 15. After a 3–2 shootout win against the St. Louis Blues, the Senators lost five more games. The underlying numbers were bubbling to the surface: the Senators were outshot in 15 of 21 games and were 24th in the league in Corsi.

On the morning of December 6, 2014, when the Senators played what turned out to be a 3–2 loss to the Pittsburgh Penguins, MacLean said, "All I know is I'm scared to death no matter who we're playing. Whether it's Sidney Crosby or John Tavares or the Sedins, I go day by day, and I'm just scared to death every day of who we're playing." He added, joking, "And sometimes I'm scared to death of who I'm playing."

The comment irked Murray. "That sent a loud message to me, whether it was in jest or otherwise, that maybe he didn't believe in the group the way we thought we believed in the group when we started the year," said Murray. "I'm not sure beyond that."

"I thought we had lost four games in a row," MacLean said. "I didn't think we had lost our sense of humor."

Two days later, Murray made the decision to fire MacLean and replace him with assistant coach Dave Cameron. "I've had some tough days lately," Murray, who had been diagnosed with terminal cancer in the summer of 2014, said. "This is one of them."

Murray continued, "Watching the team play and continue to play the same way as we did at the end of last year, where we were giving up way too many scoring chances, too many goals, too many breakdowns in the defensive part of our game…I guess from that point on—the last four, five games, certainly—we examined each and every performance as best we could, had discussions, and it just came to a point where I felt something had to be done."

Murray said he didn't like the positioning of the forwards when it came to breakouts—they left the zone too early and left the defensemen without many options to move the puck. "We've talked about that a thousand times," Murray said. "I know the red line has disappeared in our game, and whether I like that or not doesn't matter; your forwards can't disappear and not give the defensemen options to make the play. We talked about it, and nothing changed in that area. That's why I think our turnover numbers are so atrocious in so many games."

MacLean said he felt communication wasn't an issue on his part. "I thought my door was open all the time," MacLean said. "You guys saw it. It was open. Communication is a two-way street. You have to have someone that talks and someone that wants to listen. I was always prepared to listen. Listening and patience is one of my strengths. I felt we communicated what the players needed to hear. We didn't win enough games."

MacLean's farewell press conference immediately elevated itself to the best ever by a departing coach. Not many coaches quote Taylor Swift in their exit performances:

I brought with me a résumé that included playing in June. I was on one team that won a Stanley Cup, went to three Stanley Cup Finals, coached in four Western Finals. I had a habit of playing in June. That was what I tried to establish here. To play in June, your best players have to be your best players. I pushed them to be.

I leave today with my résumé fuller by three years as a head coach in the National Hockey League, a Jack Adams Award, a runner-up for a Jack Adams Award, two playoff appearances in April, which I know is a place to start. I am a better coach today and I will be better prepared for the next opportunity, and I will still coach to play in June.

My daughter Erin said to me today something about the players play, play, play and I'm going to shake, shake it off...and move forward. Any questions?

In that moment, a woman's voice cried out from the door at the back of the room. "You're the fucking best coach, Paul MacLean. I love you!" Blowing a kiss, the woman repeated, "You're the best."

Without missing a beat, MacLean gestured toward the door at the back of the room with the paper he had in his right hand and said, "That is not my daughter."

It was a "drop the mic" conclusion to MacLean's days with the Senators.

41 A Cruel End

If you're a Senators fan, you probably saw the photoshopped pictures on the Internet: Ottawa Senators goaltender Patrick Lalime, a beach ball behind him in the net. It was an awful punctuation mark for the goaltender's run with the Ottawa Senators, a five-year stint from 1999 to 2004 that saw him give the Senators the best netminding they ever had as they rose to become an NHL powerhouse.

Lalime set playoff goaltending records with the Senators, but unfortunately that is overshadowed by two goals he gave up to Toronto Maple Leafs forward Joe Nieuwendyk in Game 7 of the first round in the 2004 Eastern Conference playoffs. It was the Senators' fourth loss in five years in the playoffs at the hands of the hated Leafs in the Battle of Ontario, and it wound up costing both Lalime (traded to the St. Louis Blues) and Coach Jacques Martin their jobs.

But the end shouldn't define Lalime's time with the Senators, which was brilliant. Let's face it—the truth is Lalime didn't get a lot of help from his teammates in the postseason: In his 41 playoff starts, he had a 21–20 record. In those 20 losses, the Senators were shut out 11 times.

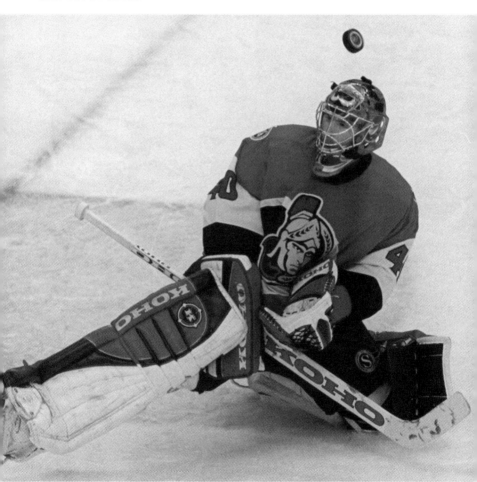

Patrick Lalime makes an acrobatic save against the Carolina Hurricanes in 2000.

Lalime, who was traded to the Senators in June 1999 by the Mighty Ducks of Anaheim for Ted Donato and the rights to Antti-Jussi Niemi, had his best days in the NHL with the Senators. He had shown promise when he started with the Pittsburgh Penguins in 1996–97 when he went 14–0–2 to start his career, an NHL record. But a bitter 904-day contract dispute with the Penguins saw him banished to the minors for two seasons and finally traded to the Ducks. He got his chance with the Senators, under Martin, where Lalime established himself as a legitimate No. 1 goaltender.

"I think [they're] the greatest memories of my career when I look back at it," said Lalime, who retired in 2011. "I had a good start in Pittsburgh with great players, but coming here, I had a chance to become a No. 1. Jacques gave me that chance. Those are the years that I was No. 1 that I enjoyed. We had so many good players. What a great place to live and to play. I always say this feels like home every time I come back here. It does. Same with the family. That's how they feel too. They feel like it's home. We could be living here no problem."

Lalime owned most of the Senators' goaltending records when he left. In a first-round win over the Philadelphia Flyers in 2002, Lalime gave up two goals in five games and had three shutouts in a row (0.40 goals-against average, .985 save percentage). He has played the most playoff games (41) and has the most wins (21). He owns a 1.77 goals-against average in the postseason and a .926 save percentage with five shutouts.

"The one thing I can say is I didn't do my job in the last game I played here, the last period I played in Toronto. That was tough to swallow as an athlete. You just feel like you let your teammates down. I'm a team guy and that hurt a lot," Lalime said.

"If you take that period away, I think for the most part in the playoffs I did pretty well," he continued. "I thought I was there, I gave my team a chance to win. If you want to look at stats, stats are there too. I heard that a lot. I think 11 out of those 20 games, I think we got shut out 11 times. But it's hockey. If you have to win 1–0, you have to win 1–0. I have to do my job. I have to stop the puck. The blame for the last game I played here, the last period, there's nowhere to hide."

Nieuwendyk's first goal was a wrister from the top of the left-wing circle that beat Lalime to the stick side to make it 2–0 at 7:41 of the first period. He scored again with 21 seconds left in the first, from just a little deeper in the circle, between Lalime's pads.

"He couldn't shoot the regular shot. He had to come in with a lot of movement on it. Ahh, well. I've seen it all," Lalime said with a rueful laugh. "It's part of sports. People have the right to their own opinion. I think at the end of the day it made me a better person, a better guy. You work through adversity, you learn about yourself, though it wasn't easy or easy for the family. After all the good memories, you have that thing going, and that takes the spotlight away from a lot of stuff."

He continued, "I look at the good stuff that happened here. I think there's a lot more of that than the last period I was here and I couldn't do the job. You live with it; it's never going to change. I think I can walk here, around town, with my head up high.… I recognize the mistakes I made…I still wish I could change that period."

42 The White Whale

If there is one player who haunts the nightmares of Ottawa Senators fans, it's Gary Roberts. Bring up the most gut-wrenching, heartbreaking losses in Senators history, and Roberts probably had something to do with many of them.

He was the central figure in some of the most bitter Battles of Ontario when he played for the Toronto Maple Leafs at the height of the rivalry in the early 2000s. Want to make a Senators fan cringe? Mimic the voice of former Air Canada Centre public address announcer Andy Frost and his drawn-out "Gaaareeee Raaaawberts" announcement that often came after another crushing goal against the Senators.

The twist in the saga was that Roberts had all kinds of intersections with the Senators and Ottawa. He did his apprenticeship under legendary Ottawa 67's coach and general manager Brian Kilrea as a 16-year-old in his first year in the OHL and won the Memorial Cup in 1984. He wound up asking for a trade in the 1985–86 season and was dealt to the Guelph Platers, where he won another Memorial Cup under Jacques Martin, who later wound up as the Senators' coach when Roberts was inflicting all that pain on them.

That Roberts was even around to terrorize the Senators in the early 2000s is a remarkable story in itself. Roberts won a Stanley Cup with the Calgary Flames in 1988–89 and had 53 goals in the 1991–92 season as he evolved into one of the NHL's top power forwards. But it appeared his career was over in 1996 when a neck injury caused him to miss the entire 1996–97 season.

It all really started in 1991 with a check from behind into the boards by Toronto's Bob Rouse that caused nerve damage. Roberts was taken off the ice on a stretcher. He only missed one game, but the condition of his neck degenerated from there. In the 1994 playoffs, he couldn't lift his right arm. He'd get back to the bench after a shift with a burning sensation ripping down his arm. "My wife at the time was cutting my food for me and I was playing in the [1994] Stanley Cup Playoffs," Roberts told me in 2012. "I had a neck collar on. I couldn't hold my stick. I literally had to pick my right arm up and put it on the knob of my stick. I would go out and stand in front of the net and try and deflect pucks. I couldn't shoot. I couldn't stickhandle. I played in that game and I was getting abused out there. I couldn't push back. Couldn't defend myself. I was totally vulnerable for a career-threatening injury, for sure." Later, doctors told him if he had fallen on his arm, further straining his damaged nerves, he risked losing the use of it.

He played just eight games in 1994–95 and wound up twice having surgery in 1995. Incredibly, he played 35 games in 1995–96 and scored 22 goals.

He was forced to pack it in for the 1996–97 season and retired at age 30. It didn't go well. "I was drinking too much. Feeling sorry for myself. I was in the prime of my career, scoring 50 goals a year, 45 a year, the prime of my career, and just like that, and holy shit, just like that my career is taken away from me," he said as we sat in his immensely successful gym, the centerpiece of Gary Roberts High Performance Training. "A little bit of feeling sorry for myself, a little bit of being mentally lost. What was I going to do with myself? I was retired for six months and I didn't like myself very much. I woke one day going, 'If I keep going like this, I might not be here when I'm 40.'"

After speaking to Lorne Goldenberg, his friend and trainer going back to his days playing in Ottawa with the 67's, Roberts tried a new active-release therapy for soft tissue with Dr. Michael Leahy in Colorado. After only a week, Roberts said he had about 65 percent of his range of motion back.

After attending the funeral for the mother of friend and former teammate Joe Nieuwendyk, Roberts decided to make some lifestyle changes. "The next day I stopped drinking and started my comeback," recounted Roberts. "[Drinking] was a big issue at the time. I didn't consider myself an alcoholic. I was drinking and feeling sorry for myself. Just…not making great lifestyle choices through nutrition and alcohol, for sure. I wanted to get healthy. Everybody in that situation, what are the two things you need to clean up? What's your alcohol consumption and how do you eat?"

Roberts launched himself into a fitness program and learned about nutrition, working with Olympic trainer Charles Poliquin, a friend of Goldenberg's. He packed on 20 pounds of muscle, some of it to protect his neck.

When the Flames didn't want to take a chance on him, Jim Rutherford, the general manager of the Carolina Hurricanes, did. He was traded to the Hurricanes and, in the best shape of his life, he went on to play another 11 seasons with the Hurricanes, Leafs, Florida Panthers, Pittsburgh Penguins, and Tampa Bay Lightning. He played another 639 NHL games, bringing his career total to 1,224.

He scored 181 of his 438 career goals after his comeback. Some of his biggest were against the Senators, particularly in 2002. The Maple Leafs were without captain Mats Sundin when they met in the second round. Roberts scored in triple overtime to win Game 2 and help the Leafs avoid going down 2–0 in the series.

Senators captain Daniel Alfredsson knocked Darcy Tucker out of the series in Game 5 with a hit into the boards, scoring the winning goal seconds later to put the Senators up 3–2 in the series.

In Game 6 the Senators were up 2–0 in the first period when defenseman Ricard Persson took a five-minute major for boarding Maple Leafs tough guy Tie Domi. Roberts scored the Leafs' second goal during Persson's major as Toronto tied the game. Roberts scored again in the second period to help the Leafs to a 4–3 win. They never looked back, winning Game 7 by a 3–0 score. Roberts had 10 points in the series, 5 goals, 5 assists, and 25 shots.

"Roberts plays hell-bent, gives nothing but his utmost; he's a winner and he gets rewards like tonight," Toronto coach Pat Quinn said after his triple-OT winner in Game 2. "Everybody wants a Gary Roberts."

As it turned out, the Senators wanted Gary Roberts. After signing with the Florida Panthers as a free agent in 2005, Roberts was on the trade block at the deadline in 2007, and the word in the Senators camp was owner Eugene Melnyk was pushing for Roberts. In another twist, Martin, fired by the Senators the previous season, was the Panthers' general manager, and the rumor was the price was high for the Senators because Martin knew how coveted Roberts was in Ottawa. Why would Martin want to help the team that had whacked him unless he could make them overpay?

Senators general manager John Muckler wouldn't pay the Panthers' price, and Roberts was traded to the Pittsburgh Penguins for prospect defenseman Noah Welch. Roberts wanted to come to Ottawa. A return to Ontario was at the top of his list, but a chance to play with the Senators or the Maple Leafs wasn't in the cards. "Ultimately, the deal on the table from Pittsburgh is the only deal that I was aware of." Roberts said.

Former Senators president Roy Mlakar said Muckler's failure to pay the price for Roberts was one of the reasons why Muckler's contract wasn't renewed after the 2007 season. [Muckler] didn't get Gary Roberts, which was his downfall," Mlakar said.

In an interesting turn, the Senators defeated Roberts and the Penguins 4–1 in their first-round playoff series as the Senators went to the Stanley Cup Final for the first time. There's some vindication for Muckler there. But the Senators probably could have used Roberts and his full-steam-ahead approach against the physical Anaheim Ducks in the Final, in which they were hardly competitive and lost 4–1.

43 A Bus, Barbed Wire, and Bones

He had no idea at that time—and certainly has no reason to know it now—but U.S. district judge C. Clyde Atkins played a role in one memorable night in the early history of the Ottawa Senators. It's a story that was off the record when it occurred and hasn't been told often since then.

Judge Atkins, in a decision in 1992, told police in Miami to stop rousting the homeless and told the city to create two "safe zones" where the homeless could sleep, eat, and bathe without being arrested. One of those safe zones was Bicentennial Park (now known as Museum Park), a 34-acre green space designed by architect Edward D. Stone as "a unique retreat from urban pressures." It became a unique retreat but not in the way it was intended. As one of the safe zones, it had 300 homeless people living in the park and on the mud flats beneath Interstate 395, just north of the park.

On a night about a year after the park was declared a homeless safe zone—after another desultory performance that saw them lose to the expansion Florida Panthers at the since-demolished Miami Arena—the Senators, only in their second season themselves, loaded onto their bus with slouched shoulders.

Back in those days, the reporters who covered the team shared their buses and planes. The Miami Arena was located in Overtown, one of the most dangerous neighborhoods in America at the time (they used to send in 150 policemen to do a sweep of the area around the rink four hours before game time). The big gate by the loading dock was topped by barbed wire; it rolled back after the game and the Senators' bus rolled into the dark and dangerous streets on its way north to the club's four-star hotel, a short drive that would go from poor to privileged in a few blocks. "I wouldn't walk it, and I was born and brought up in this neighborhood," our bus driver said at one point.

We were shortly into the ride when the bus suddenly pulled over to the curb and stopped. This was unusual. More unusual was seeing Senators coach Rick Bowness rising from his seat at the front and turning to face the players. A moment of unexpected suspense hung in the air. It was but a moment because Bowness then exploded into what was truly one of the great coach tirades I have personally witnessed. A PG-13 paraphrase: "Look at these people," he said, his voice rising as he gestured out the window toward the park, where the makeshift homes of the homeless had sprung up like dandelions in the spring. "They are sleeping on pieces of cardboard. That is all they have in this world. You make hundreds of thousands of dollars. We ask you to work a few minutes a night, and you can't even do that."

Recalling that night more than 20 years later, Bowness said the statute of limitations on it being "off the record" had expired. In the coaches' room at the Bell Centre in Montreal, where he was now working for the Tampa Bay Lightning, Bowness chuckled when the rant was brought up. Turns out the decision to have the bus pull over was not planned. Bowness said:

Absolutely not. It hit me when I saw those people living in that park. It just hit me. It was not premeditated at all.

I don't remember what I said exactly, but the message was, and I still believe this today, every day in this league is a blessing. It really is. I never wanted those young players to take this for granted. People that were living in the streets; life affected them in different ways. Maybe some of them didn't have a chance, or maybe they made some bad decisions along the way. Everybody on that bus had made the decision to be a hockey player. That was their decision.

They didn't have to be, but they decided they wanted to be a hockey player.

When they made that decision, they were damn well going to work for it and respect the league and respect their teammates and respect the game. That means you come to work every day. It goes back to that original philosophy: we're not letting them off the hook for anything. It just struck me. So I just reacted.

I do remember that, and [I hoped] the message sank in with a couple of guys. Very rarely do those things happen that you just instinctively say, "Wow, look at that," and go, "Let's stop and get that straightened out right now."

The message sank in, and not just with the players.

44 Four Goals for No. 44

You know you've done something big when they name a meal after you. A big meal. The morning after Senators forward Jean-Gabriel Pageau scored four goals—including the overtime game winner—in Game 2 of the Eastern Conference semifinal against the New York Rangers on April 29, 2017, the fine Wellington Diner featured the Pageau 4444. Four eggs, four slices of bacon, four sausages, home fries, and toast to celebrate four goals by the player who wears No. 44. "I couldn't eat all that," Pageau said.

Food became a central theme as Pageau, a local guy from Gatineau who earned the nickname the Honey Badger for his feisty style, became the first Senator to score four goals in a game. Pageau helped the Senators overcome three two-goal deficits in the

Pageau's Fantastic Four

1. Pageau picks up a wayward pass by Rangers defenseman Dan Giardi off the boards in the neutral zone, cuts in on the right wing, and beats goaltender Henrik Lundqvist with a wrist shot. Senators 1, Rangers 1.
2. After some slogging along the boards, the puck goes back to the point, and Pageau, heading for the front of the net, tips a shot by Zack Smith. Rangers 5, Senators 4.
3. Pageau shows his hand-eye coordination again, getting his stick on a one-timer by Kyle Turris to tie the game and give Pageau his second Stanley Cup Playoffs hat trick. Rangers 5, Senators 5.
4. On a two-on-one in overtime, Pageau snaps a shot under the bar to the glove side of Lundqvist. Senators 6, Rangers 5.

game, which they won 6–5 over the Rangers to take a 2–0 series lead (they eventually eliminated the Rangers in six games). Pageau finished it off with the last three goals of the game, culminating with the overtime winner.

Heading into the game, which had the uncommon start time of 3:00 PM to accommodate television, Pageau said his pregame routine was upset, if not his stomach. "Three PM games are pretty hard," Pageau said. "I thought I [ate] too much before the game. I had two chicken parm." His fiancée, Camille Beeby, had made him two helpings of chicken parmigiana. "She's the chef," Pageau said, "and I do the dishes." Pageau ate his first helping at 8:30 AM. Feeling peckish a couple hours later, he polished off the second one.

That Pageau had a big game in the playoffs shouldn't have come as a surprise. He's always saved his best for the postseason. The 25-year-old has scored 71 goals in the NHL, including the regular season and the playoffs. Twelve of them (17 percent) have been in the postseason. He scored at almost double the pace in the playoffs as in the regular season (.34 goals per game in the postseason vs. 0.18 goals per game in the regular season). He went on to score eight goals in 19 games in the Senators' run to the Eastern Conference Final in 2017.

Pageau, generously listed as 5'10" and 180 pounds, was selected in the fourth round (No. 96) in the 2011 NHL Draft from the Gatineau Olympiques of the QMJHL. He's always punched above his weight class. After three seasons bouncing back and forth between the minors and the NHL, he earned a full-time job in the NHL in the 2014–15 season.

"He's a heart-and-soul guy of our team that plays hard night in, night out…doesn't matter what game it is in the regular season, you know that he's showing up, doing everything he can for his teammates," defenseman Dion Phaneuf said. "Just great to see him get rewarded by a four-goal game, overtime winner. It's a legendary game, and he deserves every bit of credit that he's getting and that he's going to get. What a performance by him."

Said Senators coach Guy Boucher on the night of Pageau's quartet:

> Four goals, that's absolutely sick. It's not just four goals; it's the tying goal, it's the overtime one. But it couldn't happen to a better person. He's just so liked by his peers. A guy who plays at the NHL at that size…first of all, that's unbelievable, but to be able to do what he does every night, you have to respect the man, you've got to respect the player and everything he brings to the game and to our group.
>
> When you ask players who they want to play with, the No. 1 name that always comes is Pageau. It doesn't matter if it's an offensive player [or] a defensive player; that's always the name that comes up. Today was just one of these nights when you know why everybody wants to play with this guy. It's not just a big heart, it's not a lot of character. He's a good hockey player.

Senators fans feel that way. They started singing Pageau's name at Canadian Tire Centre to the tune of "Ole, Ole, Ole," popularized by Montreal Canadiens fans. "Hearing them screaming my name, I think it was just keeping me motivated to go back out there and give everything I have," Pageau said. "Obviously I got a couple of lucky bounces, but it feels really good to do that at home. It is a special moment. I'll remember that, I think, for the rest of my life, for sure."

45 Have a Pint at the Big Rig

For Ottawa Senators fans, there's no better way to toast the career of Senators defenseman Chris Phillips than to raise a pint of Big Rig Salute 1179 lager. Well, adding some pizza would make it better, but we'll get to that in a minute.

Phillips, the first selection in the 1996 NHL Draft by the Senators, played all of his 1,179 games in the NHL with the Senators, one more than Daniel Alfredsson, to become the franchise leader in that department on February 5, 2015. A dependable defenseman, Phillips was at his best when it counted most. His most memorable moment is his overtime goal in Game 6 of the 2003 Eastern Conference Final against the New Jersey Devils that forced a seventh game.

The Senators knew they were getting a character player when they drafted Phillips. He had delayed his opportunity to play in the Western Hockey League to stay at home in Fort McMurray, Alberta, to care for his parents. His dad, Garth, was legally blind, and his mother, Carol, was confined to a wheelchair by a virus.

Phillips paid his dues in his early days with the Senators. He started out wearing No. 5 before switching to No. 4, and Senators coach Jacques Martin used him as a left-winger. He was big, he could skate, and he actually scored. He had an overtime winner right before Christmas against the Montreal Canadiens in 1997. That wasn't exactly foreshadowing. He scored a grand total of 71 goals in the NHL (13 of them game winners), each accompanied by his "One-Armed Salute," inspired by Mike Peluso, a forward on the first Senators team in 1992–93. "For not having a lot of practice, it was one of the best goal celebrations ever," Alfredsson deadpanned.

"It wasn't something where I came in and said, 'This is going to be my thing, or what I do,'" Phillips explained to the *Ottawa Citizen's* Wayne Scanlan. "I scored one or two goals, and did that, and one of our trainers, Andy Playter, mentioned that that was a pretty good celebration. I also remember when the team first came to Ottawa, I was at home watching the games on TV and remember Mike Peluso doing that same kind of Senator Salute…and it reminded me of that, so I thought I'd pay a little tribute to him as well."

Phillips would go on to play on the two best shutdown duos in Senators history with Anton Volchenkov and Zdeno Chara. "I just try and lead by example," he said when asked for advice for those who might follow in his path. "Do what I do, and let them see that if you quietly go about what's asked of you, this is possible [for] anyone. I was a high draft pick but never a superstar or anything like that, just a journeyman guy who put in hard work and time. Good, long stories can come of that."

He earned the nickname the Big Rig along the way. Then he met and married his wife, Erin, and they became tireless workers on behalf of charities and fund-raisers around the national capital. Phillips, a Western guy, put down deep roots in Ottawa. Which brings us to beer.

Phillips opened his first Big Rig Brewery and Kitchen in 2012 at a cost of $5.5 million with four partners. Aided by the association with Phillips's high profile and his classy reputation, they did more than $6 million in business the first year, putting them in the top three or four restaurants in the national capital. They then opened two more establishments.

Brewmaster and co-owner Lon Ladell has created award-winning craft beers. Big Rig won the Ontario Brewing Awards Best New Brewery award in 2013. The beers at Big Rig have won 20 medals at the Ontario Brewing Awards through 2016.

One of Big Rig Brewery's creations is the Salute 1179, brewed in consultation with Phillips. "I've always liked beer," Phillips said with a laugh. "I'm still learning every day. Listening to these guys [at Big Rig], you learn something new every day."

"This is his beer. Lon created this beer with Chris's input," Big Rig sales representative Tim Feren said. "This is an homage to his career with the Sens and in the community. It's a light lager, 4 percent. This is a really, really great easy-drinking summertime beer. Great light pale, straw notes, super crisp, super refreshing. This is a really great way to finish the night off. It's going to cleanse the palate nicely with a clean hop finish toward the end. You can just let it speak for itself."

Done in by back trouble, Phillips retired on May 26, 2016. "What impressed me so much about Chris is he was so underrated when he played as probably one of the best matchup, shutdown defensemen the eague has ever had," Senators general manager Pierre Dorion said. "Chris was always a smart player. He brought great intangibles to the game, and he was a key contributor for many years to the Ottawa Senators. As late as 2014–15, he was playing 26 minutes a night…. For those who know Chris, Chris is a great guy's guy. You want to be around him. He represents loyalty. He represents what an Ottawa Senator is."

Said former teammate Mike Fisher: "He just worked and got the job done and probably didn't get enough credit for some of the things he did here. He was one of my favorites, for sure, that I played with. I don't think he got enough credit for what he's done in the community, the teammate that he was, and the type of person he is."

Oh, yes, about the pizza at the Big Rig: I'm a pizza guy, and I'd put the pie at Big Rig in the top three in Ottawa. My favorite: the Quattro Carne—a power play of bacon, sausage, salami, and pepperoni on regular crust. Cheers, and bon appetit!

46 The Lion Is Born: The Bizarre Story

The Senators lost a lot in their first few months in the NHL, including a rental van taken by the man who was their first mascot, a guy who claimed he paddled across the St. Lawrence River using a hockey stick as a rudder and illegally entered Canada hours before the Senators' opening night game. Dean Schoenewald, a native of Ocean City, New Jersey, grew up poor in a single-parent home after his dad went to jail for counterfeiting. Schoenewald told the *Philadelphia Daily News* in November 2010 that his dad, Lester, served time with Jimmy Hoffa in Lewisburg Federal Penitentiary in Pennsylvania.

A former TV weatherman and mayoral candidate, Schoenewald had a checkered run in the mascot business after he took money intended for college tuition and showed up as the Philadelphia Eagles' unofficial mascot (he made national TV when a Dallas Cowboys fan set fire to his left wing). After he flew the coop there, he did the same in San Jose for the expansion Sharks, driving cross-country in a van made up to look like a land shark.

After the Sharks gig, he convinced the Senators to let him wear their mascot outfit. Small problem: he didn't have a visa to get into

Canada to work. According to Schoenewald, whom I interviewed at a press conference for a book he was writing in November 1993, he commandeered a boat in Ogdensburg, New York, and paddled across the river to Prescott, Ontario, where his brother Joe was waiting, and snuck into Ottawa. I am not making this up.

Jim Steel, the Senators' vice president of marketing at the time, denied the Senators approved the plan to forge the St. Lawrence River. "Let's be serious. If I'd condoned anything like that, I'd be the one looking for a job," Steel said. "There's no truth to that at all. If he's writing a book, I hope he's a better writer than he was a mascot."

An excerpt from Schoenewald's book he handed out at his press conference (which I can't find any record of actually being published): "I shoved off five minutes later on what would be an exhausting hour and 20 minute paddle to Canada. I was lowered to the ice in full costume five hours later in front of a packed house and and national TV audience. ANYTHING for the team. The Lion was born!" So was a lawsuit!

The Senators fired Schoenewald in January 1993, and he sued for the $125,000 in salary he said remained on his two-year contract, $25,000 for mental distress, and $5,000 for the Stanley Cup ring he might have been able to win (he must have been too busy performing in the stands to actually see what was happening on the ice).

In the statement of defense, the Senators said Schoenewald was dismissed for abusive conduct toward Senators and Lansdowne Park staff and fans, failure to perform at all home games, and excessive and unauthorized spending on props and skits.

There was also a $25,000 counterclaim for the rental van, which was returned. "It had 250,000 miles on it," former Senators president Cyril Leeder said. "He must have driven it everywhere."

Four years later, Schoenewald was running Mascot Mania, a mascot school in Nashville, where he charged $795 for a three-day mascot makeover. He was profiled in the *Wall Street Journal*, *Sports Illustrated*, and on *CBS Morning News*.

In 2010 he was back in Ocean City, reinvented as a Christian Democrat talk show host on his website liberalfaith.com.

In 2015 he wound up in Oklahoma City using high school kids to solicit donations in the street for what he said was suicide prevention, but an investigation by KFOR-TV's *In Your Corner* team reported Schoenewald "could never show us proof [of] where the cash was going."

On January 5, 2016, KFOR News in Oklahoma City reported a Dean Schoenewald had been sentenced to 15 years for burglary, kidnapping, and threatening to shoot his son in Kingfisher County. Court records show Schoenewald showed up at his ex-girlfriend's house armed with a small pistol, duct-taped her hands, and took his son hostage. Schoenwald eventually surrendered to police and was taken into custody without harming the boy or his mother. He's eligible for parole in 2028.

47 Roger

There are so many Roger Neilson stories from his 25-year Hall of Fame coaching career in the NHL—from introducing video as a teaching tool to wearing outlandish ties to a towel on a hockey stick—but there is but one that stands out in the legend's short time with the Ottawa Senators.

To backtrack: Neilson, who had gone on medical leave from the Philadelphia Flyers after being diagnosed with bone cancer in 2000, was replaced for the playoffs by Craig Ramsay (a former

Senators assistant) and then let go by Flyers general manager Bob Clarke in one of the all-time public relations fiascos in hockey history. ("The Neilson situation—Roger got cancer—that wasn't our fault," Clarke said on TSN. "We didn't tell him to go get cancer. It's too bad that he did. We feel sorry for him, but then he went goofy on us.")

Neilson, then 66, was hired as an assistant by Senators coach Jacques Martin, completing, as often happens, the coaching circle. Neilson had given Martin his first break when he hired him as an assistant coach with the Peterborough Petes of the OHL. Martin said:

> I had a special relationship with Roger going back to my days in Peterborough. I've taken a lot of holidays with Roger, whether it was Hawaii or Vegas. In the summertime I used to always go work his hockey camp for a couple of weeks and stay at his place. Roger was special. What always impressed me and amazed me about Roger was when you talked to a player who had been coached by Roger, the feedback was always incredible. Players loved him. The energy and enthusiasm he brought to the rink every day, the positivity. His discipline. He was such an unbelievable person and such a great hockey mind.

At the end of the 2001–02 season, in a great gesture on the Senators' part, general manager Marshall Johnston had the idea to give Neilson the opportunity to coach the final two games of the season and become the ninth man to coach 1,000 games in the NHL. Martin stepped aside and Neilson went into the books as the Senators' head coach for a 4–0 win against the Boston Bruins and a 5–2 loss to the Toronto Maple Leafs. "It was well deserved and very obvious to me that it was something that would mean a lot to him, and it meant a lot to me to be able to give him that opportunity," Martin said.

In the 2002–03 season, Neilson's health deteriorated. He underwent a procedure in December in which doctors drilled holes in his skull to treat tumors in his brain.

The Senators went into bankruptcy in January, when Covanta Energy Corp. (originally Ogden Corp., which had guaranteed the Senators' loans) filed for Chapter 11 bankruptcy protection. The Senators overcame that distraction and won the Presidents' Trophy with 113 points.

They defeated the New York Islanders and former Senators captain Alexei Yashin in the first round, dropping the first game and then winning four straight, and rolled over the Philadelphia Flyers in the second round, allowing just 10 goals in six games.

The Senators faced the New Jersey Devils in Ottawa's first Eastern Conference Final. The teams split the first two games in Ottawa, with the Senators winning 3–2 in overtime in Game 1 on a goal by Shaun Van Allen and the Devils winning Game 2 4–1. The Devils won Games 3 and 4 in East Rutherford, New Jersey, by scores of 1–0 and 5–2 to push the Senators to the brink of elimination.

Before Game 5, the Senators gathered in their video room across the hall from their dressing room for what they thought would be another scouting report. Instead it was a meeting that would stick with many of them for the rest of their lives. Neilson was frail, so frail he needed to be transported in a golf cart from the Corel Centre's loading dock to the Senators' dressing room. He sat in front of the players in a track suit and ballcap, a man fading away before their eyes.

Neilson, a deeply religious man, spoke to the players about not wasting the opportunities that God puts in front of you. The room was silent but for Neilson's trembling voice. And who knows how

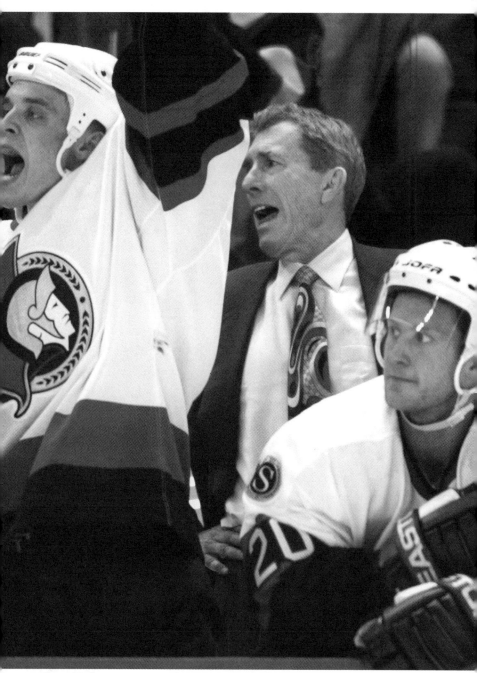

Roger Neilson: a mentor and an inspiration.

much it took out of him just to summon the energy and strength to speak?

Van Allen told me after the game: "He told us you only get so many chances. Here's a guy who is really sick, fighting the toughest battle anybody could ever fight. How on Earth did he have the guts and courage to come in and say that to us?

"He had the courage to sit in front of us in that room and give us that message. That's the type of human being he is."

"I've been in this league for 26 years and I've been with 10 different teams and I got to the Final once. Enjoy this opportunity," Neilson said, "because you never know when it will happen again."

He shuffled out of the room on his thin, unsteady legs and went home to watch the game on television.

"I don't know if anything else needed to be said. I don't think anything better could have been said," remembered Van Allen. "It just showed the character of Roger."

"Everybody knew the importance of the game, but he put it in words that really took it to you," Senators captain Daniel Alfredsson said. "What Roger's been through in his hockey career, he does put it in a good perspective, that this is a great opportunity that you guys have."

Inspired by Neilson's message and the first playoff goal for 19-year-old rookie center Jason Spezza, who also had an assist, the Senators defeated the Devils 3–1 with their most complete game of the series.

The Senators won Game 6 in New Jersey on an overtime goal by Chris Phillips but lost Game 7 at home on a goal by Jeff Friesen with 2:14 left in the third period. "We wanted to win so bad," Phillips said. "A lot of our inspiration there was for Rog. He had some really great speeches for us there, and that one, honestly, losing that Game 7 probably stung worse than losing in the Final just because of not being able to do it for Rog. That's what made that goal so big for me and the team, because of what was going on in the dressing room."

It was a heartbreaking end to their season, but Neilson's speech before Game 5 endured as one of the most touching and emotional episodes in Senators history. "I have been around a lot of things," Van Allen said, "but I don't know if I have been around anything like that before."

48 To Lift or Not to Lift

Discussions were had, opinions considered, and the decision made. To touch the Prince of Wales Trophy or not? It was the question faced by Eastern Conference playoff champions each season before heading off to the Stanley Cup Final.

In the moments after captain Daniel Alfredsson scored the biggest goal in Senators history to that point, on the afternoon of May 19, 2007, the Prince of Wales Trophy sat gleaming on a table near center ice. It was to be presented by NHL deputy commissioner Bill Daly. Alfredsson sized up the trophy, leaned in, put his right hand on it, and left it on the table. "I was going to lift it, but I didn't think it was that big," Alfredsson said. "The only thing I'm superstitious about is not being superstitious."

Senators defenseman Wade Redden picked up the trophy at the behest of Coach Bryan Murray and hauled it into the Senators' dressing room. It sat on a table by a big Gatorade jug and some orange slices. "When Alfie didn't take it, Bryan figured we might as well have it in the room. I don't know if Bryan is superstitious, but he said in Anaheim they didn't touch it and they didn't win," Redden said. "I don't think we had a plan. Obviously it's a great accomplishment, but it's not the big [trophy] we want."

When it counted the most, Alfredsson had a game that formed a cornerstone of his reputation as the Senators' greatest player. The Senators led the Sabres 3–1 in the series going into Game 5 at HSBC Arena. The Senators were in position to eliminate the Sabres, who had won their three previous playoff meetings, and advance to their first Stanley Cup Final in the modern era.

The Sabres were the Presidents' Trophy winners and the first seed in the East, and the Senators were fourth, but the Senators had played their best hockey of the season after Christmas. They eliminated both the Pittsburgh Penguins and the New Jersey Devils in five games. The Sabres had defeated the New York Islanders and the New York Rangers.

The Senators opened up a 3–0 series lead, winning the first two games in Buffalo, the second in double overtime on a one-hopper from the point by defenseman Joe Corvo. The Sabres avoided elimination with a 3–2 win in Ottawa in Game 4.

After there was no scoring in the first period, Jochen Hecht gave the Sabres a 1–0 lead, and then Alfredsson took over. He didn't get an assist on Dany Heatley's sixth goal of the playoffs, but he went hard to the front of the net and jostled with Sabres defenseman Toni Lydman, giving Jason Spezza room to set up Heatley. Alfredsson did all the work on Spezza's goal to make it 2–1 with 39 seconds left in the second period, getting Sabres goaltender Ryan Miller to overplay him before dishing to Spezza on a two-on-one. The odd-man rush was set up by Heatley dashing back to break up a Sabres rush.

Buffalo's Maxim Afinogenov tied the game on the power play at 10:58 of the third period just after a Sabres five-on-three expired and Daniel Brière hit the post, the puck going to Afinogenov. The teams went to overtime.

At 3:23 of overtime, Spezza thought he had scored, but Miller got the shaft of his stick on his wrist shot from 14 feet. Close to the halfway mark of the first overtime period, Brière won a draw in the Ottawa zone and got a shot away, and the puck wound up coming out of the Ottawa zone up the right-wing boards. Alfredsson carried it into the Buffalo zone and attracted four Sabres to him near the right point. It seemed like the Sabres, recognizing how Alfredsson was the head of the snake when it came to the Senators attack, wanted to swarm Alfredsson whenever he had the puck.

At the point, he dished the puck off to Heatley, who chipped it back to Alfredsson near the goal line. Alfredsson propelled it behind the Buffalo net, where it was rimmed around and out of the Buffalo zone by pinching Ottawa defenseman Wade Redden.

That's when one of the things that Senators team had done best in the second half of that season led to the winning goal. Senators defenseman Andrej Meszáros retreated inside his blue line and the Senators quickly reloaded. That was one of the things stressed by Murray—the quick transition. Heatley, who was playing maybe his best game as a Senator, got his feet moving on the regroup, got back, and got in position in front of the Sabres bench to give Meszáros an option.

He took Meszáros's indirect pass off the boards, took a few strides, and then slipped a backhand pass to a looping Alfredsson, who was gathering speed at center ice. Alfredsson, after a half dozen strides, hit the Buffalo blue line at almost full speed. He entered near the left-wing dot outside the line and shaded to his right, shifting from a neutral position with the puck to full forehand.

He cut between two Sabres and then made the move that made the play. Sensing pressure from the right from Hecht, Alfredsson shifted to the outside edge of his left skate and veered slightly to his left, giving himself the space to get off a shot through the screen set up by defenseman Brian Campbell. The puck beat Miller to the glove side, and the Senators were on their way to their first Stanley Cup Final.

It was a just ending for Alfredsson, who had taken all the heat the year before when he was on the ice for Jason Pominville's short-handed series winner in overtime.

As it turned out, Pominville was on the ice for Alfredsson's goal. "He deserves every little bit of praise he's getting now," Spezza said. "He's our leader. He's been phenomenal. When he was criticized in the past, it upset us all. It was great to see him score."

"A lot of people were wrongfully blaming everything on [Alfredsson]. Because he had to go through that, he certainly deserves to be the hero now," Senators defenseman Chris Phillips said.

"Right now," Alfredsson said, "it's the biggest goal I ever scored."

Later, in the Senators' dressing room, after most of the gear had been packed up, somebody realized Murray hadn't had his picture taken with the Prince of Wales Trophy. It had been packed up into its case, and Senators media-relations man Phil Legault unpacked it. Murray sat in one of the stalls, the trophy in front of him.

"Smile," somebody said.

"I can't," Murray said. "I can't get my face to relax."

After the high of advancing to their first Stanley Cup Final of the modern era, the Senators ran out of gas, falling to the Anaheim Ducks in five games.

49 A Long Way from Gothenburg

It wasn't a straight line from being a sixth-round draft pick in 1994 to the marvelous night of December 4, 2014—the night Daniel Alfredsson retired as an Ottawa Senator. After 17 years with the Senators and an awkward departure for a season with the Detroit Red Wings, Alfredsson closed the final chapter on his playing career.

After some work by Senators general manager Bryan Murray to smooth the road for Alfredsson to return to Ottawa and retire as a Senator, Alfredsson signed a one-day contract with Murray and Senators owner Eugene Melnyk. He put on the sweater he wore for his final game as a Senator on May 24, 2013, in the playoffs against the Pittsburgh Penguins and slipped his arms around the shoulders of Melnyk and Murray for a photo as many in the room applauded.

This was a significant night for the Senators and their fans—the closing of the playing career of the modern Senators' most popular star, the man who had become the face, the heartbeat, and the conscience of the franchise. He was always a person who found the right thing to say in the big moments, even if it was a truth some people didn't want to hear. Here is Alfredsson's speech from that night:

> One evening nearly 20 years ago, a young man in a small town in Sweden got a phone call that would change his life. It was an invitation to play hockey in Canada. I had never been to North America, I had a young girlfriend, Bibbi, and it was a long way from [Gothenburg] to Ottawa. But we made the leap. We began an incredible new chapter of our lives in your town starting in August

1995. Our marvelous boys were born here, and we grew from youngsters into aging parents. You made your town our town. Thank you.

It was an incredible experience to play hockey with so many great players, so many great friends over so many great seasons. I really realize that I'm a very lucky guy. Even more important to me than my time on the ice was my time in our city, meeting new people, making new friends, watching my boys grow, and most of all beginning a campaign to help change attitudes toward those struggling with mental illness. My work with the Royal Ottawa Hospital has been another high point in my life. Whatever I gave has been more than repaid in seeing the changes beginning to happen and some of the lives that I have touched. It is still an important part of my life and will continue to be so.

Some of you may remember nearly four years ago now, my body started sending me signals that all these years of hockey had a cost. My back began to act up, and I began to have the kind of issues bodies develop after years of physical work. I worked hard to fight it off, and I got some great help along the way and I got another two great seasons in Ottawa and a third one last year. But in the back of my mind, I still knew that the clock [was] ticking. Then on a Saturday morning two summers ago, I got another phone call from an old Swedish pal of mine. This call started a process that would launch the next chapter in our lives. It was a very, very hard decision to make: changing teams, uproot[ing] my family, start[ing] over again in a new place. But change helps you grow. New experiences are as important when you're young, like my children, as they were for me at 22 or even today. We've had a great year in Detroit: new friends, a new team, new adventures. Thank you, Detroit.

I've grown and learned a lot in the past 18 months. I realize[d] that you never stop learning, especially when you're open to new beginnings and new chapters. Then last season my body began to complain once more. The old injury and the hard work of recovery began all over again. I worked hard to rehab my back this summer so I could play another year. However, about three weeks ago, I realized it's time to retire. It's another hard decision.

Then I got another important phone call from Ottawa. Bryan said he and Mr. Melnyk had spoken and had an idea that I should not end my career in Detroit but with a proper retirement here in our adopted hometown. I spoke with [Detroit GM] Ken Holland about my retirement and that Bryan and Mr. Melnyk wanted me to retire as an Ottawa Senator, and Ken encouraged me to retire here. He said it's the right thing to do.

I was taken aback by this offer. I never believed that my career entitled me to any special treatment. However, Bibbi and I both agreed this was the right thing to do and it would give us a chance to say thank you to the people and the fans of Ottawa. So here we are. Today I officially retire as an Ottawa Senator, and another new chapter will begin tonight as we say good-bye to Ottawa. The future may hold some role for me in hockey again, but not this year. This is one for my family, for my own life, and for reflecting on where we've been and deciding on what's next. For now I'm just very grateful for this opportunity to say thank you and good-bye—and please, no more phone calls for a while.

Let me just say thank you to Ottawa, to the Sens, to the Sens fans, and especially to Mr. Melnyk. Thank you. And to Bryan. I really appreciate this. *Merci et à bientôt.* Thank you.

50 The Perfect Senator

The Senators have been blessed to have many memorable players wear their sweater over their first 25 years. Who was the greatest Senator is always a good discussion over a beer, because the definition of that term can be pretty wide-reaching and subjective. But who would be the *perfect* Senator? If you could take the best qualities of all the best Senators and combine them, what would that player look like?

We took a shot at it:

1. **Zdeno Chara's size:** Let's start with the toolbox before we put the tools in it. At 6'9" Chara is one of the biggest players in the game. It was always a knock on big guys that they looked slow or lumbering, but over years of work and extra practice, Chara steadily improved his mobility. His size made him imposing, and he has the longest reach in the game. That's a pretty good start.

2. **Erik Karlsson's eyes:** When it comes to seeing the game and anticipating the play, Karlsson has that quality that separates the great from the good. He's one of those players that sees things develop a second before everybody else on the ice. He also has the audacity to envision something outrageous and try it, like that saucer pass to Mike Hoffman in the 2017 Stanley Cup Playoffs against the Boston Bruins that resulted in the best goal in Senators history.

3. **Daniel Alfredsson's heart:** The longtime captain was the heart and soul of the Senators throughout the 2000s, leading with his consistent effort night in and night out, his professionalism,

and the way he approached his job. Nobody cared or tried harder.

4. **Jason Spezza's hands:** The big center could dangle with the best of them. Just ask former Montreal Canadiens defenseman Sheldon Souray and goaltender Jose Theodore. Spezza walked both of them for an overtime winner in 2005. He wasn't the greatest skater, so it was his hands that made him a prolific point producer for the Senators. He holds the franchise record for most assists in a season, with 71 in 2005–06.

5. **Karlsson's feet:** The best skater the Senators have had, Karlsson has been slowed over the years by catastrophic injuries. He had his Achilles' tendon sliced by Pittsburgh Penguins forward Matt Cooke in 2013 and underwent surgery in the summer of 2017 to repair torn tendons in his left foot. There was a stretch there when Karlsson was far and away the best skater the Senators ever had.

6. **Marian Hossa's two-way game:** He developed into one of the best two-way forwards in the game under coach Jacques Martin. Hossa was one of those special players who could have a great chance around the other team's net and then be the first forward back through the neutral zone, hounding the opposition's puck carrier. He will be a Hall of Famer, and it will be because he was so great at both ends of the ice.

7. **Dany Heatley's release:** Heatley did not need much time or room to score a goal. It was interesting that everyone in the building would know the puck was going to him and he still managed to have back-to-back seasons of 50 goals. I can't remember him scoring on a slap shot. It was just that quick little snap. He remains the only Senator to have had a 50-goal season.

8. **Mark Stone's stick:** There hasn't been a craftier guy with a quicker stick than Stone since he became a full-time player in the NHL in the 2014–15 season. His nickname should be

Cobra. From 2014–15 to 2017–18, he had 381 takeaways in 284 games. John Tavares of the New York Islanders was next over that period with 275.

9. **Chris Phillips's poise:** The player they called the Big Rig was about as calm as they come. He was a pillar for those great Senators teams through the early 2000s, playing on a shutdown pair for the most part with Anton Volchenkov. Nothing put him off his game.

10. **Chris Neil's toughness:** The presence of the winger made all his teammates a couple inches taller and a few pounds heavier. He was usually the smallest dog in the fight (he had 238 of them in the NHL) but won more than his share. His 2,522 penalty minutes are a Senators franchise record.

11. **Mike Fisher's character:** If Alfredsson hadn't done such an outstanding job of being the Senators' captain, the job could have gone to Fisher. He was an honest, hardworking player, another guy who could do whatever job was needed to help his team win. He went on to become the captain of the Nashville Predators for the 2016–17 season.

Put all those elements together, and you would have the perfect Senator. Now try to figure out how you are going to pay him.

51 Wonder Y

"The plane to go and get him was warming up on the tarmac." That, according to one person with knowledge of the situation, was how close the Senators were to making a trade for Detroit Red Wings captain Steve Yzerman.

There are at least a couple versions of this urban legend. The background: At the beginning of the 1995–96 season, Senators center Alexei Yashin was holding out. Yashin, the No. 2 pick in the 1992 NHL Draft, had signed a five-year, $4 million contract in April 1993. Two months later, when they made Alexandre Daigle the first pick in the NHL Draft, the Senators gave Daigle a five-year, $12.25 million contract.

The Yashin camp always held that they were promised by the Senators that if Yashin was the better player, they would renegotiate his contract. Yashin had 30 goals and 49 assists for 79 points in his rookie season. Daigle, also playing his first season, was second on the team in scoring in 1993–94 with 51 points. The Senators refused to open Yashin's deal. He didn't show up for training camp for the 1994–95 season, which wound up being delayed until January because of a lockout. As a compromise, Yashin was offered bonuses for team performance and game-tying and -winning goals. If he met the bonuses and averaged a point per game, his deal could be reopened. Yashin had 44 points in 47 games, and they remained in a stalemate.

The disputes continued into the fall of 1995, and Yashin again sat out training camp. The Senators started the season without their best player, and it was a disaster. Coach Rick Bowness was fired in November with a move to the Palladium looming in January.

In the background, according to one version of the Yzerman story, Senators general manager Randy Sexton was talking to his Red Wings counterpart, Jimmy Devellano, about a Yashin for Yzerman deal despite Senators owner Rod Bryden saying they would not trade Yashin. (It reminded me of what Senators GM Pierre Gauthier once told me about holdout defenseman Bryan Berard: "We're not trading him until we trade him.")

In Detroit, Yzerman had turned 30 and had sustained a torn meniscus in his knee. It couldn't be repaired, and all the cartilage was removed. Could he be the same player? The Red Wings finished first in the Western Conference three years in a row starting in 1993–94 but couldn't close the deal. They lost in the first round in 1994, then lost in the Final to the New Jersey Devils in the shortened 1994–95 season.

There was talk that the Red Wings, despite having seven future Hall of Famers in their lineup, needed a shakeup, and Yzerman, who was at odds with Coach Scotty Bowman over a commitment to team play, became the subject of trade rumors. Yzerman was playing some nights behind Sergei Fedorov and Keith Primeau at center.

As legend has it, the deal was made to swap Yashin for Yzerman, 19 for 19, and the Senators thought the deal was done. A plane was ordered to go pick up Yzerman in Detroit and bring him back to Ottawa, where he had grown up. The deal died at the Detroit end. There was talk the Red Wings ownership intervened and the Ilitches—Mike and Marian, who regarded Yzerman as one of their favorites—intervened. There was also a theory that Bowman never intended to have Yzerman traded but just wanted to scare him into toeing the company line.

Yashin sat out until January, when new general manager Pierre Gauthier arrived and signed him to play the rest of the season (46 games) for $720,000 and $12.3 million for the following four seasons. Yashin was second on the team in scoring that season despite playing only 46 games.

There have been other versions of this trade rumor: A bigger deal after Sexton was fired and Pierre Gauthier had taken over as GM, which saw Yashin, goaltender Damian Rhodes, and two first-round draft picks going to the Red Wings for Yzerman and goaltender Chris Osgood. On the face of it, this rumor seems like a gross overpayment on the part of the Senators, given Yzerman had fallen out of favor and Osgood, at that point, didn't have any Stanley Cups to enhance his résumé. There has also been speculation that Berard, another Senators holdout, and another first-round draft pick were offered for Yzerman.

There's no question there were talks between the two teams regarding Yzerman. A deal might have been close, but in the end, Yzerman stayed in the Motor City and it was the best deal the Red Wings never made. Yzerman went on to win raise three Stanley Cups wearing the Red Wings' captain's C.

52 "So You're an Expert"

Two of the biggest hits ever dished out by Ottawa Senators were by forward Chris Neil and defenseman Andy Sutton. Neil's hit was on Buffalo Sabres forward Chris Drury in the game that led to the brawl and fight between Senators goaltender Ray Emery and Sabres enforcer Andrew Peters on February 22, 2007 (covered in Chapter 35). Sutton's was on Pittsburgh Penguins defenseman Jordan Leopold in Game 2 of their first-round Stanley Cup Playoffs series on April 16, 2010.

What made Sutton's hit notorious in Senators history was not only the ferociousness of the collision but its aftermath, which resulted in one of the best clashes between a player and a reporter.

This hit was classic Sutton: A good skater for a big man (6'6", 245 pounds), he had refined the technique of coming across the ice and crushing oncoming skaters while moving sideways. Playing the left side, he would come across and make contact with his rear end or left side on the opponent. He had a long list of victims in his 13-year NHL career. The native of Kingston, Ontario, wasn't drafted and instead signed as a free agent with the San Jose Sharks after playing at Michigan Tech.

After playing with the Sharks, Minnesota Wild, Atlanta Thrashers, and New York Islanders, he was traded to the Senators at the 2010 trade deadline by the Islanders for a second-round draft pick that had previously belonged to the Sharks. The 34-year-old played 18 regular-season games with the Senators, and he had some history with the Penguins that season. On January 19 he had hit Penguins forward Pascal Dupuis from behind into the end boards. Dupuis was bloodied when his face hit the dasher. Sutton was suspended two games for that hit.

Late in the first period of Game 2, Leopold took a pass in his own zone and carried the puck up the right-wing boards. When Senators forward Nick Foligno moved in to check him, Leopold lowered his head and turned his left shoulder toward Foligno. That's when Sutton thundered in and caught Leopold in the head with his left arm. His elbow was down and both skates stayed on the ice.

Leopold went down, apparently knocked out, spreadeagled facedown on the ice. The momentum of the hit sent Sutton flying through the penalty box door. A scrum ensued, but there was no penalty assessed to Sutton for the hit. (Rule 48—which introduced a penalty for hits from the lateral or blind side in which the opponent's head was targeted—wasn't introduced until 2011. This would have been a perfect example of that.)

After the game, Sutton came out to face the media, accompanied by Senators media-relations man Phil Legault. There were a couple questions asking Sutton to talk his way through the hit. He adopted a classic defense, parrying the questions and pointing out a hit on Senators forward Jarkko Ruutu earlier in the game deserved more attention. "The hit on Jarkko was way worse," he said. "I got suspended for hitting Pascal Dupuis earlier this year for that exact same hit, so I don't know why mine is going to be hotly contested."

At that point, a reporter from Pittsburgh asked, "You didn't know your elbow came up and hit him in the head?"

Sutton turned and bristled. "Are you asking me, or are you telling me?"

"I'm asking you."

"Are you an expert?"

"No, it was on the replay."

"So you're an expert."

"No, it was on the replay."

"So you saw it? You're saying you saw it and you're an expert?"

"Yes."

"You're not an expert."

"I saw it. I'm asking you, did you know you got your elbow up?"

"You're telling me I got my elbow up?"

"It was on the replay."

"You're an expert? You know it was up?"

At that point, Sutton looked at Legault, who was standing by his right shoulder, with a "Do you believe this?" look, and Legault cut off the interview with, "OK, that's it, guys. Thank you."

It was a masterful performance by Sutton, who never admitted to anything and avoided the trap of "anything you say could be used against you."

It might have been the best stick handling of his career.

53 Buddha Power

Tom Chorske was in the midst of another miserable season with the Ottawa Senators in 1996–97. The previous 18 months had been the low point of his NHL career for the 30-year-old, just three months after the high point: winning the Stanley Cup with the New Jersey Devils. The Senators claimed Chorske on waivers on the eve of the 1995–96 season.

The Devils had fairly earned their reputation as the NHL's buttoned-down franchise under general manager Lou Lamoriello, conservative in demeanor and play. Inside the Devils dressing room, the players had taken to calling it the Firm, a reference to the 1993 Sydney Pollack–directed legal thriller (and John Grisham novel) of the same name, about a rigorously controlled law firm. Lamoriello was the Devils' general manager from 1987 to 2015. Only two men served their teams longer: Conn Smythe and Art Ross.

In his first four months with the Senators, Chorske had three coaches, two general managers, two presidents, and two home arenas. Chorske, a former first-round pick of the Montreal Canadiens (No. 16 in 1985) left the controlled environment on the edge of the New Jersey swamp and was thrown into the quicksand that was the Senators. The Senators had won 33 games in three seasons; the Devils had won 109.

"I thought I was the kind of person who could kind of roll with the punches, and that I was going to be able to turn it into a positive and be a leader. I wasn't able to do it because of all the turmoil and the chaos," Chorske admitted. "I was doing nothing. I was just bewildered at what was going on." There's rolling with the punches, and then there's getting hit with a sledgehammer.

Sweet Revenge

As the 1995–96 season wound down, the Senators didn't have much going for them. Things were looking up with some of the changes wrought by new general manager Pierre Gauthier and coach Jacques Martin, who were brought in halfway through the season, but they were going to miss the Stanley Cup Playoffs for the fourth straight year of their existence.

Their last game of the season was an afternoon game against the New Jersey Devils, the team that had waived Tom Chorske at the beginning of the season. "They needed to win to get into the playoffs, and we beat them on a Saturday afternoon and I scored two goals," Chorske said. "Although it was kind of a negative, being vindictive, that was another memorable moment in my career.... All they had to do was beat us and they were in. We showed up with nothing to lose. I don't know, the hockey gods were with us and we got some bounces. They got real tight going into the third and they couldn't do it."

Chorske hung in there. He managed 15 goals, tied for fourth on the team, in 1995–96. With the arrival of general manager Pierre Gauthier in December 1995 and Coach Jacques Martin about a month later, and the move to the Palladium in January 1996, things started to shift for the positive for the Senators. Chorske got off to a slow start in 1996–97 with four goals in 29 games before the All-Star break.

While wandering around San Francisco during the All-Star break, Chorske and his wife, Kristie, were checking out a touristy neighborhood. They wandered from shop to shop, and they happened upon one that had a display of Buddhas. Legend has it that rubbing the Buddha's belly brings forth luck, fortune, and prosperity. Maybe even goals. "They had Buddhas for riches or financial gain, different Buddhas for different fortunes," Chorske remembered. "I think I grabbed the one for good luck."

Buddha would not seem to have much connection to hockey, but it worked for Chorske. With Buddha looking down from his stall in the dressing room or riding shotgun in his shaving kit on the road, Chorske went on a tear in the second half of the season. He had the best scoring stretch of his career: 14 goals in 39 games. All but two of his goals were at even strength; one was on the power play and one was shorthanded. Six goals in each of February and March when the Senators became, for the first time, a real team. Only Alexei Yashin, with 16, had more goals than Chorske after the All-Star break.

Chorske said of the Buddha:

> I had it in my stall and I carried it around with me. As we were going into the playoffs, you guys came around my locker and said, "What do you attribute your late push to?" and I turned and said, "I picked up this Buddha on All-Star break, and maybe that had something to do with it." It was all on after that.
>
> Some of the Buddhists were not happy. That was not what Buddha was supposed to be about—helping athletes win sporting events—but it was fun. It was one of [the most] memorable things [of] my career being part of that thing.

The Senators were 13th and last in the Eastern Conference in January, nine points out of the last playoff spot, but with Chorske heating up and Buddha in their corner, the Senators started to climb up the standings. The Senators and their fans rallied around Buddha, and for the first time in five years, there was legitimate excitement about something that was happening on the ice. The Senators finished 10–4–2, which included three straight one-goal wins to cap the season, the last a 1–0 win over the Buffalo Sabres and goaltender Dominik Hasek to thrust them into the playoffs for the first time.

Backup goaltender Ron Tugnutt had taken over from Damian Rhodes, who was out with an ankle injury. Tugnutt said:

> I remember going into every game knowing we were going to win. Even going into a place where I had never won before, a team that had owned me like Detroit, the second-to-last game of the year. That was the one that set us up to get in, actually. [Defenseman Wade] Redden scored the winning goal there.
>
> My mind-set going in was, "Oh, these guys own me. I play brutal here." That time going in it was, "We got this." Sure enough, we won, and that's the only time I think I won in Detroit. What I remember was when we were walking in there, we knew we were going to win. It was an awesome feeling. We were just a bunch of young guys having fun. "We're awesome, man," and Buddha was leading the charge. It was a distraction that everybody needed. Everyone just kind of laughed about it. It kept everybody loose. "Guys, we're good. We've got the Buddha, man."

What became of the Buddha? Chorske's not sure. "It's gone. It disappeared from my shaving kit long ago," he said. "It's too bad. It's a little relic I'd like to have."

54 *Siriously*

It was something Senators fans already knew. In February 2013 if users of the new Apple iPhone accessed the Siri "intelligent assistant"—which provided answers to questions—and said "Show me a picture of God" or asked "What does God look like?" the female voice answered, "I don't know what Daniel Alfredsson's appearance is." That wasn't totally true, because a small head-and-shoulders photo of the Senators captain, along with his statistics, appeared along with a text version of Siri's answer.

Alfredsson, the Senators' all-time leader in goals, assists, and points—and the heart and soul of the team for 17 years—was the most popular Senator in the modern history of the franchise. On radio station TSN 1200, the rights holder for Senators broadcasts, people were regularly encouraged to join the "Church of Alfie," and "Praise Alfie!" was frequently heard over the airwaves after another of Alfredsson's clutch goals.

There was a variety of theories about why Siri would equate Alfredsson with the Greatest One. Alex DeVries, an engineer, suggested to the CBC that an 18-year-old *Sports Illustrated* article that included the sentence "God was watching over Helen Alfredsson," in reference to the Swedish golfer, could partly be responsible. (I remember Senators director of personnel John Ferguson, when the Senators drafted the unknown prospect in 1994, saying he thought Helen was Daniel's cousin, but they were actually not related.)

DeVries explained that Siri searched the Internet to find matches between words, but one article probably wasn't enough to make Alfredsson identified as God in Siri's opinion. "My money is on that it's a good prank that somebody has pulled within Apple. That would be my guess," he said.

Marc Saltzman, the author of *Siri for Dummies*, told the *Ottawa Sun* he thought making Alfredsson the answer to the command "Show me a picture of God" was a ruse committed by a smart Senators fan. "It could just be an Easter egg hidden by the development team," Saltzman told the *Sun's* Doug Hempstead. "It is very funny."

When the media showed up at the rink for practice after the Siri answer had become a hot topic, Alfredsson handled it all like he did everything: coolly and with a touch of humor. "I don't know what to think, to be honest. Some the guys told me that this morning," he said in an aw-shucks way. "I don't know. I guess I have to get to work to decide who the next Pope is." (Pope Benedict XVI had resigned that week, becoming the first pontiff to step down in 600 years.) Alfredsson, a first-liner, was always good with the one-liner.

It wasn't long before Apple got clued in, and Siri now replies to "Show me a picture of God" with, "Here are some images of God I found on the web." None of them are of Alfredsson. But if you ask, "Was Daniel Alfredsson ever God?" the first entry Siri comes up with is from YouTube: "Daniel Alfredsson Is God Says Siri." Maybe that will live on for eternity.

55 A Legend Steps Down

On an April day in 2016, not far down the Ottawa Valley from where a young coach started cutting his teeth behind a bench, a chapter was closed on a 35-year NHL career. Senators general manager Bryan Murray, almost two years into a battle with terminal colon cancer, announced he was stepping down and ending his career as a full-timer in the NHL. He had gotten up in the morning and gone to work for an NHL team almost every day since November 11, 1981, when he was named the coach of the Washington Capitals, his first NHL job.

Murray, after consulting with Senators owner Eugene Melnyk, ended his 10-year run as Senators general manager that day and named assistant general manger Pierre Dorion to succeed him. "I guess I've been struggling with it for the last month in particular," Murray said. "I thought about it; I met with Eugene. We had a long discussion about where we're going, what we're doing, and I just felt at the time, and I suggested ahead of time, in all likelihood it would be the right time," he said.

"I think having Pierre in position to do the job and take it over and be a strong general manager was important, obviously," he continued. "There really wasn't any other consideration. Knowing that and how I feel and how much time I've taken away from my family...*tolerant* is an underused word, but putting up with me wanting to be the young man still in hockey, I just felt that after much discussion, it was time to pull the plug." Faced with his health situation and confident in Dorion as his successor, Murray slipped into the role of advisor.

On that April day there was a lot of reminiscing about Murray's career and his legacy. Murray said he knew how he would like his life and work in the NHL to be remembered. "Well, I'd like to think I had respect. I treated people fairly. I communicated well. I love the game. I put a lot into the game," he said. "In turn, I think I gave back a lot of respect. I had some great, great players, many Hall of Famers, many unbelievable people I've worked with. I hope I'm remembered as a pretty good hockey guy who was a decent person."

In addition to the Senators, he was general manager of the Detroit Red Wings, Florida Panthers, and Mighty Ducks of Anaheim, as they were known then. The Panthers, in 1996, and the Ducks, in 2003, advanced to the Stanley Cup Final. He owned a 620–465–131–23 record as a coach in the NHL, including 107–55–20 with the Senators. He was hired to coach the Senators on June 8, 2004, and was behind the bench to guide the Senators to the Stanley Cup Final in 2007. The Senators lost to the Ducks in five games, to a team Murray had a big hand in building during his time there from 2001 to 2004.

That's one thing you can say about Murray, and it's probably the biggest compliment you can give a hockey guy: he took every franchise to heights it hadn't experienced or hadn't experienced in years. The Red Wings were known as the Dead Things, and he helped lay the foundation for future Stanley Cups there. In Florida, he took a three-year-old expansion team and got them to the Stanley Cup Final in 1996. In Anaheim, he put down the foundation for their 2007 Stanley Cup championship.

After two seasons behind the Senators' bench, he was named Senators general manager in the summer of 2007. In his nine seasons as general manager, the Senators made the Stanley Cup Playoffs five times, advancing to the second round in 2013.

Wrote Melnyk in a statement:

> Bryan Murray is a legend of the game and I know his portrait will one day find itself in the Hockey Hall of Fame. Words cannot express my thanks to Bryan and the tremendous support of his wife, Geri, and their two daughters, Heide and Brittany. Bryan's leadership and grace on and off the ice [have] always been exceptional, and I am very happy that Bryan will continue to be a senior member of our hockey operations.

Murray said he would like to be stepping down in better circumstances. The Senators had missed the playoffs for the second time in the past three seasons in 2015–16. "Leaving after a disappointing year, that's maybe the hardest part. You always want to try and leave on the up, and that wasn't to be this year, but I really feel good about the talent level that [will be] on the ice in the future," Murray said. "I was adamant that when I stepped aside to let someone else take over, that we all feel good about the future here. I think it's a very bright future. I think we will be competitive for years to come." The Senators went to the Eastern Conference Final the next season, losing in Game 7 in double overtime against the Pittsburgh Penguins.

Dorion had a good perspective on what Bryan Murray had meant to many up-and-coming NHL executives who got their start under Murray's influence. Murray filled a lot of roles for Dorion as he no doubt did for many before him: boss, mentor, and father figure. Dorion's father, Pierre Sr., was a hockey lifer. He was the chief scout for the NHL's Central Scouting Bureau and worked for the Toronto Maple Leafs. He died of a heart attack in 1994. Dorion said:

> In my eyes, my father was the greatest human being I ever met. He passed away at a young age. Having Bryan Murray in my life has filled a personal need that nobody outside of my dad could.
>
> To me, Bryan is the second-greatest man I've ever known. In the past nine years working together, whether it was many lunches, formal or informal, and the many conversations, it was always about doing the right thing. Working nine years with Bryan has been one of the greatest things in my life, especially in the last seven years, when I've worked with him on an everyday basis.

The Senators, and the NHL, were poorer not having Bryan Murray as part of the show.

56 Turn Back the Clock at the Cattle Castle

Even on a sultry summer afternoon, with sunlight streaming through windows, a Senators fan could stand in the center of the floor under the gleaming dome of the Aberdeen Pavilion in downtown Ottawa and imagine the sound of skates on natural ice. Maybe they're the skates of first Senators superstar "One-Eyed" Frank McGee grinding on the ice in pursuit of the Stanley Cup.

The Aberdeen Pavilion, also known as the Cattle Castle, was opened in 1898 as the centerpiece of the Central Canada Exhibition, Eastern Ontario's harvest fair, and was home to sheep, cattle, and other four-legged creatures. When the frigid winter arrived, it was home to the two-legged stars of the Ottawa Senators at the turn of the 20th century, nicknamed the Silver Seven, and the first Ottawa dynasty with Stanley Cup victories against all comers between 1903 and 1906. The Cattle Castle is the oldest building to have hosted a Stanley Cup championship, according to the City of Ottawa website.

McGee, who lost an eye when he was hit by a puck in 1900, was the Silver Seven's scoring star with a five-goal game during the eight-game regular season and scored a hat trick in Ottawa's first Cup-clinching victory in a two-game total goals series against the Montreal Victorias in 1903. Which is what spawned the Silver Seven moniker. For the victory, the Senators were awarded silver nuggets by team executive Bob Shillington, because cash would have voided their amateur status.

From 1903 through 1906, the Cattle Castle saw the Silver Seven successfully rebuff 11 challenges for the Stanley Cup. One of the most famous was against a team from Dawson City in Canada's

Yukon. The Dawson City Nuggets traveled by dog sleigh, steamer, and train, and even had to walk when warm weather thawed northern roads.

It was a vicious, bloody match according to newspaper accounts (players on each team exchanged blows to the head with their sticks), with Ottawa winning the first game 9–2.

In the second game, Norman Watt of Dawson City (who had knocked out Ottawa's Art Moore with a stick over the head in the first game after being hit in the mouth) was quoted in newspaper reports saying, "McGee doesn't look like too much." In one of the greatest "Oh, yeah?" moments in hockey history, McGee scored 14 goals in Ottawa's 23–2 win in the second game of the challenge to win the Cup. At one point, McGee scored eight goals in a row in a span of less than nine minutes. McGee, who was killed in action in the First World War, helped put the Aberdeen Pavilion on the hockey map, and his life and death mirrored the intersection of both at the Cattle Castle.

In addition to its role as the centerpiece of Ottawa's fairgrounds, the Cattle Castle was a mustering point for Canada's military in both world wars. The building was designed by architect Moses C. Eddy and based on London's Crystal Palace. It was built at a cost of $75,000 and named for the governor general of Canada.

In the 1990s, the building had fallen into disrepair, and in 1992 it looked like the Cattle Castle and memories it contained would be razed. But the Ottawa City Council reversed a decision to destroy the structure and instead moved it to a new location and spent more than $5 million to restore the gleaming, domed building. It is now a jewel of a reinvigorated Lansdowne Park and complements a new football stadium for the Canadian Football League's Ottawa REDBLACKS along with residential and retail units.

The Cattle Castle has hosted concerts, conventions, and events such as the Brier Patch, the social center of the Brier, Canada's national curling championship. The Aberdeen Pavilion was designated a National Historic Site of Canada in 1983 because it is the only large-scale exhibition building surviving from the 19th century. For Senators fans, it was worth saving for the memories.

57 "We're Gonna Kill 'Em"

In the parlance of sports, there is "bulletin board material" and then there is "put up a giant 4K multimedia presentation right outside your opponents' dressing room" material. Unfortunately for the Senators and their fans, owner Eugene Melnyk opted for the latter in 2004.

To set the scene: the Senators, who had lost three straight times to the Toronto Maple Leafs in the postseason Battle of Ontario (2000–02), were feeling about as confident as could be expected given the history of the rivalry and the circumstances in their first-round series in 2004.

The Senators were coming off a run to the Eastern Conference Final the year before in which they had suffered a crushing loss to the New Jersey Devils in Game 7. They had slipped a little from their 113-point performance that won them the President's Trophy, finishing the 2004 season with 102 points, one behind the Maple Leafs. That set up a first-round meeting between the fourth and fifth seeds.

Ottawa's Marian Hossa scored a pair of goals to break a 2–2 tie in Game 1 at Air Canada Centre, and the Senators went on to a 4–2 win. Senators killer Gary Roberts scored both goals in Toronto's 2–0 win in Game 2 as goaltender Ed Belfour delivered a 31-save shutout. Belfour stopped another 37 shots in Ottawa in Game 3 to help the Maple Leafs to another 2–0 win and a 2–1 series lead. Roberts scored again in Game 4, but Hossa had his third goal of the series, and Daniel Alfredsson, Todd White, and Chris Phillips scored for a 4–1 Senators victory to tie the series.

The Senators' offense dried up again in Game 5 back in Toronto (a familiar theme for those Senators teams in the early 2000s), and Belfour had his third shutout of the series, facing 21 shots in the Maple Leafs' 2–0 win to put the Senators on the brink of elimination.

Mike Fisher scored one of the biggest goals in Senators history in double overtime of Game 6 to keep the Senators alive. Winger Antoine Vermette worked the puck down low in the right-wing corner, and with Chris Neil jamming the front of the net, Fisher set up on the far side of the crease to Belfour's right. Vermette came out of the corner and put a pass through the slot that Fisher tipped in at 1:47 of the second overtime period to give the Senators a 2–1 win.

Melnyk was fresh to the NHL ownership business, having purchased the Senators out of bankruptcy before the season started. When he crossed paths with a reporter after Game 6, he was, of course, asked for a prediction for Game 7. "We're gonna kill 'em," he said. "We're going to go in there and beat them on their own ice in front of their fans!" Oh, boy.

There's something to be said for trying to show confidence in your team. There's something to be said for showing that you are behind your guys. But given the history between the teams, the pressure the Senators were already feeling to close out a Battle of Ontario, and Ottawa's 0–3 record in Game 7s to that point in their young history, it was about the worst thing to say.

Of course the Senators lost the game, and it wasn't even close. Joe Nieuwendyk scored two awful goals on Senators goaltender Patrick Lalime in the first period, the Senators lost 4–1, and the path of the franchise was altered.

You can debate to what extent a statement by somebody who wasn't even involved in the game could affect the outcome. But you are left with this, from Maple Leafs tough guy Tie Domi: "A big inspiration [for us to win] was Eugene Melnyk's comments."

A couple days later, Senators coach Jacques Martin was fired by general manager John Muckler, and by the end of June, Lalime had been traded to the St. Louis Blues.

58 Full Circle

The first time I heard Eugene Melnyk's name come up in connection with the Ottawa Senators was at the NHL All-star Game in Florida in 2003.

The Senators were bankrupt, and while owner Rod Bryden meticulously worked on putting together a new proposal to reacquire the team, the future of the team became a topic at All-Star weekend in early February. Melnyk's name was brought up as a potential owner in a question to NHL commissioner Gary Bettman.

Six months later it was official: Melnyk, the founder, chairman, and chief executive officer of Biovail Corp., a Mississauga-based pharmaceuticals company, was the new owner of the Senators. He purchased the franchise and the Corel Centre for $127 million US ($100 million for the team and $27.5 million for the debt-laden arena).

At first blush, it looked like Senators fans had their prayers answered: an owner with deep pockets and a passion for hockey after years of the franchise being operated on a skate string, though with remarkable results given the budget constraints. "It's got to be run like a business," Melnyk said in the early going, "but the bottom line is it's got to be fun."

Melnyk endeared himself to Senators season-ticket holders right off the bat with a free concert featuring the Eagles, the Rock & Roll Hall of Fame band from Los Angeles. "We wanted to do something special. We want people to be enticed to be here and not threatened. That kind of mind-set is going to change," he said, a reference to pleas over the years for Senators fans to buy tickets to keep the team in Ottawa. "I think a lot of it has to do with people just not being emotionally tied because of the threat that the team may leave," Melnyk said. "I'm guaranteeing you the team is going to be staying in Ottawa now."

Melnyk spent to the salary cap for the first eight years of his ownership, but in 2011, there was a shedding of contracts: popular veterans Chris Kelly and Mike Fisher were traded as an austerity program was undertaken by general manager Bryan Murray.

In an interview with the *Ottawa Citizen* in 2013 in a piece titled "On the Senators' New Financial Reality," Melnyk said the team had moved to the middle of the pack when it came to spending. "I think where we are now is…it's a very fine, a fine line. It's very easy to sit back and say, 'Oh, why doesn't Melnyk spend more? He doesn't spend, he doesn't spend.' Well, hold on a second, first things first, we spend right down the center," he said. "We're not the New York Rangers, we're not the Toronto Maple Leafs, and I'm trying to keep ticket prices reasonable, because there's a very delicate balance between ticket pricing, attendance, and being able to put a competitive team on the ice."

When Melnyk bought the Senators, his Biovail stock was worth $1.5 billion. But later that year, Biovail came up short of forecasts—a significant amount of Biovail product being lost in an accident involving one of its trucks was partially blamed—and the stock value dropped by more than half. Melnyk resigned as Biovail's CEO in 2004 and lost control of the company to a competing slate of directors. He sold his stake in Biovail and invested in other companies (Melnyk got about $20 a share when he cashed out. Midway through 2015, the stock price for Biovail, now known as Valeant Pharmaceuticals, peaked at more than $200 a share. It has since crashed to about $20.

The Senators' new financial reality precluded keeping captain Daniel Alfredsson and adding another top-six forward in the summer of 2013, so Alfredsson left as a free agent to join the Detroit Red Wings. That angered many Senators fans, and Murray traded the Anaheim Ducks prospects Jakob Silfverberg and Stefan Noesen, and a 2014 first-round draft pick (which the Ducks used to take Nick Ritchie) for forward Bobby Ryan.

Melnyk became an increasingingly controversial figure over the years with his comments. While they were made out of passion— "I'm a hockey fan, and fanatically a hockey fan," he described himself in 2017—the timing of the comments often made life more difficult for the Senators.

In 2004 before Game 7 of a first-round series against the Toronto Maple Leafs, after an emotional double-overtime win by the Senators in Game 6, Melnyk, asked for a prediction for Game 7, said: "We're gonna kill 'em." The Senators lost.

In 2009, responding to some calls for the Senators to "blow up" the team and do a rebuilding, he responded: "Anybody that says we should blow up this organization should get their own bomb and blow themselves up."

In March 2016, when asked why the season under Coach Dave Cameron had gone badly, Melnyk replied: "No idea. Bryan and I sit there and we just nod our head. We can't get it. We get it now. I remember back in December some of those games, three in a row that we lost by a goal we were leading. It was inconsistency and some stupidity," said Melnyk. He then brought up Cameron's decision to start rookie goaltender Matt O'Connor in the home opener after the Senators opened with two games on the road: "I go back to the very first game. You put in the second goalie. What was that about? On opening night and the guy gets clobbered. It's not fair to him, not fair to the fans. Just a lot of little tiny mistakes that all of a sudden escalate and get serious and get in people's heads." That comment made Cameron a lame-duck coach, and he was fired shortly after the end of the season.

Melnyk used the Senators to do some tremendous work in the community. He was one of the first owners to have games at which members of the military were honored, and his Eugene Melnyk Skate for Kids has brought almost 2,000 kids to the rink over the years for an early Christmas complete with a new helmet, Senators sweater, and skates.

But all of his good work and that of the Senators has been overshadowed by controversy. His firing of Senators president Cyril Leeder in January 2017—a man who was responsible for bringing the franchise to Ottawa, and an immensely popular and respected

The embattled Eugene Melnyk.

member of the community—drew criticism from the mayor of Ottawa, Jim Watson.

There was no better example of Melnyk's comments causing more harm than good than what he said about the Senators' future in Ottawa at the club's Alumni Classic on the eve of the NHL's signature event, the Scotiaback NHL100 Classic, the outdoor game between the Senators and the Montreal Canadiens to mark the NHL's centennial. Melnyk grabbed the headlines by raising the possibility of the Senators moving if attendance didn't approve. Before the Senators alumni took to the outdoor rink on Parliament Hill, Melnyk said:

> I love the game of hockey. If it doesn't look good here, it could look good somewhere else. But I'm not suggesting that right now. What I'm saying is, I would never sell the team.
>
> [Moving is] always the possibility, with any franchise. If you open a grocery store and nobody comes, but one opens two blocks down and there's a line outside, where are you going to have your store?
>
> Here, we're fighting every day to sell a ticket. Honest to God. And when you get to the third round of the playoffs and you're begging people to buy a ticket, something's wrong with that picture. We're just hoping that changes, that's all.

NHL commissioner Gary Bettman didn't like the controversy overshadowing the league's showcase centennial event. "If you're asking me if I was happy about the swirl of attention that those comments got while we were basically closing out our centennial celebration, the answer is no," Bettman said. "[But] how what he said was portrayed was blown out of proportion, because he never said, 'I'm moving,'" Bettman added. "What he said was, 'I need a new building, and for the long term if things [get] bad, I'll have to deal with it.'"

On that national stage, Melnyk's comments became the story of the weekend. The irony was not lost on the fans: the owner who came in 2003 and said the fans would not be threatened and denied the franchise would be moved was doing just that in 2017.

59 Forsberg

You thought this chapter was going to be about Peter Forsberg, didn't you? Well, there was a time when it might have been possible that Forsberg, the winner of the Hart Trophy as the NHL's Most Valuable Player in 2003, could have had a profound effect on the Senators' future. Forsberg was selected No. 6 in the 1991 NHL Draft by the Philadelphia Flyers, a surprisingly high selection based on the pre-draft predictions, which had him going late in the first round or perhaps even in the second round.

In 1992 Forsberg, who had stayed in his native Sweden to play after he was drafted, was traded to the Quebec Nordiques by the Philadelphia Flyers as part of the package that included goaltender Ron Hextall, defensemen Steve Duchesne and Kerry Huffman, and forwards Mike Ricci and Chris Simon, two first-round draft picks, and $15 million for Eric Lindros.

When Alexandre Daigle emerged as the potential No. 1 pick in the 1993 draft, the eyes of Nordiques owner Marcel Aubut got bigger than Bonhomme Carnaval's (Google it). Aubut, a man of huge appetites, loved to make the grand, bold move (like trading Lindros twice, but that's another story), and he fancied Daigle, the most hyped Quebecois prospect since Mario Lemieux, as the centerpiece of his new and suddenly remade Nordiques.

There were numerous advances made by Aubut in pursuit of Daigle, offering Forsberg for the first pick in the 1993 draft, but the Senators were convinced Daigle was their man. Daigle went on to have a journeyman career, while Forsberg became a superstar and helped lead the Quebec franchise, which moved to Denver to become the Colorado Avalanche after the 1994–95 season, to their first Stanley Cup in 1996 and another in 2001.

Could he have had a similar impact in Ottawa? He wouldn't have had anything close to the Colorado supporting cast around him in Ottawa for years to come. The acquisition of Patrick Roy in December 1995 from the Montreal Canadiens was the true tipping point that made the Avs Stanley Cup contenders.

As his star ascended, there was also the question of whether the Senators, who were a budget team through Forsberg's prime, could have even afforded a player of his stature. (We know the answer to that one. Forsberg averaged $10 million a year for the five-year period between 1999 to 2004.)

No, the Forsberg who wound up having the biggest impact on the Senators is Anders Forsberg. When Senators general manager Bryan Murray, who had been the GM of the Detroit Red Wings from 1990 to 1994, took over the Senators in 2007, he was looking for another set of eyes in Europe. He turned to Detroit Red Wings scout Hakan Andersson (the guy who identified Pavel Datsyuk, Johan Franzen, and Henrik Zetterberg, among other players, for the Red Wings) for advice.

Andersson recommended Forsberg, paying it forward (former Red Wings scout Christer Rockstrom, who left the Wings to go to to the New York Rangers, had recommended Andersson to the Red Wings). Murray hired Forsberg for the 2007–08 season.

In the three seasons he worked for the Senators, they drafted defenseman Erik Karlsson, forward Andre Petersson, and goaltender

Emil Sandin in 2008, forward Jakob Silfverberg and goaltender Robin Lehner in 2009, and forward Marcus Sorensen in 2000, all from Sweden. Forsberg also played a key role in the decision to trade the Senators' first-round draft pick in 2010, No. 16, to the St. Louis Blues for Swedish defenseman David Rundblad. He had been picked by the Blues 17th overall in 2009. The Blues used the pick to take forward Vladimir Tarasenko, who had a 40-goal season in 2015–16.

Forsberg was in the process of leaving the Senators to coach Skelleftea in the Swedish Elite League, where Rundlbad was playing. Forsberg compared Rundblad favorably to Karlsson, who was still in Sweden at the time. "He reminds me of Karlsson, but he's bigger," Forsberg said at the time. (Hey, not every pick is going to be a home run.)

Rundblad didn't pan out. He played just 113 games in the NHL before returning to play in Europe after the 2015–16 season, when Tarasenko was scoring his 40 goals. But the Senators got good value for him, dealing him to the Phoenix Coyotes for center Kyle Turris, who was a mainstay for the Senators for six seasons before he was traded as part of the blockbuster deal that brought center Matt Duchene to the Senators from the Colorado Avalanche on November 5, 2017.

Just putting the Senators onto Karlsson, of course, is enough to put Forsberg in the Senators scouts' Hall of Fame (which we just created this moment). It's not like Forsberg plucked Karlsson out of some snowbank in Gothenburg, but he did take up Karlsson's cause and campaigned the hardest for the Senators to draft him. "He wasn't in the backwoods, playing on an outdoor rink," Senators general manager Pierre Dorion said during an off day during the 2017 Stanley Cup Playoffs, when Karlsson—playing on one foot, it turned out—was dominating and helping carry the Senators into the Eastern Conference Final. "Every team saw him. He played in [the big tournaments] in February and April. Every team that had five scouts would have seen him there, so he was not 'discovered' by anyone."

With Forsberg leading the way, Dorion said the Senators' European scouts, which included Mikko Ruutu and Vaclav Burda at the time, pushed Karlsson up their list. He got as high as seventh on the Senators' final list, and Murray moved up from the 18th pick to take Karlsson 15th when the Senators started to get antsy.

After he had a significant influence on the Senators in the three years he worked for the club, Forsberg indeed left to become the coach of Skelleftea in Sweden's top league. He then coached Modo for two years before leaving to join the Buffalo Sabres as a scout in 2015. The connection there was Tim Murray, with whom Forsberg had worked with the Senators. Murray became the Sabres' general manager in 2014. After Murray was fired by the Sabres, Forsberg became an advisor to Mora IK of the Swedish league in the 2017–18 season, according to eliteprospects.com.

Forsberg's part in the selection of Karlsson will be his legacy with the Senators.

 **Fergy**

As one of the toughest players whoever put on a sweater in the NHL, the late John Ferguson brought immediate respect to the Montreal Canadiens in the 1960s. As one of the sharpest evaluators of talent as an executive, he brought immediate credibility to the Ottawa Senators in the first days of the franchise in the 1990s.

Fergy got into a fight with Ted Green of the big, bad Boston Bruins 12 seconds into his first NHL game, and despite not being the biggest guy (shorter than six feet tall and less than 200 pounds) but armed with massive fists, he became the Canadiens' policeman. While he walked the beat from 1963 to 1971, each of the Canadiens gained a couple inches and 20 pounds, and the team won five Stanley Cups.

He was one of the first power forwards in the game. He transcended being just a tough guy. He averaged 18 goals a season in his career, at a time when scoring 20 was something. He had 1,216 penalty minutes in 500 regular-season games.

In his first season, Ferguson rode shotgun for Canadiens great Jean Beliveau, and the captain won the Hart Trophy. "The most formidable player of the decade and possibly in the Canadiens' history," was the way Beliveau described Ferguson in Beliveau's 1994 autobiography, *My Life in Hockey*. "For us, Fergy's greatest contribution was his spirit. He was the consummate team man and probably intimidated as many of us in the dressing room as he did opponents on the ice. You wouldn't dare give less than your best if you wore the same shirt as John Ferguson."

Ferguson, who grew up in Vancouver and was a great lacrosse player too, was also respected in horse racing circles. In *The Habs*, by Canadiens broadcaster Dick Irvin, Bruins goalie Gerry Cheevers, a guy who knew his way around the track as well, recalled the one time Ferguson said something approaching conversation on the ice. It happened when Triple Crown favorite Hoist the Flag broke his leg preparing for the Kentucky Derby in 1971. Cheevers recounted to Irvin:

> I saw Fergy coming in for the rebound off the backboards. I know there's going to be a hit, a collision, so I've got to prepare for it. I'm saying that I'm finally going to lay this guy out for a change, right on his keister. So I turned quickly, I go right at him, and suddenly he yells, "Cheesy! Hoist the Flag broke his leg this morning!" Which he did. I said, "What?" but he kept right on coming and laid me

Ferguson puts on an Ottawa Senators hat after being named the team's director of player personnel in March 1992.

out flatter than a pancake. That was the only time he ever talked to me in his whole career.

After his playing days, Ferguson became an executive and was respected for his scouting abilities. He was an assistant coach with Team Canada 1972 in the Summit Series and famously pointed out to Bobby Clarke that Russian forward Valeri Kharlamov "[is] killing us." Clarke slashed Kharlamov in the ankle, and the series swung the Canadians' way.

Fergy moved on to become the coach and general manager of the New York Rangers and then the Winnipeg Jets when they were in the World Hockey Association. He helped rebuild the team when it entered the NHL in 1979, before his time in the tough Smythe Division with the Jets ended in 1988. He worked as president of Windsor Raceway between his hockey gigs. He loved to combine a hockey scouting trip with a visit to a nearby track, his two passions intertwined.

For a guy whose game was based on grit and intimidation, it was interesting that Ferguson loved skill as a talent evaluator. You might have thought such a tough guy would have sneered at the skillful Europeans, like some others did in the 1980s, but Ferguson embraced them. When he was the general manager of the Rangers, he lured Ulf Nilsson and Anders Hedberg, among the first Swedes to come to play in North America and who had starred on a line with Bobby Hull, away from Winnipeg (unfortunately, Ferguson wound up being let go by the Rangers and wound up with the Jets months later, a victim of his own machinations).

Ferguson used the Jets' first pick (No. 10) in the 1988 NHL Draft to take Teemu Selanne, who went on to a Hall of Fame career. He also brought Thomas Steen to the Jets at a time when Europeans weren't embraced the way they are now.

Ferguson joined the Senators as director of player personnel in 1992, bringing much-needed experience, contacts, and credibility to the startup. John Owens, the Senators' vice president of corporate communications and a coworker of Ferguson's, said he was a down-to-earth man. "I remember years later I was at the Toronto airport on the moving [walkway]. John is coming the other way. He turns around and runs back just to say hi," Owens said. "I remember thinking, *You're a legend. Jesus. And you're running back to say hello to me.*"

Remembered Senators founder Bruce Firestone: "John knew two things—hockey players and horses—and he said to me once that they were a lot alike: 'You just have to look at their teeth and ankles.'"

Ferguson pushed for Alexei Yashin to be drafted by the Senators in their first draft. Yashin (337 goals, 444 assists for 781 points in 850 games) is second in points among players in the 1992 draft behind only Sergei Gonchar (220 goals, 591 assists for 811 points in 1,301 games). In typical Ferguson fashion, he always said what was on his mind (it was one of this best qualities), and he took a stand with Yashin in his early contract disputes with the Senators, which greased the skids for his departure in 1995.

Ferguson's crowning moment for the Senators was making a passionate case to take Daniel Alfredsson in the sixth round (No. 133) of the 1994 NHL Draft. "John Ferguson Sr. was talking about Alfredsson long before people had any idea how good Alfredsson was…even internally. People had no idea how good the guy was going to be when he got over here," John Ferguson Jr. told Bruce Garrioch of Postmedia when the Senators retired Alfredsson's No. 11 in December 2016.

"[Fergy] found Alfie. Insisted on Alfie," Owens said. "He was going to quit if we didn't draft him. He was so high on that kid."

Ferguson wasn't around to see Alfredsson honored. He was diagnosed with prostate cancer in September 2005 and passed away in July 2007 at age 68. He was working for the San Jose Sharks, doing what he loved: scouting.

"There was no more passionate competitor—as a player, as a coach, or as an executive—than John Ferguson," NHL commissioner Gary Bettman said in a statement when Ferguson lost his battle. "He was tough; he wanted the best for his teams, his teammates and his players, and his country, and would stop at nothing to try to help them win. His fight against cancer was every bit as fierce as his competitive drive on and off the ice."

His legacy in hockey was great and looms large with the Senators. Senators fans should think of Ferguson every time they look up and see Alfredsson's No. 11 hanging from the rafters of Canadian Tire Centre.

61 Hit Hogtown

All Senators fans should, at least once, make a trip to Toronto to cheer on their team against the Maple Leafs at the Air Canada Centre. It shouldn't be that much of a culture shock, because Senators fans are used to being surrounded by a sea of blue at the Canadian Tire Centre in Ottawa. Maple Leafs fans are frequent visitors to Ottawa, where tickets are cheaper and, most important, available.

Senators fans should make their move as early as possible to try and get tickets to see their team in Toronto, because tickets can be a tough get. In early 2018 you were probably looking at about $140 a ticket in the secondary market. Pricey? You bet. But for a one-time trip to the scene of some of the biggest games in Senators history (though they often didn't have the outcome Senators fans wanted) and a chance to dip into Toronto's considerable list of things to do, it can be worth the price.

Like a trip to Montreal to see the Senators play the Canadiens at the Bell Centre, getting there is half the fun. Taking the train is the way to go. The trip will take you from Ottawa right into Union Station. (Which will never be finished, will it? Every time I've been there over the last 25 years, some part of it is being renovated.)

Union Station, at Front St. and Bay St., is a National Historic Site of Canada since 1975 and is Canada's biggest and most impressive train station in the beaux arts style, constructed largely out of limestone from 1914 to 1920. The Great Hall has a floor of Tennessee marble.

Union Station has access to the Toronto subway and the PATH system, a network of pedestrian tunnels, elevated walkways, and at-grade walkways that is more than 19 miles (30 kilometers) long.

According to the *Guiness World Records*, the PATH system is the largest underground shopping complex in the world, with more than 4 million square feet of retail space.

The ACC is connected to Union Station to the south. That's one of the good things about a trip to Toronto. If you can get a hotel not too far from the rink, you don't have to go too far to do a lot in addition to taking in a hockey game. Within walking distance of the ACC, you can head west and check out the CN Tower, which at 1,815.3 feet was the world's tallest tower until 2009 (it's now third). Ripley's Aquarium of Canada is also located not far from the base of the tower.

There's also lots of hockey history to be had in Hogtown. Just across at the street from Union Station is the Hockey Hall of Fame (www.hhof.com). During hockey season, it's open Monday to Friday from 10:00 AM to 5:00 PM, Saturday from 9:30 AM to 6:00 PM, and Sunday from 10:30 AM to 5:00 PM. Admission ranges from $13 to $19. You can check out the Stanley Cup, go head-to-head with animated goaltenders and shooters, call your own play-by-play of some of hockey's biggest goals, and see 3-D films in one of two theaters.

If you're up for a 30-minute walk from Union Station, you can head for the old Maple Leaf Gardens, where the Maple Leafs played from 1931 to 1999. The Maple Leafs won the Stanley Cup there 11 times, the last in 1967, but you probably knew that. Elvis Presley performed there in 1957, and the second game of the legendary Summit Series between Canada and the USSR was played there in 1972.

One of my favorite pre- and postgame hangouts is Hoops Sports Bar & Grill, a short walk away from the ACC, at 125 Bremner Blvd. It's a solid sports bar with 19 beers on tap.

If you want a more upscale experience, you can go to Real Sports Bar and Grill in Maple Leaf Square, but be warned: it is the natural habitat of some of the tassle-loafered Maple Leafs fans Senators fans love to mock.

A good craft beer spot is the Amsterdam Brewery on the Queen's Quay, within walking distance of the ACC. It's the city's oldest independent brewer, established in 1986. I'm an IPA guy, so I go for the Boneshaker IPA.

You can check out the dining options inside the Air Canada Centre at www.aircanadacentre.com. One of the spots worth visiting if you are a beer fan is Suds in the Six (Section 116), which has a selection of local craft beers.

62 Watch Your Step

On St. Patrick's Day in 1994, in the second season for the Senators, we reporters went out for a postgame beer (it wasn't green) in San Jose after a rare Senators win (2–1 over the Sharks, in which newcomer Dan Quinn scored both goals). This was the Senators' third win in 24 games—a stretch that included 13- and 12-game winless streaks, respectively—and ended a nine-game losing streak.

Things were grim, and here was a rare night on the road for the Senators to celebrate a victory (the Senators were 6–31–5 on the road that season, and they won three of them in a row in early November).

The reporters were in a sports bar not far from the rink and, as was the case frequently back in those days, some of the Senators players came into the same place to grab a postgame drink and some dinner. Senators forward Andrew McBain was one of the players who came in, a guy back then who made it fun to go to the rink when victories and good news were few and far between. The Beaner, as he was called by his teammates, had a quick and often self-deprecating sense of humor. He was a first-round pick of the Winnipeg Jets (eighth overall in 1983) and a good player (608 games in the NHL; 301 points, including back-to-back 30-goal seasons with the Winnipeg Jets and a single-season high of 77 points).

His most valuable contribution to an expansion team made up of retreads and castoffs was his one-liners. He was sitting in his corner stall one day at practice. "How's it going, Andrew?" he was asked. "I'm suffering from GMS," he said. "GMS?" "Give Me Somebody," he cracked about his linemates.

On this night in San Jose, we wound up at the end of the bar watching a sports blooper show on one of those projector TVs that cast its images on a silvery pull-down screen that wavered and shimmied whenever anyone even walked by it.

Suddenly the images were inside the old Chicago Stadium—apparently as dangerous inside as the neighborhood outside—watching McBain in a game against the Blackhawks almost exactly a year earlier. He had gotten into it with Chicago forward Jocelyn Lemieux near the end of the second period and was sent to the dressing room. The fun part was having McBain right beside me, providing the play-by-play as he got tossed out of the game. At the old Chicago Stadium, the visiting team entered and exited the ice through a gate behind one of the nets. You turned left and went down about a dozen stairs to the dressing room.

McBain, after jawing with Hawks goaltender Ed Belfour, arrived at the door and the elderly gentleman who sat at the top of the stairs stooped and hauled the gate open. "Right now, the old guy warns me to watch my step," McBain narrated as he arrived at the top of the stairs. "I said to him, 'I've been in this league for 11 fucking years. Don't tell me to watch my fucking step." At which point, of course, McBain slipped and started a downhill plunge, with his arms pinwheeling wildly.

The next time we were in the Stadium, the players came out of the dressing room for the morning skate, and someone had taken some tape and stuck the following message on the ascending stairs: WATCH YOUR STEP, it said one stair, and then on the next, it was followed by, THIS MEANS YOU, BEANER.

63 Player 61

A rivalry between teams doesn't reach its full and appropriate level of unpleasantness until it is incubated in the heat of the playoffs. For the Senators' first 20 years, most Ottawa fans would have put the Toronto Maple Leafs, the Pittsburgh Penguins, and even the Buffalo Sabres near the top of the list of the Senators' most hated rivals, ahead of what should have been the most natural.

That would be the Montreal Canadiens, the Senators' closest geographical rival and a team with fans who, frankly, can be quite easy to dislike. It is a different dislike than that felt for Maple Leafs fans, who count among themselves a disproportionate number of drunken boors who travel to Canadian Tire Centre and give all of Leaf Nation a bad rep.

Canadiens fans have a haughtiness that can make them tiresome, particularly since they love living in the past. (There's a reason for this old joke: How many Canadiens fans does it take to change a lightbulb? Five. One to change it and four to talk about how great the old one was.) They haven't been to a Stanley Cup Final since 1993, though they won that one and can still lay claim to being the last Canadian franchise to have lifted the Cup.

The seed for a rivalry between the Senators and Canadiens looked like it was planted in the first game of the modern era between the two teams, when the upstart Senators made their return to the NHL with a 5–3 win against the eventual Stanley Cup champions on October 8, 1992, at the Ottawa Civic Centre.

But for much of the Senators' existence, the fortunes of the two teams went in opposite directions. When the Senators evolved into a league power in the early 2000s, the Canadiens were in one of the worst stretches of their existence. Seats were empty at the Bell Centre, and they were put up for sale with no takers until George Gillett came along and got them for a song in 2001. (He paid $275 million CDN for an 80 percent interest in the iconic hockey club and 100 percent ownership of the Bell Centre. Gillett sold the package for more than $500 million in 2009 to the Molson family).

When the Senators were building up to winning the Presidents' Trophy in 2003, the Canadiens were in a stretch when they missed the playoffs four out of five seasons. In the 2013 season, both teams took advantage of a season shortened to 48 games by a lockout to make the playoffs. The Canadiens were the second seed as Northeast Division champions and the Senators were the seventh, setting up their first postseason meeting. It didn't take long for things to go sideways.

Halfway through Game 1, Senators defenseman Eric Gryba caught Canadiens forward Lars Eller with his head down at the Montreal blue line as he took a pass from Canadiens defenseman Raphael Diaz. Gryba caught Eller in the head with his shoulder and Eller went down hard, bleeding heavily. It was an ugly scene. Gryba got kicked out of the game and wound up with a two-game suspension. The tone for the series was set. The Senators scored three times in the third period and won that game 4–2.

Senators coach Paul MacLean and Canadiens coach Michel Therrien engaged in some great back-and-forth, which immediately made the series a classic. MacLean defended Gryba for doing his job, mentioned how players in earlier eras had been taught to keep their heads up, and put the blame on "Player 61" (Diaz), and said if Eller should be mad at anybody, it was Player 61 for giving him a suicide pass.

"Everyone was blaming my player for doing what he's supposed to do," MacLean said. "All I did was point out what happened. I feel bad for the kid that got hurt, but that's what happened. It was a hockey play that went bad for him. If that's being harsh or cruel… that's too bad. Grow up."

"Inappropriate comment," Therrien said. "No respect for the player on the ice who was bleeding. No respect for his family in the stands. When he compared that to a hockey hit, the comparison he made was with the '70s, '80s, and '90s. This is why we've got new rules, to avoid those hits when a player is vulnerable. That's why we've got rules…. That was a lack of respect to Lars Eller and his family, and I'm never going to accept that. Never."

Canadiens forward Brandon Prust then delivered the quote of the series, which is saying something: "I don't care what that bug-eyed, fat walrus has to say," he said of MacLean.

The Canadiens bounced back to even the series with a 3–1 win in Game 2, and the scene shifted to Ottawa.

Did I say the MacLean-Therrien feud made this an instant classic? Wait. It got better. With Senators center Jean-Gabriel Pageau on his way to his first playoff hat trick, the Senators were ahead 4–1 in Game 3 at Scotiaback Place after a goal by Ottawa's Kyle Turris with 13 minutes left in the third period. On the next faceoff, Montreal's Ryan White and Ottawa center Zack Smith exchanged whacks, with White giving Smith a two-handed chop to the back of the leg that sent Smith to the ice.

It was on. The players paired up on the ice while the crowd went wild. The fights:

Senators defenseman Jared Cowen vs. White (decision Cowen).

Smith vs. Montreal defenseman Francis Bouillon (decision Smith).

Ottawa's Chris Neil and Canadiens forward Travis Moen (decision Neil).

Senators forward Matt Kassian vs. Canadiens forward Colby Armstrong (decision Kassian).

Senators defenseman Chris Phillips vs. Montreal defenseman Jarred Tinordi (draw).

There were eight game misconducts.

"It's a war tonight," legendary CBC play-by-play man Bob Cole said, "and Ottawa has taken over the game."

With 17 seconds left in the game, MacLean tried to gather his players by the bench to tell them to play it out without further incident, but the referees wouldn't let him, so he called a timeout. "My only recourse was to take the timeout because I didn't want anyone to get hurt," MacLean said. "Things had gotten dumb enough as it was."

"We were beaten by a better team, but a timeout with 17 seconds left…it's rare that you see that," Therrien said. "You let the players dictate the game. As a coach you never want to humiliate a team, but that's exactly what MacLean was trying to do. To me, that was a total lack of class."

The Senators won the fights, the game and, ultimately, the series (4–1).

"When I was walking out of the rink that night," remembered Smith, "I had a lot of people telling me that was the best game they ever saw."

You need some fire to forge a rivalry. The Senators-Canadiens rivalry is burning now.

64 Sparky

November 1995 in Ottawa was like something out of a Gordon Lightfoot song. The gales of November came early. They sunk the SS *Edmund Fitzgerald* in 1975 and they took the Ottawa Senators down in 1995. It wound up being a miserable time in a dark season.

The Ottawa Senators, in their fourth season since their return to the NHL, had actually gotten off to a decent start and were 5–3 after a 5–4 win over the Los Angeles Kings on October 26. When the calendar turned, they won their first game in November but would not win another that month. Coach Rick Bowness, the expansion team's first coach, didn't make it past November 21. After an eight-game losing streak that dropped the team's record to 6–13, Senators general manager Randy Sexton fired Bowness. "We needed to provide a spark," Sexton said in explaining the unpopular move. A legend was born.

Sexton turned to Dave "Sparky" Allison (who hated that nickname, by the way), who was promoted from the Senators' American Hockey League farm team in Prince Edward Island, to become the Senators' second coach. He launched one of the most colorful, if not successful, two months in the team's history.

Allison, 36, was a journeyman as a player. A native of Fort Frances, Ontario (where he played minor hockey with the Kenora Thistles, who are one of the great names in hockey), he played his junior hockey with the Cornwall Royals of the QMJHL. He had 423 penalty minutes in his last season, to lead the league.

He signed as a free agent with the Montreal Canadiens in 1979 just as their run of four Stanley Cup championships was ending. Allison spent a decade in the minors but for three games with the Habs in the 1983–84 season. Three games, 12 penalty minutes.

He turned to coaching in 1989–90 with the Virginia Lancers of the East Coast Hockey League and had stops with the Albany Choppers of the IHL and Richmond Renegades of the ECHL before taking over the Kingston Frontenacs of the Ontario Hockey League for the 1992–93 season. His teams were decent but not great, hovering around the .500 mark.

The Senators hired him to coach their AHL farm team in 1994–95, and the team had a 41–31–8 record in his first season. They were 10–11–2 to start the 1995–96 season when he got the call from Sexton.

It was a tumultuous time. The Senators were playing at the Civic Centre, with a move to the Palladium coming up in January. Behind the scenes, Senators owner Rod Bryden and Sexton were under tremendous pressure from Ogden, the arena management company that had guaranteed the financing of the Palladium and would manage the building, to turn things around. They were going to have almost twice as many seats to sell in a couple months, and another last-place team wasn't going to do it over the long term.

The expectation that a coaching change could turn things around ignored the fact that the Senators were a horrible team. It was a mix of over-the-hill veterans, journeymen, and kids. It was an old man's league then, nothing like it is today, where 20- and 21-year-olds are the stars of the game and the foundation of franchises. They had 13 players 28 or older play for them that season.

Daniel Alfredsson, the future best player in club history, was a 23-year-old rookie and must have been wondering what had possessed him to leave Sweden. Alexandre Daigle and Radek Bonk were 20, Pavol Demitra 21, Alexei Yashin 22. There was potential there, but it was a long way off. The Senators had no stars in their prime. So Sexton pulled the trigger. Poor Dave Allison just didn't know at which end of the gun he was standing.

The voluble redhead swept in and immediately became a hit with the media. "Hey, I'm not inventing a cure for cancer here. The last time I saw the puck, it was the same size in PEI as it is here," he said. "I know there are going to be trials and tribulations. No question. But if we tackle our problems head-on, honestly, and don't carry any grudges, I believe we can rectify them. If not, I'll hop in my blue truck and head home."

Allison, a tough, honest, hardworking player who had his cup of coffee in the NHL, had made it back as a coach. "Basically this is a great job," he said. "And it was a great job when I was coaching in PEI and when I was coaching in Cornwall and when I was playing in Muskegon. About the only difference now is I have bottled beer instead of draft."

At the morning skate before the Senators were to play the Colorado Avalanche in a nationally televised game on December 9—the Avs had just made a blockbuster trade to acquire goaltender Patrick Roy from the Montreal Canadiens three days earlier—Allison was asked if he was excited to be behind the bench for such a high-profile game. His answer was an a cappella version of the theme song from CBC's *Hockey Night in Canada*: "Duh, duh, duh, duh, duh, dah..." The Senators lost that game (7–3), as they did most of the games under Allison.

Among his other quotables:

"Hope is something for people with terminal illnesses. We don't need hope. We'll score some goals. We scored some dandies in practice today."

"I'm not all of a sudden going to become Attila the Hun. About all we can do is work hard to be successful. That's all I can do."

He did get to coach in the first game at the new Palladium on January 17, 1996, but after the Senators won but two games for him (2–22–1), he was fired a week later by new general manager Pierre Gauthier and replaced by Jacques Martin.

"I wanted experience. That's why there were changes," Gauthier said in an interview for this book. "I've had to make changes, and I had to bring in experienced people."

That was Allison's downfall. He lacked experience—he had but one year coaching at the AHL level, remember—and the Senators were a mess that cried out for structure. Allison wasn't a bad coach, just inexperienced and in over his head at that point in his career. You don't coach for 30 years without having something on the ball. In 2017–18 Allison started his fourth season in the United States Hockey League with the Des Moines Buccaneers.

For a guy who lasted only two months and had just two wins, Allison left a colorful legacy.

65 Tuckered Out

The Tucker hit. When it comes to Senators fans, that's all you have to call it.

Senators fans didn't have a lot to cheer about when it came to the Battle of Ontario against the Toronto Maple Leafs at the turn of the century. The Senators won a few games and a few battles the four times they met their archrivals from the Centre of the Universe in the Stanley Cup Playoffs between 2000 and 2004, but the Maple Leafs always prevailed in the end. Perhaps the best and most satisfying battle won by the Senators, as short-lived as the joy might have been, came with a couple minutes left in Game 5 of the second round in 2002.

To set it up: The Senators, the seventh seed in the Eastern Conference, defeated the second-seeded Philadelphia Flyers 4–1 in the opening round, with Ottawa goaltender Patrick Lalime holding the Flyers to two goals in five games with a performance for the ages. The Maple Leafs, seeded fourth, eliminated the fifth-seeded New York Islanders in seven games to set up the third meeting in the Battle of Ontario. The Maple Leafs–Islanders series was one of the dirtiest in recent memory. There were vicious hits, mostly by the Maple Leafs. Toronto forward Gary Roberts railroaded Islanders defenseman Kenny Jonsson into the boards with a hit that would be worth a significant suspension today.

Toronto forward Darcy Tucker took out the knee of Islanders star Mike Peca with a low hit (it would be called clipping today) that destroyed Peca's knee. Never mind that the hit came about two seconds after Peca had gotten rid of the puck (in one of those odd twists, Peca and Tucker would wind up teammates four years later with the Maple Leafs and sit beside each other in the dressing room).

Lalime's outstanding play carried over to Game 1 against Toronto, a 5–0 Ottawa win at Air Canada Centre. The Maple Leafs won Game 2 in overtime and the Senators took Game 3 in Ottawa 3–2. The Maple Leafs bounced back with a 2–1 win in Game 4 to send the teams back to Toronto tied 2–2.

Game 5 at Air Canada Centre was tied 2–2 with two minutes to go when the Senators got some sustained pressure in the Toronto zone. When the puck came around the right-wing boards, Tucker moved to corral it. Senators Captain Daniel Alfredsson approached Tucker from behind and launched him into the boards with a thrust of his left arm.

The puck went to the point where Ottawa defenseman Sami Salo's shot deflected behind the Toronto net to Ottawa forward Juha Ylonen. With Tucker writhing on the ice and Toronto fans incensed there was no penalty, Alfredsson took a pass from Ylonen and scored what turned out to be the winning goal with 2:01 to go in the game.

"You can look at it yourselves. It was a pretty tough hit," Toronto coach Pat Quinn said after the game. "I didn't particularly like it, especially as to how the hit happened and then the results after that. Quite frankly, I'm full of anger." Asked if he was surprised it was Alfredsson who delivered the hit, Quinn replied: "He's been pretty active in those hits, usually from behind." Tucker said he sustained a broken bone and a dislocated shoulder.

Fast-forward a dozen years later when Alfredsson announced his retirement from the game. Tweeted Tucker (@16DarcyTucker): "Guess I should book my trip to Ottawa December 4th I'm sure Alfie would want me there on the big day. #waitingbythephone"

Tucker also wrote a guest column for Sun Media on the occasion of Anderson's retirement. He wrote:

> After all the battles I had with Daniel Alfredsson over the years, I carry no animosity toward him. Although my shoulder does at times.
>
> Back in Game 5 of the 2002 playoffs, Alfredsson slammed me into the boards late in the third with the score tied 2–2. While I separated my shoulder on the play and no penalty was called, Alfredsson kept going and, seconds later, scored the game-winning goal. There was criticism that it was a hit from behind, but I'll leave that for others to debate.
>
> We had our skirmishes during all those memorable Battles of Ontario, sure, but I have a lot of respect for the man. He did a lot of great things for the city of Ottawa

beyond just playing the game. Animosity is carried within the context of playing in a number of series like that against each other, but at the end of the day, you have to have a lot of respect for someone like that.

That's what made Daniel Alfredsson who he was: One of the top competitors I ever faced in the game. And for that, I truly respect him.

66 And a Sixth-Round Pick...

They are the faceless numbers in the list of transactions, those draft picks that are part of trades in the NHL. Sometimes it's a first-round pick and a big part of the deal. Sometimes it's a late-round pick most people dismiss as insignificant.

Here's a look at the top 10 picks who were part of Senators trades over their first 25 years and wound up being somebody whose sweater you might have wanted to buy.

1. **July 8, 2009:** The Senators traded goaltender Alex Auld to the Dallas Stars for a 2010 sixth-round pick. The Senators used the No. 178 pick to take a winger with questionable skating from the Brandon Wheat Kings of the Western Hockey League. Mark Stone finished tied with Johnny Gaudreau of the Calgary Flames for the rookie scoring lead in 2015 and finished second to Aaron Ekblad of the Florida Panthers in voting for Rookie of the Year.

2. **June 20, 2008:** The Senators traded the No. 18 pick in the 2008 draft and their third-round pick in 2009 to the Predators for their first-round pick, No. 15. The Predators drafted

Mark Stone in game action in 2018.

goaltender Chet Pickard. The Senators selected defenseman Erik Karlsson, a two-time Norris Trophy winner and future Hall of Famer. The third-round pick in 2009 turned out to be Taylor Beck, just in case you were interested. After time with six NHL franchises, he signed in the Kontinental Hockey League for 2017–18.

3. **June 23, 2001:** The Senators resolved their Alexei Yashin contract hassle problem by shipping him to the New York Islanders for defenseman Zdeno Chara, forward Bill Muckalt, and the No. 2 pick in the 2001 draft, which they used to take center Jason Spezza. He went on to have 687 points in 686 games with the Senators. It turned out to be a franchise-changing trade even with Muckalt failing to score a goal in 70 games in the 2001–02 season. A remarkable deal given the market for Yashin was small, like "only the Islanders were interested" small.

4. **September 24, 1997:** The Senators traded goaltender Kirk Daubenspeck to the Chicago Blackhawks for their own sixth-round pick in the 1998 draft—it had been traded to the Blackhawks as part of a package for Mike Prokopec—and future considerations. The Senators used the No. 161 pick to take Chris Neil. He played 1,026 games, all for the Senators, the 10ᵗʰ-most in his draft class.

5. **February 25, 1993:** The Senators sent defenseman Brad Miller to the Toronto Maple Leafs for a ninth-round pick (No. 227) in the 1993 draft. The Senators took Pavol Demitra. He is fifth in points for players taken in 1993, with 768 points in 847 games. He died when the aircraft carrying the KHL's Lokomotiv Yaroslavl crashed on September 7, 2011.

6. **March 19, 1996:** The Senators traded Kerry Huffman to the Philadelphia Flyers for the 239ᵗʰ pick (third-to-last) in the 1996

draft. Hello, defenseman Sami Salo, who played 878 NHL games (15th-most in that draft) and scored 99 goals.

7. **February 24, 2011:** The Senators traded Alexei Kovalev to the Pittsburgh Penguins for a conditional pick, which wound up being in the seven round, No. 203. The Senators took forward Ryan Dzingel, who has at times been a top-six forward for the Senators.

8. **June 23, 2001:** The Senators acquired fourth- and seventh-round draft picks in the 2001 draft from Tampa for a previously acquired third-round pick from New Jersey. The Senators used the seventh-round pick to take Jan Platil. The Lightning used the third-rounder for Evgeny Artyukhin. The Senators used the fourth-round pick to select goaltender Ray Emery. Say what you want about the controversial goaltender, but he helped them to the 2007 Stanley Cup Final.

9. **March 1, 2017:** The Senators traded center Curtis Lazar and defenseman Michael Kostka to the Calgary Flames for defenseman Jyrki Jokipakka and the Flames' second-round pick in 2017 (No. 47), forward Alex Formenton. He was 17 years old when training camp started in 2017 and played his way onto the team before being returned to junior after playing one game.

10. **August 29, 2008:** Sometimes the Senators just wound up being part of one of those lost afternoons when you try and follow the bouncing pick. Here we go. The Senators acquired a first-round pick from the Tampa Bay Lightning (previously acquired from the San Jose Sharks as part of a deal for Ottawa native Dan Boyle) along with Filip Kuba and Alexandre Picard for defenseman Andrej Meszaros. Then on February 20, 2009, the Senators traded Dean McAmmond and that first-round pick (No. 26 overall) they got from the Lightning to the New York Islanders for Chris Campoli and Mike Comrie. The Islanders traded that first-round pick to the New Jersey Devils,

who traded it to the Columbus Blue Jackets, who traded it to the Anaheim Ducks, who used it to take right-winger Kyle Palmieri. Got all that? Palmieri wound up with the Devils after all when he was traded there for a couple picks in 2015.

67 Rate the GMs

Through 2017, there have been eight men who have had the title of Ottawa Senators general manager. They all made good, sometimes great, moves and bad, sometimes horrific, moves. Who did the best job? It's a great debate.

Here's my ranking:

1. Pierre Gauthier, 1995–96 to 1997–98

Gauthier arrived when the Senators were in the midst of perhaps their greatest calamity. They had gone through two coaches in the fall of 1995, were floundering spectacularly, and were poised to make the move from the 9,500-seat Civic Centre to the 20,500-seat Palladium. They were sorely in need of credibility.

He made one of the biggest trades in Senators history, shipping out malcontent defenseman Bryan Berard, goaltender Don Beaupre, and forward Martin Straka in a three-way deal with the Toronto Maple Leafs and New York Islanders that brought back goaltender Damian Rhodes and Wade Redden.

He fired Coach Dave Allison and replaced him with Jacques Martin, who remained behind the bench for nine years and took the Senators to great regular-season, if not playoff, success.

Gauthier, in his sometimes quirky way, gave the Senators respectability. In the three drafts he ran (1996–98), the Senators selected eight players who played at least 300 games in the NHL. That's pretty good.

Best move: Hiring Jacques Martin as coach.

Worst move: Trading Pavol Demitra for Christer Olsson. Who? Exactly.

2. Marshall Johnston, 1999–2000 to 2001–02

Hired by Gauthier as director of player personnel, Johnston was a great evaluator of talent. He took over after Rick Dudley left for the Tampa Bay Lightning and days later traded forward Ted Donato and the rights to forward Antti-Jussi Niemi to Anaheim for goaltender Patrick Lalime.

Marshall resolved the almost yearly Alexei Yashin contract renegotiation crisis by finally trading him to the New York Islanders in 2001 and spectacularly won the deal. He acquired defenseman Zdeno Chara, who would go on to win the Norris Trophy (unfortunately not with Ottawa) and the second pick in the 2001 NHL Draft, center Jason Spezza, a point-a-game player (mostly with Ottawa). Johnston helped add to the nucleus started by Gauthier and was a pretty good teller of jokes too.

He had another strong drafting record. He selected forwards Martin Havlat and Chris Kelly in 1999, defenseman Anton Volchenkov and forward Antoine Vermette in 2000, and Spezza, defenseman Tim Gleason, goaltender Ray Emery, defenseman Christoph Schubert, and forward Brooks Laich in 2001.

Best move: Yashin for Chara and the No. 2 pick in the 2001 NHL Draft (which he used to take Jason Spezza), even if he had to take forward Bill Muckalt, who didn't score a goal in 70 games.

Worst move: Taking Bill Muckalt.

3. John Muckler, 2002–03 to 2006–07

Muckler came in at a time when the Senators were ascending but lacked confidence. The veteran of Stanley Cup victories with the

Edmonton Oilers came in and told the Senators it was okay to want to win the Stanley Cup. He gave them some swagger, and it paid off with a trip to their only Stanley Cup Final, in 2007.

Muckler's biggest trade was sending forward Marian Hossa, who had just been signed to a new contract, and defenseman Greg de Vries, to the Atlanta Thrashers for forward Dany Heatley in August 2005. Hossa went on to what will be a Hall of Fame career, but Heatley had back-to-back 50-goal seasons and helped the Senators to that Cup Final in 2007.

Most of Muckler's deals were tepid swaps at the trade deadline that wound up being inconsequential. (Remember Peter Bondra, Tyler Arnason, and Oleg Saprykin? Probably not.)

Muckler's drafting record as general manager was poor, which was partly a function of the Senators getting really good and dropping down the list. The highest pick they had for Muckler was No. 9 in 2005 (the lottery year after the lockout), and it was squandered on defenseman Brian Lee, who played 209 games and was out of the league at age 25.

Forward Patrick Eaves (29th in 2003), defenseman Andrej Meszáros (23rd in 2004), Lee in '05, and forward Nick Foligno (28th in 2006) were the first-round picks during Muckler's watch.

Best move: Hiring Bryan Murray as coach.

Worst move: Acquiring forward Peter Bondra for forward Brooks Laich and a second-round pick on February 18, 2004. Bondra had five goals in 12 regular-season games and none in the Senators' seven-game loss to the Toronto Maple Leafs in the first round. Laich went on to a solid 12-year career with the Washington Capitals, including three straight 20-goal seasons. Some might argue his worst move was not acquiring Senators antagonist Gary Roberts in 2007, which cost him his job, according to legend.

4. Bryan Murray, 2007–08 to 2015–16

The Senators' longest-serving GM took over from Muckler after the run to the Stanley Cup Final in 2007 and had to oversee a downsizing of the organization in 2011, moving veteran forwards Mike Fisher and Chris Kelly. He loved the big deal and traded for and signed winger Bobby Ryan, and he made another big deal to get defenseman Dion Phaneuf, saving the Senators some money at the time but saddling the team with Phaneuf's long-term deal and diminishing skills. Goaltender Ben Bishop for good ol' Cory Conacher and a fourth-round pick (Tobias Lindberg) was another loss. He was forced into a couple corners after trade demands by first Heatley and then Spezza, so it's tough to come down hard on those forced deals. But he had his wins too: defenseman David Rundblad traded to the Phoenix Coyotes for No. 1 center Kyle Turris, and acquiring Bishop for a second-round draft pick.

Trading goaltender Brian Elliott for Craig Anderson was another victory. Anderson gave the Senators a strong stretch of great goaltending, though year-to-year consistency was an issue. Negotiating Daniel Alfredsson's return to Ottawa so he could retire a Senator was another good move. He had a run of four pretty good drafts from 2008 to 2011, with future NHL GMs Pierre Dorion and Tim Murray doing the scouting. The 2008 draft alone produced five players (defenseman Erik Karlsson, defenseman Patrick Wiercioch, forward Zack Smith, forward Derek Grant, and defenseman Mark Borowiecki). In 2009 the Senators took defenseman Jared Cowen, forward Jakob Silfverberg, goaltender Robin Lehner, defenseman Chris Wideman, and forward Mike Hoffman. He scooped forward Mark Stone with pick No. 178 in 2010 and selected center Mika Zibanejad, forward Stefan Noesen, forward Matt Puempel, forward Shane Prince, center Jean-Gabriel Pageau, defensman Fredrik Claesson and forward Ryan Dzingel in 2011. Potential future star defenseman Thomas Chabot and forward Colin White were taken with the No. 18 and No. 21 picks in the 2015 NHL Draft, Murray's last before he stepped down and handed the job to Dorion.

Best move: Trading a third-round pick to move up in the 2008 draft to take Karlsson.

Worst move: Signing Ryan to a seven-year, $50.75 million contract in 2014.

5. Pierre Dorion, 2016–present

It's a pretty small sample size for Dorion, and within his first two seasons as general manager, there were wild swings in the club's performance.

Best move: Trading for goaltender Mike Condon in November 2016. With the status of No. 1 goaltender Craig Anderson up in the air after his wife, Nicholle, was diagnosed with cancer and Andrew Hammond out with an injury, Dorion acquired Condon from the Pittsburgh Penguins for a fifth-round draft pick in 2017. Condon came in and played in 27 straight games. He helped the Senators stay competitive and make the playoffs. They wound up playing 19 playoff games, making a few bucks for the owner.

Worst move: Trading popular center Kyle Turris, a first-round draft pick in 2018 or '19, 2017 first-round pick Shane Bowers, a third-round pick in 2019, and Hammond for center Matt Duchene. While there was doubt Turris would re-sign in Ottawa, the Senators were 6–3–5 at the time and finished 28–43–11, missing the playoffs.

6. Randy Sexton, 1993–94 to 1995–96

One of the franchise's original founders, Sexton replaced Mel Bridgman after he was fired at the conclusion of the Senators' first season. Sexton himself was fired shortly into his third season, with the Senators headed for their fourth-straight last-place finish.

Best move: Listening to Senators director of player personnel John Ferguson and drafting that Swedish kid, Daniel Alfredsson, in the sixth round of the 1994 NHL Draft.

Worst move: Firing Coach Rick Bowness and replacing him with Dave Allison. It was a disastrous move that hastened Sexton's own firing.

7. Rick Dudley, 1998–99

He left for the Tampa Bay Lighting after one season. Compensation was Lightning captain Rob Zamuner and a second-round draft pick, which was packaged up in a deal that wound up landing Senators defenseman Tim Gleason (the pick turned out to Tobias Stephan) and three exhibition games, in which the Lightning would play Ottawa, with the Senators keeping the revenues. Forward Andreas Johansson also went to the Lightning.

Best move: Acquired forward Ted Donato for a fourth-round draft pick in 1999 (Preston Mizzi). Johnston turned Donato into Lalime, who became the best Senators goaltender to that point.

Worst move: Any of the other six trades he made while Senators GM.

8. Mel Bridgman, 1992–93

A No. 1 pick in the NHL draft by the Philadelphia Flyers in 1975, he played 14 seasons for five clubs. A graduate of the prestigious Wharton School of Business, Bridgman's first and last GM job was with the Senators. He lasted one season.

Best move: Picking up defenseman Norm Maciver on waivers. He went on to become the Senators' leading scorer in their first season.

Worst move: Three times taking ineligible players in the expansion draft. "Ottawa apologizes," was not a good start in the NHL.

68 "It's Alexei Yashin!"

People did double takes. On a frigid Friday night in December 2017, walking along Wellington St. in front of Parliament Hill in full equipment and his No. 19 jersey, his skates tucked under his arm, was former Senators star Alexei Yashin. People stopped. They stared. They circled back.

"That's Alexei Yashin!"

"Yash, great to see you back in Ottawa."

"Can I take a photo?"

"Can we take a selfie?"

"Will you sign this, please?"

He accommodated everybody, including a young man who was getting flustered as his cold fingers fumbled in the cold air with a plastic baggie full of hockey cards. "Keep walking with us. When you find it, I will sign it," Yashin said.

Yashin had played in the Senators Alumni Classic on Parliament Hill, part of the NHL's Centennial celebrations, and rather than getting changed in the freezing dressing rooms under the stands, he opted to walk the couple blocks back to his hotel in all his gear, including his trademark turtleneck and a black balaclava. The walk took him three times longer than it should have as he stopped to sign autographs and take pictures with the people who flocked around him.

Yashin, the first draft pick in Senators history (he was the No. 2 pick in the 1992 NHL Draft) was a controversial figure because of numerous contract battles while playing for the Senators from 1993 to 2001, including sitting out the 1999–2000 season.

The problems started after his first season in 1993–94. It was a "he said, he said" situation. Yashin believed his contract would be renegotiated if he emerged as the team's top player (he led the Senators in scoring that season with 79 points (30 goals, 49 assists). Yashin had signed a five-year, $4 million contract in April 1993. Fellow rookie Alexandre Daigle had signed a five-year, $12.25 million contract after he was selected first in the 1993 NHL Draft in June. Daigle was second on the team in scoring in 1993–94, with 51 points. That's when the trouble started. Yashin believed he was promised he would make as much or more than Daigle.

The Senators weren't buying what Yashin was selling when it came to renegotiation. Yashin sat out the beginning of the 1994–95 season, which wound up being delayed until January because of a lockout. He then sat out a seven-day training camp. A compromise was struck: Yashin was offered bonuses for team performance and game-tying and -winning goals. If he met the bonuses and averaged a point per game, his deal could be reopened. Yashin had 44 points in 47 games and they remained in a stalemate. "I'd like to go through a summer without a dispute with Alexei," Senators owner Rod Bryden said. He wouldn't get his wish.

Yashin sat out training camp again in 1995 and demanded a trade. "Alexei will play hockey in the NHL with us or Alexei will will not play hockey in the NHL or anywhere else until 1998," Bryden said. "We're not going to trade him." Yashin sat out until January, when new general manager Pierre Gauthier arrived and signed him to play the rest of the season (46 games) for $720,000 and $12.3 million for the following four seasons. Yashin was second on the team in scoring that season despite playing only 46 games.

There was no question Yashin was far and away the Senators' most productive player. He led them in scoring each of the next three seasons, in which he averaged 80 points, capping off the run with a 94-point season in 1998–99, 38 points more than Shawn McEachern, who finished second on the team.

Yashin finished second in the voting for the Hart Trophy behind Jaromir Jagr of the Pittsburgh Penguins, and that prompted another monumental holdout. Yashin, entering the last year of his contract, in which he was to earn $3.6 million, wanted $11.5 million a season.

He sat out the entire season with the belief that he would be a free agent at the end of it. Bryden wasn't having any of that. He took Yashin to arbitration, hoping for a ruling that Yashin would still owe the club another year of service. Senators general manager Marshall Johnston, stuck in the middle of the battle, made this announcement: "It is our view, supported by the NHL, that under the terms of the standard players' contract and the collective bargaining agreement, as well as under the accepted principles of contract law, Alexei is obligated to deliver to our club one more full season of play under the terms and conditions of his contract."

Yashin spent the season he sat out practicing in Europe with the EHC Kloten of the Swiss League with his old Russian coach, Vladimir Yursinov.

In June the arbitrator sided with the Senators. Yashin owed the team another season. "If a player chooses not to play at all, then that is the player's decision," arbitrator Lawrence T. Holden Jr. wrote in his decision. "What the full performance concept requires is that the player render performance for the full term of years specified...without illegally holding out if the player wants to obtain the negotiated benefit of free agency."

Yashin played the 2000–01 season for the Senators, and he didn't dog it. He had his second 40-goal season and 88 points to lead the Senators in scoring again. Having made their point, the Senators washed their hands of Yashin and traded him to the New York Islanders in June 2001 for the No. 2 pick in the draft, which the Senators used to take future star Jason Spezza; a big, raw defenseman named Zdeno Chara; and Bill Muckalt, a forward who would go without a goal the next season.

The Islanders signed Yashin to a 10-year, $87.5 million contract. "I'm very happy, very much looking forward to a change of place. I'm looking forward to playing for an organization which seems like they really want me to play for them," Yashin told the *Ottawa Citizen* after the deal was announced. "The most important thing I would like to say to the fans, my teammates, the coaching staff and the organization is I want to thank them. I know sometimes it was not easy for them, but I enjoyed every minute with them, and every moment I tried to do my best. It's too bad it didn't work out."

Yashin had wondered what kind of reception he would get during his postcareer return to Ottawa on this cold December 2017 night to play in the Alumni Classic, but he received a warm welcome from the crowd. Said Alfredsson: "I thought it was great. I know he likes Ottawa. This was really good for him to get the welcome he did and know in the future he's always welcome."

"Ottawa is a part of my life, and I have good memories here," Yashin said. "It was nice to wear my jersey." Then he stopped for another round of selfies with a group of girls as they waited for a light to change.

The Islanders, by the way, bought Yashin out of the last four years of his contract in 2007. They paid him between $2.2 million and $4.2 million per season not to play for them until he finally came off the books in the summer of 2015.

The White Monster

It wasn't a pretty place, but it was a nice place to visit. The unique Ottawa Civic Centre, the home of the expansion Ottawa Senators for their first two and a half seasons and 121 games, wasn't kind to the home team. The visitors? They knew they were going to win;

the only questions were "By how much?" and "How many points would they get?"

The Senators had a 24–85–12 record in their home rink from 1992 to 1995, and it brought to mind the famous quote from former Vancouver Canucks coach and brilliant broadcaster Harry Neale: "Last season we couldn't win at home. This season we can't win on the road. My failure as a coach is I can't think of any place else to play." That was the Senators, but it was all rolled into one season, over and over.

Tom Chorske had a unique perspective from having played at the Civic Centre as both a visitor and a member of the home team. The forward visited with the New Jersey Devils when the Devils were building toward a Stanley Cup championship in 1994–95. After the Devils won the Cup, he wound up playing at the Civic Centre for the Senators for the three months at the end of 1995 before the Senators moved into the Palladium out in the West End in January 1996.

"As a visiting player, the facility was subpar, and it sounds bad, but you knew it was not going to be a difficult night, probably," Chorske said. "There was not a lot of pushback on those nights. You were just skating around and pretty much moving the puck up the ice around them and getting lots of chances. I can remember scoring a couple of goals there against [Senators goaltender] Craig Billington. I had played with Craig in New Jersey, and we were good friends."

The Civic Centre was a stopgap remedy for Terrace Investments after they successfully won an NHL expansion franchise in 1990. Their successful bid included plans for a new 22,500-seat rink in Ottawa's West End, but that wasn't to be ready until late 1993. Financing issues delayed the start of construction of the Palladium until July 1994, so the Senators wound up calling the Civic Centre home for a couple more seasons than planned.

This wasn't uncommon: The Hartford Whalers played in the 7,444-seat Springfield Civic Centre from 1978 to 1980, until the Hartford Civic Centre (in a mall—talk about quirky) was completed. The Calgary Flames played in the Stampede Corral from 1980 to 1983, with a capacity of about 8,000, until the Saddledome was built. The San Jose Sharks played in the Cow Palace (capacity: about 11,000) until their new rink was built. And the Tampa Bay Lightning called the Expo Hall at the Florida State Fairgrounds home in 1992–93 for their first season in the NHL. It held 10,425.

The Civic Centre was built as part of a Centennial project in 1967. After the Auditorium had been torn down, the city needed a new rink, and with the football stadium at Lansdowne undergoing a renovation, somebody had the bright idea to amalgamate the two.

The rink had a...well...unique configuration. As a cost-saving measure, it was built under the north grandstand of the football stadium. Being shoehorned in there meant the roof was way lower on the south side of the rink, the solution to which was a large wall, painted white, that imposed itself on the south side of the arena. There was just one level of seats on the walled side, while the north side of the bowl had two sections extending to the ceiling. It was basically three-quarters of a bowl.

After the bid to Bring Back the Senators was successful, the Civic Centre underwent an extensive renovation. New seats were installed and the dressing room areas were refurbished, though they were still barely up to NHL standards. "What we put up with for locker room facilities, I'm not sure the [collective bargaining agreement] would allow today," Senators defenseman Brad Shaw told Sportsnet with a laugh.

Most important, Terrace Investments installed 42 private boxes that were retrofit around the top of the building at a cost of around $3 million. That brought attendance to 10,500 for NHL games. The boxes turned out to be a good deal for the Senators. They rented them out for $65,000 a season, so they had paid for themselves very early into the second season. As Senators founder Bruce Firestone points out in his book *Don't Back Down*, those boxes generated about $6.3 million in profit during the two and a half years the Senators played at the Civic Centre.

Firestone said the Senators made $9.8 million before interest, taxes, and amortization that first year in the Civic Centre, which isn't hard to believe. The team's payroll (including the farm team) was $6.5 million. That will get you a second-line center these days, and maybe not even a good one.

The Senators' best night at the Civic Centre was their first one when they beat the Montreal Canadiens 5–3 to win their first game back in the NHL on October 8, 1992. It was pretty much all downhill from there. They didn't win another home game for six weeks.

Both the NHL and the Civic Centre were small places back then. The room for the scouts and media used to be down at ice level, and there was only one small elevator, so it was always a trek to walk up to the press box. The route took you across a hallway between the two dressing rooms to some stairs that went up to the concourse level and then up to the press box through the luxury suites.

The workbench where the players would prepare their sticks was outside the visitors room, and many a casual but informative conversation was had with a player by that bench. Things were different in a lot of ways. One evening, Washington Capitals defenseman Al Iafrate was sitting on that workbench. He was an imposing figure with his "skullet" (bald on top, party in the back) and bicep tattoo, which few players had back in 1992–93. It was after the warmup, and he was bare-chested, wearing his hockey pants, socks, and skates. He was smoking a cigarette. He raised his cigarette between two fingers and saluted a greeting. That's something you just don't see today.

Speaking of the Civic Centre press box, the best one-liner I heard in there (and if you've ever spent any time in the company of cynical sportswriters, that's saying something) came from the late, great Jim Kelley, a Hall of Famer with the *Buffalo News.*

Like everything at the Civic Centre, things were cramped in the press box. To increase the capacity of the press box, they put in a back row on some risers. The people who sat in the back (usually the visiting media) would hit their heads on the ceiling. There was barely room to turn around. There was always the danger the legs of your stool could slide off the riser backward and send you tumbling against the back wall.

Jim, who was a good-sized man, came into the press box one night and began the battle to get set up in the back row. There was the sound of the stool legs scraping and some heavy breathing as he tried to turn around and hang his coat up on a hook. Finally, a sheen of sweat on his brow, Jim settled onto his metal stool. He slumped slightly. "You don't walk into this press box," he said with a heavy sigh, "as much as you put it on."

70 A Last Game of Keep-Away

As his last warmup before an NHL game wound down, Daniel Alfredsson grabbed the puck and started to stickhandle among the Ottawa Senators on the ice. It was a giant game of keep-away, the way he had finished hundreds of practices during his 17 seasons with the Senators. It was a fitting ending to Alfredsson's last day as a Senators player on December 4, 2014.

Earlier in the day, Alfredsson had announced his retirement at a press conference after he signed a ceremonial agreement that allowed him to retire as a member of the Senators. Wearing his No. 11, Alfredsson skated with the Senators in the warmup before the game against the New York Islanders. With the Foo Fighters' "My Hero" playing over the sound system, the fans cheered as Alfredsson grabbed the puck and stickhandled his way through a few of the other players. It was a touching moment as Alfredsson, who had played the 2013–14 season with the Detroit Red Wings, returned to the city where he started his NHL career to say thank you and good-bye to Senators fans.

"Oh my God, that could've been one of my best skates ever," Alfredsson said afterward. "Just basically knowing that this is the last time I get to experience this and in this atmosphere. I couldn't have played, I'm not in good enough shape. But I skated a couple laps, and you feel like, 'Maybe a few shifts.' It gets the juices flowing, the energy that's in the rink. It's incredible."

It was a feel-good moment after an unsuccessful negotiation to keep Alfredsson with the Senators had preceded his departure as a free agent in the summer of 2013 to play for the Wings. Many fans were embittered by his leaving.

Alfredsson said he had made the decision that if he was able to play the 2014–15 season, it would be with the Red Wings, but each time he tried to increase his workouts, his back gave him problems. "I worked hard to rehab my back this summer so I could play another year. However, about three weeks ago I realized it's time to retire," he said. "It's another hard decision."

Senators general manager Bryan Murray worked hard to smooth over the damage after Alfredsson's departure, and during a drive around the Detroit area when the Senators were visiting the Wings on November 23, the wheels were put in motion for Alfredsson to retire as a Senator. After talking it over with his wife, Bibbi, Alfredsson said he decided to accept the Senators' offer. "I was taken aback by this offer. I never believed that my career entitled me to any special treatment," Alfredsson said the morning of his last skate. "However, Bibbi and I both agreed this was the right thing to do and it would give us a chance to say thank you to the people and the fans of Ottawa. So here we are."

"We're just happy to have him back," said Senators defenseman Erik Karlsson. "It always felt like the right decision to retire him as a Senator. I know that's what he's always wanted and that was his plan for a very long time. He left for one year, and that's the way it was; he had a lot of fun and we had a lot of fun, and now we're here together again. Unfortunately, he's going to hang them up."

"Without question, Daniel has been the greatest player that this city has ever seen in many, many different ways," Senators owner, governor, and chairman Eugene Melnyk said. "As a player on the ice, as a leader on the ice, as someone who interacted with the fans any time, he was always available. For any charitable work, he was always available. For media, he was always there. That's a rare commodity to have in an organization like ours. Being the longest-serving captain in what is really an infant franchise is phenomenal, for 13 years being our captain."

"It's as good an ending as anyone can hope for," Alfredsson said. "I'm very happy that it turned out the way it did and I was able to get this opportunity. I thanked Bryan [and Mr. Melnyk] earlier. They made this happen, and for that I'm very grateful."

Alfredsson said the ceremony and reception from the fans was better than he expected. "I didn't expect my retirement would be this big a deal," Alfredsson said. "The way I've been welcomed back has been almost surreal. I don't know how to thank everybody more than saying thank you. It means a lot to me and to my family, obviously, and to my kids as well. I'll be forever grateful."

The Senators were led onto the ice for the warmup by goaltender Craig Anderson, who stopped, turned, and stood by the gate. The other players followed him out and formed symmetrical rows. Alfredsson was last on the ice as the crowd cheered and chanted his name. He raised his stick in a salute to the crowd. After a couple laps, Alfredsson dropped to the ice and stretched with Karlsson and longtime teammates defenseman Chris Phillips and forward Chris Neil.

Alfredsson started the butterfly drill and took a pass from Phillips and fired a shot to Anderson's glove side, which he stopped. Some of the crowd booed. There were cheers when Alfredsson scored on his next shot on Andrew Hammond, called up from Binghamton of the American Hockey League before the game to replace injured Robin Lehner.

After the game of keep-away, the Senators re-formed their two lines leading to the gate at the end of the bench, leaving Alfredsson to take some more slow circles, stick raised, fans chanting his name. As he skated off the ice, he raised his hands and applauded the crowd.

In the interlude between the warmup and the start of the game, highlights of Alfredsson's career with the Senators were shown on the video board. Drawing the biggest cheers were Alfredsson's lampooning of Toronto Maple Leafs captain Mats Sundin tossing his stick into the crowd at Air Canada Centre and Alfredsson's controversial hit on Maple Leafs forward Darcy Tucker in the 2002 Stanley Cup Playoffs, which left Tucker dazed on the ice and Alfredsson scoring the winning goal.

Alfredsson came back out before the opening faceoff and circled the ice as the crowd again poured down chants of "Alfie! Alfie! Alfie!" His family joined him at center ice, and he addressed the crowd. "Thank you for all the great times and all the beautiful memories," Alfredsson said. "They will connect us with all of you forever.... Now the plan for me is to take some time off, spend some time with my family," Alfredsson told the crowd. "Let's not say good-bye. *Merci. À bientôt.* Thank you."

The memorable night finished with the fans saying thank you. As the clock hit 11:11 each period, the chant went up again: "Alfie! Alfie! Alfie!"

71 Hit the Road

The road trip can be a wonderful place for a Senators fan. It has been my experience that road trips require a proper place to either prepare for the prospect of watching the Senators in an enemy rink or to properly put things in perspective and dissect the experience postgame.

In my 30 years crisscrossing North America to cover the Senators and other sports events, I have had the pleasure of stopping into a great number of such places. In consultation with some of my colleagues, many of whom have much more experience than me (hello, Pat Hickey) we have come up with a list of fine establishments that will add to your road-trip experience. Hell, they might even be the highlight.

I provide this list (with addresses) with one warning: we sportswriters tend to like more, shall we say, grittier types of places that might be slightly off the beaten path. Less kind people might refer to them as "dive bars." I prefer to think of them as gathering places with character. Commonalties: attentive, professional staff; brews ranging from PBR to fine craft; shuffleboard; tattoos; and for the most part proximity to the rink, for whatever value you attach to that.

With a stick tap to old friend Scott Burnside, and with a warning that you frequent these establishments at your own risk, here we go.

Anaheim: Doheny's Tavern Grill and Sports Bar—13062 Chapman Ave., Garden Grove, CA 92840

Arizona: Overtime Lounge—5304 N. 59th Ave., Glendale, AZ 85301

Boston: The Fours—166 Canal St., Boston, MA 02114

Buffalo: Swannie House—170 Ohio St., Buffalo, NY 14203

Calgary: The Unicorn—223 8 Ave. SW, Calgary, AB T2P 1B9

Carolina: London Bridge Pub—110 E. Hargett St., Raleigh, NC 27601

Chicago: Rossi's—412 N. State St., Chicago, IL 60654

Colorado: PS Lounge—3416 E. Colfax Ave., Denver, CO 80206

Columbus: High Beck Tavern—564 S. High St., Columbus, OH 43215

Dallas: City Tavern—1402 Main St., Dallas, TX 75202

Detroit: Detroiter Bar—655 Beaubien St., Detroit, MI 48226

Edmonton: Sherlock Holmes Pub—10012 101A Ave. NW, Edmonton, AB T5J 0P5

Florida: Elbo Room—241 S. Fort Lauderdale Beach Blvd., Fort Lauderdale, FL 33316

Las Vegas: Champagne's Cafe—3557 S. Maryland Pkwy., Las Vegas, NV 89169

Los Angeles: Hank's Bar—840 S. Grand Ave., Los Angeles, CA 90017

Minnesota: 8th Street Grille—800 Marquette Ave., Minneapolis, MN 55402

Montreal: Hurley's Irish Pub—1225 Crescent St., Montreal, QC H3G 2B1

Nashville: Beer Sellar—107 Church St., Nashville, TN 37201

New Jersey: Don't bother with anything around the rink. Your best bet is to see the next entry.

New York (Islanders and Rangers): Nancy Whiskey Pub—1 Lispenard St., New York, NY 10013

Philadelphia: Las Vegas Lounge—704 Chestnut St., Philadelphia, PA 19106

Pittsburgh: Shale's Café—1208 Fifth Ave., Pittsburgh, PA 15219

San Jose: The Old Wagon Saloon & Grill—73 N. San Pedro St., San Jose, CA 95110

St. Louis: Hair of the Dog—1212 Washington Ave., St. Louis, MO 63103

Tampa: The Hub Bar—719 N. Franklin St., Tampa, FL 33602

Toronto: Hoops Sports Bar & Grill—125 Bremner Blvd., Toronto, ON M5J 3A8

Vancouver: Winking Judge Pub—888 Burrard St., Vancouver, BC V6Z 1X9

Washington: Irish Channel Restaurant & Pub—500 H St. NW, Washington, DC 20001

Winnipeg: King's Head Pub—120 King St., Winnipeg, MB R3B 1H9

72 The Captains

When it comes to Senators captains, the conversation pretty much begins and ends with No. 11, Daniel Alfredsson, who held the job for 14 years, from 1999 to 2013, and set the gold standard.

That's not taking away anything from the other men who wore the C. Laurie Boschman, the Senators' first captain, was 32 years old when he arrived through the expansion draft in June 1992, finding out he had been taken by the Senators from a customs agent on his way home from New Jersey to Winnipeg for the summer.

He handled a season in which the team lost 70 games with class while continuing to push and motivate his teammates. He was reserved when dealing with the media but had a reputation as somebody who could give and take it with the best of the chirpers.

Boschman almost singlehandedly saved the Senators from going the entire season without a road win when he scored three goals on April 10, 1993, on Long Island to give the Senators a 5–3 win over the Islanders, ending the Senators' 38-game road losing streak. Not surprisingly, after all that, he retired after the season.

It took three guys to take over the job the next season, with forward Mark Lamb and defensemen Brad Shaw and Gord Dineen—three solid veterans—rotating the captaincy for the 1993–94 season.

Randy Cunneyworth was signed as a free agent in July 1994 and was named captain of a team that was beginning to transition from being composed of castoffs and journeymen to featuring good, young players drafted by the Senators. Cunneyworth, one of the classiest guys to play the game, took on an important role in setting an example for the likes of Alexei Yashin, Alexandre

Daigle, Radek Bonk, and the other young players who would come along, such as Wade Redden and Chris Phillips. "I thought we had a group of players that were really good people," former Senators coach Jacques Martin said. "A captain like Randy Cunneyworth was near the end of his career, but [he was] such a respected leader and such a well-respected player and person by his teammates."

Politics played a big role in Alexei Yashin taking over the captaincy when Cunneyworth departed as a free agent in 1998. Despite his unpopularity with fans because of his frequent contract battles, Yashin was given the captaincy as a political move to try and smooth the waters. That led to Senators forward Vaclav Prospal putting voice to an opinion that was probably held by a lot of people after Yashin sat out the 1999–2000 season. When Yashin was forced to return after an arbitrator ruled he owed the Senators another season to fulfill his contract, Prospal said: "He was thinking about himself, and at the time he was the captain. There's no captain in the NHL that lets his team down like that."

There were a lot of people, even within the Senators circle, who thought Alfredsson should have been named captain after Cunneyworth, and it finally happened when Yashin held out in 1999. A wrong was made right. "As a franchise, especially when it struggled early, you're looking for a reason for legitimacy and to establish yourself," former Senators president and one of the franchise founders Cyril Leeder said. "I think that's what Alfredsson really did. He became the face of the franchise, somebody that the people could really relate to, cheer for, and like."

It was the combination of player and person that made Alfredsson such an effective leader. He brought the blue-collar mentality of his hometown, the port city of Gothenburg, to the rink every day. He was one of the first on and one of the last off the ice at practice, leading the legendary games of keep-away at the end of every practice.

The Captains
Laurie Boschman 1992–93
Mark Lamb, Brad Shaw, Gord Dineen 1993–94
Randy Cunneyworth 1994–98
Alexei Yashin 1998–99
Daniel Alfredsson 1999–2013
Jason Spezza 2013–14
Erik Karlsson 2014–18

He was there every day to answer questions from the media, whether things were going well or the team was struggling. Sometimes his answers were a little too honest for some people's liking. The best example came in the spring of 2013. After the Senators went down 3–1 in their best-of-seven series against the Pittsburgh Penguins, Alfredsson was asked if the Senators could come back to win three straight and the series. "Probably not," he said. "Their depth and power play right now, it doesn't look too good." That "probably not" soundbite became a buzz phrase in Ottawa.

He was often at his best in the Battle of Ontario, which endeared him to Senators fans and made him public enemy No. 1 to Toronto Maple Leafs fans. There was the famous hit on Darcy Tucker in Game 5 of the second round in 2002 that led to Alfredsson scoring the winning goal to give the Senators a 3–2 series lead (only to lose in seven games).

That was bad enough, but the move that really defined Alfredsson as the Senators' leader in the Battle of Ontario came a couple years later. Toronto captain Mats Sundin, one of Alfredsson's best friends, was suspended one game for throwing a piece of his broken stick into the stands at Air Canada Centre. The game Sundin sat out was against the Senators, and in that game, Alfredsson broke own his stick. He started to skate with the remaining part of the shaft in his hand and faked throwing it into the stands. That drove the Maple Leafs fans nuts. "I understand players not being too happy, but I know Mats," Alfredsson said. "I was trying to make a joke, but it was bad timing."

It became tradition then for Maple Leafs fans to boo Alfredsson every time he touched the puck. It became the case at Canadian Tire Centre as well, where the building would often be packed with Maple Leafs fans.

It became a tribute to Alfredsson's unpopularity in Toronto that whenever an opposing player would step to the foul line during a Toronto Raptors basketball game in the Air Canada Centre, they would put a picture of Alfredsson on the big video board to get the crowd to boo in an attempt to distract the shooter.

Alfredsson thrived no matter what the environment. "What separates him from other players is he was able to put aside whatever was happening and perform at a high level," Martin said. "No matter what happened, he kept working and playing at that high level.... What amazes me is his positive attitude through all those years."

The many and varied qualities Alfredsson bought to the team, both on the ice and off, also made him a great candidate for the captaincy. "Down by a goal or up by a goal, I could play him in all situations and count on him to do the right thing," Martin said. "He was the whole package."

Leeder and former Senators GM Randy Sexton once made a list of the qualities they wanted in their ideal captain. Leeder said:

> If you wrote down what you wanted the ideal Senator to be, it wouldn't be as good as Alfie. It wouldn't be as good as he was. We did that. Randy had a checklist of what he wanted the captain to be, and Alfie was better than that.
>
> Make Ottawa your home, part of the community, do everything right on the ice, set a good example, say the right things publicly...and he's just a good person too.

Daniel is still the face of the franchise. When you think of the Senators, you think of Daniel Alfredsson.

73 Crazy Night in Buffalo

In early March 1994, the Senators packed up their 10–48–8 record and four-game losing streak for a seven-game, 15-day road trip that would see them crisscross North America. It seemed unlikely, but it was true: this edition of the Senators was looking as inept as the the first-year team of the season before, which finished with a 10–70–4 record. The 1993–94 Senators would finish with a minus-196 goal differential, three worse than the first-year team.

The road trip took them to Boston, Quebec City, Philadelphia, Anaheim, Los Angeles, San Jose, and Buffalo. It covered 7,494 miles, and that only seemed to equal the number of goals the inept Senators gave up through the first five games of the trip (they were actually outscored 31–6).

After they defeated the almost-as-inept San Jose Sharks 2–1 on St. Patrick's Day, they packed up for the finale in Buffalo. The win had not done much to improve the mood around the Senators, the finish line for a miserable season a short distance away. Teams traveled on commercial flights then, and the mood didn't improve when Flight 488 from Pittsburgh to Buffalo was delayed. A flight attendant with the passenger manifest in her hand said they were waiting for a connecting passenger. The name on the manifest: Kelly Chase. Chase, the St. Louis Blues' tough guy? Said one Senator: "Yeah, I had dinner with him when the Blues were in Ottawa, and he heard the Senators were interested in him. He said,

'If they ask about me, tell them I have a drug problem.'" Ottawa wasn't a popular destination then. A few minutes later, a petite blond woman came aboard and took her seat near us. Meet Kelly Chase, pharmaceutical salesperson from Buffalo. The flight got under way, and the Senators finally arrived in western New York road-weary and cranky.

The Sabres were headed for a fourth-place finish in the Northeast Division with a scrappy lineup, which wasn't unusual then. They had five players who would have more than 100 penalty minutes for the season: Rob Ray (274), Brad May (171), Randy Moller (154), Matthew Barnaby (106), and Wayne Presley (103).

The Senators weren't in a mood to go quietly. Ottawa's Bill Huard and Moller fought four minutes into the game. Senators tough guy Dennis Vial and May squared off two minutes after that. After a relatively quiet second period (six roughing minors, two for interference, a slashing, a holding, and a boarding penalty), after which the Sabres led 4–2, all hell broke loose in the third period.

Vial fought Ray six minutes into the third. Buffalo's Ken Sutton and Ottawa's Andrew McBain dropped them two minutes later. Ray and Huard fought at 16:19. Vail and Sabres leading scorer Dale Hawerchuk, no choir boy, swung their sticks at each other and were penalized with less than three minutes to go. But things went sideways with seven seconds left when the Senators accused Buffalo defenseman Craig Muni of going after the knee of forward Evgeny Davydov. Senators coach Rick Bowness smashed a stick and hurled it onto the ice. He then twirled a white towel in mock surrender and got kicked out of the game. He jawed with Sabres goaltender Dominik Hasek as he left the ice. "I just wished him good luck in the playoffs," Bowness said.

When play resumed, Vial shot the puck across the ice and into the Sabres bench in the general direction of Sabres coach John Muckler. Vial had run by the Buffalo bench with his elbow out earlier in the season, just missing Hawerchuk and catching Sabres winger Scott Thomas, *Slap Shot*–style.

"I was only trying to ice the puck. I couldn't send the puck up the sideboards, so I shot it across the ice. It just happened to hit their bench," Vial explained.

"Vial was firing it at me because I told Vial exactly what I thought of him," Muckler shot back. "Vial can't hit the net. Maybe he can hit the bench."

"Everybody in the rink saw the shot coming, so that wasn't so bad," May said. "But it was ridiculous. I know Dennis, he's a very tough guy, tough as nails, and he probably has the biggest heart on the Ottawa team. He doesn't have to do something like that."

Vial was suspended for one game.

What a finish to a miserable road trip.

74 Dean and Gord Part I

Dean Brown and Gord Wilson have been the radio voices of the Ottawa Senators from day one when CFRA became the first official broadcaster of Senators games in 1992.

Brown, a native of Warren, Manitoba, was working in London, Ontario, when CFRA program director Al "Puppy Dog" Pascal was driving around listening to the radio looking for new talent and heard Brown doing sportscasts. John Badham had been hired to be the sports director at CFRA and the voice of the Canadian Football League's Ottawa Rough Riders. Brown was hired to do the Riders pregame show, patrol the sideline, and do general sports reporting three days a week.

Within a season, Brown had moved up into the booth to do color after Geoff Courier, Badham's broadcasting partner, departed for Saskatchewan. The next year, 1985, Brown became the voice of the Riders when Badham left to broadcast Toronto Argonauts games. When Terrace Investments won the bid to bring the Senators back to Ottawa, Brown became a hockey play-by-play man.

Here are Brown's top five memories from the Senators' first 25 years, in his own words.

1. Opening Night
Whenever anyone asks me this question, this is always my answer. The winning of the franchise was huge. The first draft, the first entry draft, the first camp, the first preseason games…for me, all the firsts pale in comparison to the first game against the Montreal Canadiens at the Civic Centre. It is still so clear to me. Gord and I shoehorned into that tiny home radio broadcast booth. I remember just looking at all the faces there. So many of the faces I knew because the building was so small and we were close enough, from our perch, to see those faces. I always remember the feeling [of] "It's real." In the NHL! My city was now an NHL city. I was working in the NHL full-time. I look back now and appreciate everything [my family and I] have because of this game, and it still seems like the longest of shots and the greatest lottery win ever. It was one of the most surreal nights of my life and still is.

2. December 30, 1998
Gord and I were in Buffalo for a game. I was in the booth getting ready, and I got a phone call. It was from my wife, Mauri. We were pregnant and she was due in a few weeks. That day she had gone in for a normal checkup. The doctors found that she had escalating levels of uric acid building up in her body. It would not harm the baby, but if she didn't deliver soon, her kidneys could be destroyed.

They were inducing her. Mauri told me, "If you want to see this baby being born, you better make tracks."

I packed up my stuff and told Gord he was on his own. I raced to the elevator and went downstairs wondering how in the world I was going to get from Buffalo to Ottawa at 6:00 on a Wednesday night. The elevator door opened and there was Senators defenseman Lance Pitlick. He was injured and not playing. I told him my story and that Gord needed a color man. That was the night Lance Pitlick debuted as an NHL color analyst.

When I got downstairs, I found our veteran bus driver, Teddy. He knew everyone. If anyone knew how to get me home, it would be Teddy. He said, "Let me make a call." At that time, the Knox family owned the Sabres. Mr. Knox was in Florida, so his limo driver was at home. Within 20 minutes he picked me up. On the drive to Toronto, I booked one of the last two seats on the last Air Canada flight to Ottawa that night. The wonderful woman on the phone put me through to the airport desk after booking my flight. That lady said she would be waiting for me at the curb to rush me through security (which you could still do back then).

They held the flight for 10 minutes for me, and I made it home in time to see my first child the moment he arrived in the world. Thanks to my mad dash from Buffalo, I was able to meet Connor Brown the moment he took his first breath.

3. The Skates

Back in the early days of the franchise, many of us who traveled covering the team still played rec hockey, until the time constraints of an NHL season just made that impossible. Back in those days, equipment manager Ed Georgica would carry one extra bag, and it would be filled with our skates and gloves. Players weren't as superstitious or persnickety about their sticks as they are now, so we were allowed to use some of them. After the team's morning skate, we would play shinny before it was time to return to the hotel and work. Often the coaches would also stay and play.

One day in St. Louis in their old building, head coach Rick Bowness had his father, Bob, along for the trip. Rick's dad was a great player back in the old Senior hockey days for the Maritimes.

Rick had one of those relationships with his father that they make Hallmark movies about. Rick's father was a wonderful man. He was also battling cancer at the time. I was talking to Rick's dad during the morning skate and telling him about our shinny games. He said he'd love to play one day. I suggested *this* would be a great day for that. He hadn't brought any gear, though. I told him I was going back to the hotel to work and he could use mine.

Rick and his father (along with everyone else) played for more than an hour in that smelly, old, beautiful arena in St. Louis. The day went on, the season went on, and eventually Rick's dad passed away.

I came to the rink a few weeks later for practice and brought my skates with me. I gave them to Rick, and he looked at me like I was losing it. I told him these were the last skates his dad ever wore and I could get another pair. Rick started to mist up, said thanks, and went into his office. I don't know if Rick still has those skates or not.

4. The Power of the Pen

Back in the days when we had a budget to give interview guests a small gift in return for their time, we had these beautiful Mont Blanc pens from a sponsor. Since Gord did the interviews then and still does now, he was the one tasked with trying to get an interview with Red Wings coach Scotty Bowman while we were in Detroit.

Scotty was infamous for being very stingy with his time for interviews, especially from the visiting radio guy. So Gord did the smart thing: he gave the Red Wings media-relations person one of the pens and asked if he would give it to Scotty as a gift and ask if an interview was possible.

Moments later, Gord alone was whisked into Scotty's office and he got that coveted one-on-one interview with Scotty. The next time the Senators played Detroit it was back in Ottawa, and again there was a crowd of reporters all asking for Scotty. He walked by them all and straight to Gord and asked if he had any more of those pens. Gord said yes, and that meant another exclusive one-on-one interview with the great Scotty Bowman.

I, like everyone else, was left outside during their private time, but I remember chuckling as all the Detroit reporters wanted to know who this Gord guy was and how the hell he got to keep having these private sessions with Scotty. They never knew Scotty just couldn't say no to a free Mont Blanc pen.

5. Pat Burns

My Pat Burns story is similar in some ways to the Scotty Bowman story except the trigger was not a pen but rather a Craven menthol. I knew Pat from the few times my radio station had sent me to do a story on the then-Hull Olympiques of the QMJHL or to cover one of their playoff runs.

I knew Pat and he knew me, but we were never really friends. When he got to the NHL, it was kind of the same. We knew each other but not as pals or confidants. He didn't give me any scoops or have off-the-record conversations with me. But that's exactly what other members of the media thought when he became coach of the Toronto Maple Leafs.

First time we were in Toronto after he had taken over, the media was all huddled in an area outside the coach's office waiting for him. His door opened, and he pointed at me and said, "Dean, can I talk to you for a moment?" Of course I followed him into his office while the rest of the media wondered why I was selected and why I was getting a one-on-one.

As soon as I sat down in his office, Pat said, "You got a smoke?" In those days I still smoked, and he had been telling everyone that he didn't. I said yes, and we shared a couple smokes and chatted about the league, the teams, people we knew in common. I asked, "Why me?' thinking I was special in some way. In that direct way Pat would speak, he didn't make up a story to make me feel special. He just said, 'You're the only guy here who smokes my brand.'

This went on, over and over until Pat actually really, really quit smoking and so did I several years later. Ironically, we never really got to know each other through hockey, but we did through a horrible, horrible habit.

I suppose though the *method* of connection is not as important as actually *making* a connection. I will always cherish those smoky conversations with Pat.

75 Dean and Gord Part II

Gord Wilson has seen more Ottawa Senators games live than anybody. By his count, he can recall missing only five Senators games, regular-season and playoffs, through 2017.

A native of Montreal whose father was in the air force, he moved to Ottawa as an infant. His radio career started at CKOB in Renfrew, where he was "an engineer, copywriter, salesman, commercial producer, disc jockey, and did the news, sports, weather, and farm reports."

After nine months there, he got a shot with CKBY/CKOY in Ottawa working overnights. Eighteen months later, when colleague Dean Brown over at CFRA got his chance to move from the sideline up into the booth for Ottawa Rough Riders broadcasts, Wilson moved to CFRA.

In 1990 Wilson was the first to report back to Ottawa from Palm Beach, Florida, that Ottawa was returning to the National Hockey League when Terrace Investments was awarded an expansion franchise. He became the color man in 1992.

Here, in Wilson's own words, are his five top memories from his time in the broadcast booth; in dressing room; and on planes, trains, and buses with the Senators.

1. The Beer Bottle Breakout

It took place in St. Petersburg, Florida, during an off day after yet another disappointing Senators loss. A few of us media types had some free time to go wondering about, and we ended up on a pier overlooking the ocean. On that pier was a restaurant, and there we found head coach Rick Bowness and assistant coach Alain Vigneault. A few empty beer bottles sat with them.

They asked us to join them, so we happily did.

After about half an hour of discussing the loss from the day before, and us having all the answers and solutions to the team's problems, the head coach finally had enough. "You guys don't know what you're talking about," Bowness said, and then he proceeded to give us a hockey lesson about the Senators "system."

One beer bottle went to one side of the table, another over to the other side. Once Bowness got his Coors Light team aligned, Vigneault arranged his empty Buds. I think somebody's arm may have served as a blue line. After 10 minutes of a lot of slurred words and clanking empties, we all felt much wiser. The Sens didn't win too many more games after that lesson, nor did they break out of their own zone any better, but at least those of us in attendance on that sunny day in St. Pete's had a better understanding of what they were trying to do, thanks to Rick and Alain's Beer Bottle Breakout.

2. We're Not Worthy

This took place on April 10, 1993, in the bowels of the Nassau Veterans Memorial Coliseum on Long Island. It was game 81 of an 84-game schedule, and the 40th road game of the year. The Senators to that point hadn't won a game away from the Ottawa Civic Centre. But it all changed that night when Senators captain Laurie Boschman scored three goals in leading the Senators to a 5–3 win. When Boschman was named the first star of the game and finished his postgame interviews, he was the last to get to the team bus.

Upon his arrival, all his teammates dropped to their knees, raised their hands in the air, and chanted "We're not worthy!" It was a classic moment for a team desperate to find anything positive during a season that saw Ottawa finish with a record of 10–70–4.

The Sens, by the way, lost their remaining two road games.

3. A Fist Pump for Kevin

Another of my favorite on-ice moments came when the Senators were in New Jersey facing the Devils. It was the 1999–2000 season, and Kevin Dineen was a member of the Sens. It was his only year with the club. During his one game against future Hall of Fame goalie Martin Brodeur, Dineen stepped in over the Devils' blue line and fired a shot toward the Devils' net. Harmless enough. The puck was going wide but came close enough that it grazed the outside of the net behind Brodeur.

Dineen saw the netting move and instantly thought the puck went in. In one quick motion, Kevin dropped to one knee and gave a big fist pump, but before he could finish this wonderful celebration, he realized the puck had gone into the corner and play was continuing.

The Devils would eventually ice the puck. Dineen would have to get off the ice, but he had to do so by skating by the New Jersey bench. He knew he was in for the razzing of his life, and that's what he got.

To add insult to injury, following the game, the Senators' bus got delayed on the tarmac at the Newark airport. As Dineen sat on the bus talking on his cell phone, his teammates got off the bus, and when they got his attention, all dropped to one knee and celebrated Kevin's imaginary goal with a big fist pump.

4. The Mystery of Room 750

What happens on the road is supposed to stay on the road, and this story has for a number of years. But the statute of limitations has expired on this one, so here goes.

The scene is again Long Island, and the season is 1995–96. The team was staying at the Long Island Marriott, which was basically a parking lot away from the rink. Some details are a little sketchy, but let's say I was staying in room 650. I went to bed around 10:00 PM but was awakened at 11:00 by some rather loud amorous activity in the room above me. This went on for at least an hour. And when I say loud, I mean screams of ecstasy to beat the band. It was most impressive.

Shortly after midnight, the quiet returned and I was able to get back to sleep. At 2:00 AM the nocturnal noises returned from up above. Again, very impressive. I was now very proud of whoever was staying in room 750.

When I arrived at the rink for the morning skate, the first person I ran into was athletic therapist Conrad Lackten. I smiled and said, "Hey, how is room 750?"

He said, "I'm not in 750. I'm in room 819."

I told him about my night, and we had a good chuckle. The next person to walk up to us was defenseman Stan Neckar. Conrad immediately asked him how he enjoyed his stay in room 750. He told Stan that he kept him up all night because of all the sexual noise coming from the room. Stan immediately got defensive and said, "I was in room 718! Jaroslav Modry was in 750!"

Mystery solved. And Modry became one of my off-ice heroes.

5. Thank You, Bob Rae!

And thank you, Bill Huard, for this story. Billy was a tough player for the Sens in 1993–94 when the Ontario provincial government was led by the NDP's Bob Rae. The federal Conservative government had introduced the Goods and Services Tax in 1991, a nationwide tax that affected the purchase of just about everything, including newspapers. A 25-cent paper now cost 27 cents because of the GST that was implemented by the Conservative government.

While in Calgary, Alberta, we watched Billy Huard pull out a quarter to buy a paper. When the clerk asked him for the extra two cents, which Bill didn't have, he tossed the paper back and responded, "Well, thank you, Bob Rae!"

On that same trip, farther west in Vancouver, the Senators had just wrapped up a rather grueling practice at the old Pacific Coliseum, which was nestled in a beautiful location with the ocean almost across the street and the mountains in plain view. With everyone completely out of breath, Bill leaned over to the late E.J. McGuire and, while gasping for air, asked the assistant coach: "Geez, what altitude are we at? I can barely breathe."

E.J.'s response was short and to the point: "We're at sea level, you dope."

76 Go Back to 1927

When the Ottawa Senators hosted Game 3 of the 2007 Stanley Cup Final on June 2, it was 80 years and 50 days since the Senators had last hosted a Stanley Cup Final game. The Senators won on both those dates, but the victory on April 13, 1927, wound up being a little more significant: while the modern-day Senators beat the Anaheim Ducks to avoid going down 3–0 in the 2007 Final, the old Senators won their 11th and last Stanley Cup.

The game between the old Senators and the Boston Bruins was played at the Ottawa Auditorium, a 7,500-seat barn that sat at the corner of O'Connor and Argyle Streets, where the Taggart Family YMCA stands now. The Aud was built in 1923 to replace the Arena, which stood at the end of Laurier St. (where Confederation Park is today). The Arena had hosted the 1910 and 1911 Stanley Cup challenges and the 1920 Stanley Cup Final.

There were 10 teams in the NHL in 1927, evenly split between Canadian and American Divisions. The Senators finished first in the Canadian Division with a 30–10–4 record, six points ahead of the Montreal Canadiens. The New York Rangers won the American Division with a 25–13–6 record, ahead of the Boston Bruins (21–20–3). The Senators got a bye into the Stanley Cup semifinal and defeated the Canadiens. The Bruins defeated the Chicago Blackhawks and then the Rangers to advance to the best-of-three Final. It was the first time the Stanley Cup Final was played in both Canada and the U.S.

Can you imagine this happening today? After the first game of the Final in Boston was declared a 0–0 draw (they played 20 minutes of overtime, but the ice became unplayable), NHL president Frank Calder decided the Final would be no more than five games with overtime limited to 20 minutes. If they were tied after overtime of the fifth game, they would share the title.

In Game 2 King Clancy, Frank Finnigan, and Cy Denneny scored for the Senators in a 3–1 win. Denneny scored on a setup from Clancy in a 1–1 tie in Game 3.

The Senators, boosted by fresh legs (they dressed Frank Finnigan and Hec Kilrea on the wings with Frank Nighbor at center), won the Cup with a wild 3–1 victory to win Ottawa's last Stanley Cup. Finnigan scored ("Finnigan was on the puck like a hawk after a hen," the account in the *Ottawa Evening Citizen* said), and Denneny, the hero for Ottawa, had another pair. "Cy may not be as speedy as he was a few years back, but his stick has lost none of its cunning," reported the *Citizen*. Goaltender Alex Connell "lived up to his previous reputation of being a marvelous net guardian."

Senators captain George Boucher and Boston's Lionel Hitchman were kicked out of the game for a fight Ottawa police had to stop. Boucher had jumped in after Hitchman and Ottawa's Hooley Smith slashed at each other and then "squared away to finish the affair under Marquis of Queensbury rules." Hitchman was bleeding from the mouth, according to the newspaper account. Smith then butt-ended Boston's Harry Oliver over the eye. "The action on the part of Smith [was] entirely uncalled for but was doubtless the result of the offender completely losing control of his temper," the *Citizen* wrote. The legendary Eddie Shore came to Smith's aid.

The 1927 Stanley Cup Champion Ottawa Senators

Goaltender
1 Alex Connell

Defense
2 Edwin Gorman
3 George Boucher
4 Alex Smith
9 King Clancy
14 Milt Halliday

Forwards
5 Cy Denneny
6 Frank Nighbor
7 Hooley Smith
8 Frank Finnigan
10 Hec Kilrea
11 Jack Adams

Both Smith and Shore were kicked out of the game. "It was four man hockey to the finish," the *Citizen* account said.

After the game, referee Jerry Laflamme was grabbed by Bruins coach Art Ross on his way to the dressing room and assaulted by Boston's Billy Coutu. The Bruins had "squawked" throughout the game and were particularly upset about a high-sticking call Laflamme had assessed to Sailor Herbert. (There was a two-referee system in place, and the Bruins felt Laflamme had overstepped his authority by calling the penalty in the other referee's end. Sound familiar?)

"It was really a disgraceful ending to the greatest season in the history of hockey," the *Citizen* reported, "as it was the first time during the long and tiring season that an official had been assaulted either on or off the ice and it is as hoped for the good of the game which is so popular in Canada and in may cities across the border President Calder will mete out proper punishment to the offenders." Coutu was given a lifetime suspension from the NHL.

The *Ottawa Evening Citizen* speculated in its editions of April 14, 1927, "that each member of the Ottawa hockey team, winners of the Stanley Cup, [would] receive in the neighborhood of $1,200 extra salary as a result of winning the world's championship. This, it [was] believed, [would] be a new high record for players' shares." The Bruins were to receive about $800, according to a "high authority."

Congratulations poured in for the Senators, but the one "which pleased the boys the most" was sent to the residence of owner Frank Ahearn.

```
President Frank Ahearn, the Ottawa Hockey Club,
Canada
    Both of us are delighted at the splendid
success of the Ottawa team. Please give our warm
congratulations to all.
                                    Evelyn Byng
```

The players voted unanimously that their first toast out of Lord Stanley's bowl would be to the governor general of Canada and his wife, Lord and Lady Byng, who, two years earlier, had donated the trophy in her name to honor the league's most gentlemanly player. "We only regret they were not here to watch the game last night, for they were among our most vocal supporters and warmest friends," Ahearn said.

Reported the *Citizen*: "The result of the series plainly demonstrated that the Senators fully earned the highest honors in hockey."

77 No Pun Intended

Monday, January 4, 1993, was an unseasonably warm winter day, during which rain pounded down on Ottawa. The inclement weather matched the mood of the city's hockey fans and its hockey team, which was sitting in last place in the National Hockey League with a pathetic 3–35–3 record, five points behind the next-to-last-place San Jose Sharks.

This was a floundering team, a team destined to set records for futility in its first season, a team in need of help. A team so bad that a 23-year-old old man with no background in hockey, who could barely stand up on skates, figured he could help. Vincent Pun, a graduate in economics from the University of Western Ontario and an aspiring tennis pro, thought playing hockey for the Senators would be a good way to stay in shape for the winter. He had been following the Senators' miserable season, and despite not having played organized hockey, he looked at the standings and figured the Senators could use his help. "I have to do something in winter," he said. "It's better than a 9-to-5 job. I figured I had a better chance here. I think the key is to make a lot of mistakes so you can learn from them."

The Senators, losers of nine games in a row, were to practice at the Kanata Recreation Complex. Pun headed to the rink, stopping off at a Canadian Tire store on the way to purchase a thousand dollars worth of hockey equipment. He showed up at the rink ready to pitch in and help the local team.

It was the first time he had worn full equipment. With the price tags still attached to some of his new, stiff gear, wearing a bandanna and glasses and with the steel blades of his skates throwing up sparks on the cement stairs in the stands, he was welcomed down to the ice by Senators forward Mike Peluso, one of the first players on the ice that day. "I knew he didn't know much about hockey, because he was running in the bleachers in his skates," Peluso said. "If he's never been on skates before, he's doing well."

Senators defenseman Norm Maciver skated out for practice and saw Pun staggering around the ice. "We thought they were filming some TV show or something," Maciver said in an interview for this book. "I remember getting on the ice right before practice started. I was like, 'What's going on? Who is this guy?' Then we heard the story. Only in Ottawa. That was too funny."

Pun could barely stand up. After a few minutes on the ice, he was waved off by Senators assistant coach E.J. McGuire, citing insurance concerns. Afterward, in the Senators' dressing room, Pun's audition led center Mark Freer to remark: "He skates like Brad Marsh," a reference to the Senators' veteran plowhorse defenseman. "I heard that," said Marsh.

Senators coach Rick Bowness wasn't happy. "If anybody does that again, I'll lock the doors and we won't allow the public into practice," Bowness said. "We'll bar the public. This is why a lot of teams don't allow the public into practice. You always get guys trying that. This isn't senior hockey; this is the National Hockey League."

After he was shooed off the ice, Pun changed his skates in the stands and shuffled off. "I understand," he said. "They were polite."

It was just another day in the life of the Senators in their monumentally bad first season, a season when the man in the street figured he could be a man on the ice…even if he could barely stand up.

78 One for the Rhodes

Damian Rhodes always seemed like that guy who had trouble believing he got into the cool party. After playing college hockey at Michigan Tech from 1987 to 1990, he didn't view himself as an NHL prospect. When he got a chance to play his first game with the Toronto Maple Leafs in 1991, he told the *Hockey News* he thought it might be the only NHL game he would play. "Toronto just kind of took a chance on me," he said. "I spoke to [Leafs PR director] Bob Stellick once, [and he] told me, 'We never expected you to make the big team.'"

Stuck behind Maple Leafs goaltender Félix Potvin, Rhodes seemed destined to be a backup, which appeared to suit him fine. But on January 23, 1996, new Senators general manager Pierre Gauthier swung a big deal and Rhodes was suddenly thrust into the role of No. 1 goaltender.

When Rhodes arrived on the scene, his teammates told him the team didn't have a coach. Dave Allison was fired the same day as the big trade between the Maple Leafs, Senators, and New York Islanders that saw the Senators get Rhodes and defenseman Wade Redden. Rhodes told his teammates he didn't know if he was ready to be a No. 1 goaltender.

But Rhodes, playing behind the structured system put in place by new coach Jacques Martin, helped turn the Senators from a struggling franchise into a respectable team. He lived up to the stereotype of the quirky goaltender, rocking a leopard-print jock strap and dying his hair blond in preparation for the Senators' 1998 run to the playoffs and a first-round meeting with the New Jersey Devils.

The dye job earned him notoriety and nicknames, Billy Idol and Gunther (who worked in Central Perk on the television show *Friends*) among them. It also earned him a 10–4–2 record with a 1.81 goals-against average post-coiffure compared to 13–17–5 and 2.23 while going au naturel. "My confidence is pretty good right now, but we'll see what happens when we start," he told *Sports Illustrated*'s Michael Farber on the eve of the playoff series against the Devils.

Rhodes went dyed head–to-head and beat Devils goaltender and future Hall of Famer Martin Brodeur. Rhodes has said that performance is the one of which he is most proud. But Rhodes's most memorable single night with the Senators came on January 2, 1999, when he became the first goaltender to be credited with a goal and a shutout in the same game in a 6–0 win against the Devils.

Rhodes became the fourth goaltender in NHL history to be credited with a goal when, during a delayed penalty against New Jersey, Devils defenseman Lyle Odelein passed the puck from deep in the Ottawa zone into his own net at 8:14 of the first period. Since Rhodes was the last Senator to touch the puck, he was awarded the goal by referee Don Van Massenhoven. The other three NHL goaltenders credited with goals before Rhodes were Ron Hextall of the Philadelphia Flyers, Chris Osgood of the Detroit Red Wings, and Brodeur.

"I guess I should go out and buy a lottery ticket, huh? I probably couldn't shoot the puck all the way down the ice," Rhodes said after the game. "[Senators forward] Shaun Van Allen said I should have let in a goal so I could have the winner. That goal was like the cherry on top. But the shutout is definitely better. It's better to stop goals than to score them."

Odelein had to watch the puck slide back toward the open net. "It's a tough way to get your first goal of the year," said the defenseman. "Unbelievable, man. It just went so slow. You just sit there watching it, and you [know] it [is] going to go in. From then on, it was just, wow, unbelievable."

Senators forward Andreas Johansson scored two goals in the game, but he was more excited about Rhodes's scoring exploit. "I was cheering more than anyone," said Johansson, who was in the Senators' fantasy hockey league. "Rhodes gave me nine points today. Five for the shutout, three for the win, and one for the goal."

In the game before his remarkable double, Rhodes had taken a pair of unsportsmanlike conduct penalties, which was not overlooked by at least one other player on the ice that day. Ron Tugnutt, backing up Rhodes, watched the puck slide down the length of the ice and into the New Jersey net. Tugnutt turned to Senators assistant coach Perry Pearn on the Ottawa bench. "Friday he's a goon. Today's he's a sniper. I can't compete with that," Tugnutt said to Pearn. "When I saw that puck go in, I knew it was going to be his night. I could have been eating doughnuts, maybe a steak. There was no way I was going in."

79 Tugger

In 1995 Ron Tugnutt was 27 years old and playing in the American Hockey League with the Portland Pirates, the farm team of the Washington Capitals. He was making $75,000 a year. Things weren't going well. He didn't know where his career was going, but it didn't look good. He had been the backup to Patrick Roy in Montreal with the Canadiens the previous two seasons and had been offered $500,000 to play another season, but on the advice of his agent, he had turned it down. "'It will always be there,' I was told. Well, the year ended and didn't end well for me."

No offer was forthcoming for Tugnutt, not that he had been happy playing behind Roy. "He was only a couple of years older than me, and there was zero chance I was ever going to play because he would tell me I wasn't going to play," Roy said. "He was a tough partner. You almost had to be like a dog, submissive. 'You are the Almighty.' He didn't have all the accolades by then in his career, but he had a few already. He was where I wanted to be, and I wanted to push to get that. It was him telling me I wouldn't be able to push him; it was him telling me when I was going to play, what games I would play."

Tugnutt continued, "I played a game in Florida because he wanted to go golfing. That was his mental break. He's the star of the team. It seemed to work for him. Maybe he earned it."

But Tugnutt did marvel at Roy as a goaltender. "I have to tell you, was he ever good. Oh, my God, he was so good," Tugnutt said. "I remember telling my dad, 'I'm sick of this shit. I'm sitting on the bench just watching him play every night.' My dad says, 'Well, you might want to watch a little bit more. He's pretty good.'"

With no job in the NHL, Tugnutt signed with the Caps and went to the minors. "I was terrible in the minors," Tugnutt said bluntly.

Then things changed. The Caps sent goaltender Olaf Kolzig down on a rehab stint. "He went 3–0 on the last-place team, had two shutouts, and was Player of the Week. They sent him down for conditioning, and I went up and sat on the bench and watched Jim Carey play," Tugnutt said.

When he left to return to Portland, Caps general manager David Poile told Tugnutt they would not be offering him a contract at the end of the year. "'You've done nothing. It's up to you if you want to save your career,' he told me," Tugnutt remembered. "That week up in Washington, traveling on a plane, not a bus, I went down with a new fire in my eye. I had a young family. The money I was making in the minors [was] not going to cut it. I need[ed] to have a good second half. That got me back in."

With Barry Trotz as coach and Tugnutt fired up to save his career in hockey, the Pirates went on a rip. They ended up losing in the 1996 Calder Cup Final in seven games to the Rochester Americans.

Tugnutt might have been told he wouldn't get a contract, but after his remarkable second-half run, he suddenly had value. The Caps had to protect their position and made him a qualifying offer to keep him as an asset. The Caps would have the right to match any subsequent offer from another team. "I was sitting there thinking I was going to be a free agent and I could go anywhere, and next thing you know I got an offer. That was brutal," Tugnutt said. "I wasn't supposed to get an offer. That's business, right? When I went down there, I wasn't worth anything."

With Kolzig and Carey, who won the Vezina Trophy in 1996, ahead of him, Tugnutt saw he was doomed to remain in the minors. Enter Senators general manager Pierre Gauthier, who was looking for a goaltender to back up Damian Rhodes. Gauthier had been part of the Quebec Nordiques organization when they drafted Tugnutt at No. 81 in the fourth round of the 1986 draft.

On March 21, 1991, Tugnutt made 70 saves, the second-most in a regular-season game, in a 3–3 tie against the Boston Bruins. The Nordiques were headed to a last-place finish. Gauthier knew Tugnutt understood what it was like to play on what amounted to an expansion team.

In 1993, when Gauthier was working in Anaheim, the Mighty Ducks picked up Tugnutt up in the expansion draft from the Edmonton Oilers. "I owe that guy a lot. If I knew his address, I'd be sending that guy a Christmas card every year," Tugnutt said of Gauthier. "He was a big fan of mine and kept giving me opportunities, which was nice."

Gauthier gave Tugnutt what turned out to be his best opportunity in Ottawa. Gauthier came up with a clever way to get Tugnutt from the Capitals, a reverse *Godfather* approach, you could call it: he made the Caps an offer they could refuse.

Gauthier put this unusual deal on the table: he offered Tugnutt more money to play in the minors than in the NHL with the Senators. He would get $300,000 US to play in the minors or $275,000 CDN to play in the NHL. Explained Gauthier: "I said, '[Poile's] not going to want to pay that for his backup to play in the minors.' I took a chance that he wasn't. I told Ron, 'It will be you and Rhodes. I don't think he's going to match. I can't afford U.S. money in the minors; I'm really tight. That's my guarantee you're in the NHL.'"

"I remember clearly, when we talked about the contract, I said, 'I don't care,'" Tugnutt said. "I [didn't] care what they [gave] me. I just want[ed] to go back to the NHL. They [could have given] me an American League salary, I [didn't] care. I just want[ed] to go to the NHL."

An inspired Tugnutt played some of his best hockey for the Senators. With his battling style, he helped lead them to the

Stanley Cup Playoffs for the first time in 1997 after Rhodes went down with an ankle injury with 22 games to go.

Tugnutt went 10–4–2 down the stretch and had perhaps his greatest moment when he shut out the Buffalo Sabres 1–0 on the last night of their regular season to put the Senators into the postseason.

The Senators lost that first series to the Sabres in seven games, the winning goal in Game 7 coming on a shot by Derek Plante at 5:24 of overtime that ticked off the tip of Tugnutt's catching glove.

Tugnutt had a 72–51–25 record with the Senators with a .906 save percentage and a 2.32 goals-against average. He became one of the heroes of those first Senators teams that were actually good. Tugnutt was a battler. He wasn't the biggest guy or the most athletic, but he won fans and his teammates over with his competitiveness.

He was traded to the Pittsburgh Penguins in 2000 for Tom Barrasso (and wound up playing for the Penguins in a five-OT 2–1 loss to the Philadelphia Flyers on May 4, 2000), signed a nice free-agent deal with the Columbus Blue Jackets that summer ($10 million for four years), and finished up with the Dallas Stars in 2003–04. His career ended after sustaining knee and groin injuries. It was a pretty good run for a guy who had thought his career might be over and pondered retirement almost 10 years earlier.

"You've got to stay positive. Everything happens for a reason. If I had maybe taken that 500 grand deal [in Montreal], I might have been done with my career sooner because that year in the minors made me a better goalie," he said. "Even at 27. At 27 my true playing days started after Portland. That's when I became a true NHL goalie. That's when I knew I belonged. Before that, I wasn't good enough."

Smitty

If you look up in the rafters at Canadian Tire Centre, you will see the banners commemorating the nine Stanley Cups won by the Senators in their first iteration, prior to and after the formation of the NHL in 1917.

There are banners marking the Senators' Presidents' Trophy, which they won in 2003, and their Eastern Conference championship they won in their run to the Stanley Cup Final in 2007.

There are two other banners bearing the numbers that have been retired by the Senators: No. 8, worn by Frank Finnigan—who scored the last Stanley Cup–winning goal for the Senators in 1927 and who was a big supporter of the Bring Back the Senators campaign—and No. 11, which was worn by former captain Daniel Alfredsson from 1995 to 2013.

If you look to the north upper deck, there is one other tribute: a memorial to Brian "Smitty" Smith, a former NHLer and CJOH sportscaster who was gunned down on August 1, 1995, by Jeffrey Arenburg, a schizophrenic who thought the television station was broadcasting his thoughts. The Canadian Tire Press Box on the north side is named in Smith's honor.

A native of Ottawa, Smith played junior hockey in Brockville for the Junior Canadiens and went to the Memorial Cup in 1960. He started his pro career with the Hull-Ottawa Canadiens. He then played the 1963–64 season in Europe under the assumed name Bobby Smith because Smith was wary of Eddie Shore, the tyrannical coach of the Springfield Indians, who owned his rights. He played in Austria until the International Ice Hockey Federation figured out what was going on and suspended him.

He played for Shore from 1964 to 1967 and was a teammate of Ottawa 67's legend and Hall of Famer Brian Kilrea. They were part of the Indians team that went on strike against Shore in 1966, enlisting the aid of lawyer Alan Eagleson.

Shore eventually sold the team to Jack Kent Cooke, who owned the Los Angeles Kings, who were beginning to play in the NHL in 1967. Smith and Kilrea were part of the original Kings roster when they began play in the NHL. Smith scored 10 goals that season, two of which were against his brother, Gary "Suitcase" Smith.

Smith kicked around the minors the next season before playing one last time in the NHL with the Minnesota North Stars. He finished his pro career with the Houston Aeros of the World Hockey Association in 1972–73. A broken jaw sustained early that season hastened his retirement. He joined CJOH (now CTV Ottawa) in 1973.

Smith was a tireless booster of Ottawa. As a kid, he attended Camp Minwassin, run by the Boys and Girls Club of Ottawa since 1924 and situated on Mink Lake in Eastern Ontario, near Eganville. He became a supporter and fund-raiser for the Boys and Girls Club. The camp was renamed Camp Smitty in his honor after his death. An annual golf tournament in Smith's name has raised millions for Camp Smitty and sent close to 3,000 kids to the camp.

Smith was an enthusiastic supporter of the Bring Back the Senators campaign when there was mostly cynicism in the media about the bid. From the Camp Smitty website:

> When the Senators started their quest to get an NHL team, Brian was the first and almost only media personality to think it was possible and became a strong supporter of the bid. Brian also narrated the video that the Senators presented to the NHL Board of Governors to secure the franchise. The Senators have certainly recognized Brian's

place in Ottawa sports history with all their wonderful tributes, highlighted by the hanging of a banner to "Brian Desmond Smith, Smitty-18" (at the Civic Centre and now at Canadian Tire [Centre]). The press box is also named after Smitty, and a portrait with his L.A. Kings sweater hangs on the 2nd concourse not far from his plaque as a member of the Ottawa Sports Hall of Fame.

Arenburg was waiting in the parking lot with a .22 caliber rifle when Smith, on his way to host a charity golf tournament for the Children's Wish Foundation, rushed out of the building. Smith's face was the first Arenburg recognized.

Arenburg was found not criminally responsible for Smith's murder and spent nine years in the Oak Ridge Division of the Mental Health Centre Penetanguishene (now Waypoint Centre for Mental Health Care) before being released. After he was out, Arenburg had other incidents: He assaulted a U.S. border guard and spent a year in jail. He spent another six months in jail after a speeding incident in Quebec (he called the judge an idiot and was found guilty of contempt). He eventually wound up back in Ottawa and was living alone when he died of a heart attack in June 2017.

He killed Brian Smith but not his spirit. "[Brian] was a mentor to many of us. Talented and much loved in our community. He was that kind of guy. If you knew him, right away you liked him," Terry Marcotte, who learned from Smith and took over as CJOH sports director years later, said in a tribute to Smith on the 20th anniversary of his death. Also mentored by Smith was TSN's James Duthie.

"Your greatest legacy is to be remembered, and not only is he remembered by his family and friends," his widow, Alana Kainz, told CTV Ottawa, "he's remembered by the whole community, and the spirit of Brian is in this community to this day."

One other way Brian Smith's legacy lives on: his organs were donated to 12 people across Canada.

81 "Maybe Friday"

It's a good debate: who is the best player to have worn a Senators sweater? The leading candidates are forwards Daniel Alfredsson and Marian Hossa, defenseman Zdeno Chara, and goaltender Dominik Hasek. Hasek is already in the Hockey Hall of Fame; Hossa and Chara will be there one day, and probably Alfredsson too. My choice: Hasek gets the title based on his two Hart Trophies, six Vezina Trophies, and two Stanley Cups.

But when it comes to his time with the Senators, Hasek and his recalcitrant adductor muscle will always be at the bitter core of the franchise's unfulfilled potential and wistful "what might have been" season in 2006.

The 41-year-old's arrival in the summer of 2004 as a free agent was one of many sweeping and stunning changes made by general manager John Muckler that off-season in the wake of the Senators losing to the Toronto Maple Leafs in the playoffs for the fourth time since 2000. Another loss to the hated Leafs in the Battle of Ontario led to Muckler blowing up the team. Coach Jacques Martin was fired and replaced by Bryan Murray. Goaltender Patrick Lalime was traded to the St. Louis Blues, creating the opening for Muckler to bring in Hasek, whom he had worked with in Buffalo.

Hasek's Hall of Fame of career was already memorably intertwined with the Senators even before he signed as a free agent in the summer of 2004. At the height of his powers, he was in net for the Buffalo Sabres in April 1997 when Ottawa's Steve Duchesne beat him for the only goal of the game and propelled the Senators into the Stanley Cup Playoffs for the first time.

In one of the more bizarre turns—and a foreshadowing of what was to come about a decade later—Hasek pulled the chute on the Sabres against the Senators in the playoffs that spring. Hasek pulled himself out of Game 3 of their first-round playoff series against the Senators with a knee injury he sustained trying to stop the late Sergei Zholtok on a power play in the second period.

Hasek's career path ultimately led him to Ottawa. The lockout of 2004–05 and the cancellation of the season only allowed the Senators' loss to the Leafs to ferment and further raise expectations for 2005–06. Muckler's off-season moves looked like gold through the first four months of the season.

Under Murray's guidance, the Dany Heatley–Jason Spezza–Daniel Alfredsson line—nicknamed the Pizza Line because it helped contribute to fans getting a slice of pizza when the Senators scored five goals—was ripping it up. Heatley would become the first Senator to score 50 goals in a season, and both he and Alfredsson would top 100 points. The team went on to become first in goals scored and third in goals allowed.

Hasek, on the downside of his career and having undergone surgery on his groin that spring, was still a force. As the Olympic break approached, he had a 28–10–4 record with a goals-against average of 2.09 and a .925 save percentage. More important, he still possessed the aura of a multiple Vezina and Hart Trophy winner and gave the Senators a swagger they had never before possessed. The Senators were a legitimate Stanley Cup favorite. "When he was here and playing, there was a confidence level and a compete level no one else at that time could give us," Murray said. "He was one of the best in the time he played the game. I can remember when he played for Buffalo and watching practice one day, and when practice was over…all the players stayed on the ice for 35, 40 minutes,

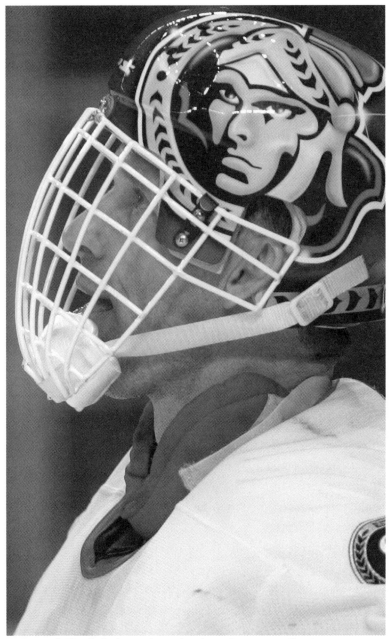

Is Dominik Hasek the best to have played in a Senators uniform?

and I don't think anybody scored on him. Shootout. Slap shots. One-timers. He just wouldn't let anything in."

At the Turin Olympics, in the first period of a game against Germany, Hasek hurt himself. "When I made a save I felt a really sharp pain and I knew right away that it [was] bad," Hasek said. "It's hard to describe; it's a little bit different than in the past… it's like three or four inches from the experience I had before." At that time, Muckler reported it to be a "slight strain to the adductor muscle group" and added: "It came right out of the blue. You always think the worst. Fortunately, that's not the way it turned out." Unfortunately that's *exactly* what it was: the worst.

"Of course I'm worried, I'll be honest," Hasek said upon returning from Turin. "But on the other hand, I want to do all the best to get on the ice as soon as possible, and I hope I can be in the same shape I was during the season. But I have to admit, I am worried. It's a difficult situation for me."

As the weeks went by, the frustration with Hasek's inability to play grew. It became a running joke. When Hasek was asked when he might return, he replied "Maybe Friday." It has become a buzz phrase whenever Hasek's name is mentioned in Ottawa. "When he got hurt in the Olympics, we couldn't understand why he didn't come back and play, because he seemed to be able to do everything, stretch, until it came [to] game time," Murray said. "I watched him in the weight room, in the dressing room, do everything that a goaltender had to do and more and not play. That was really, really frustrating."

"I have to feel well. I have to practice hard and get into the game. If I cannot do it, I cannot play," Hasek said.

The Senators finished with 113 points, matching the franchise record set in 2003, but entered the playoffs with an inexperienced Ray Emery in goal. They beat the Tampa Bay Lightning in five games but went down 3–0 to Hasek's old team, the Buffalo Sabres, losing two of those games in overtime.

Behind the scenes, Muckler, Murray, and his teammates were pleading with Hasek to return and give the team a spark. Alfredsson, Wade Redden, and Martin Havlat had a meeting with Hasek. Hasek told TSN's *Off the Record* that he told his teammates he wouldn't "cheat them." "I could stand in the net, but we'll lose 6–2," said Hasek. "I walked away from the table."

Murray summed it up:

> Ray didn't give up bad goals, but he didn't make big saves. It became very obvious as we got deeper into the playoffs we were better than most teams we played, but we had to really fight to win the hockey game. There will always be that question. When he got hurt in the Olympics, was it so severe that he couldn't come back? I never questioned a player in my life until Dominik.
>
> We just needed him to go in the net and stand there. He would have made a difference in the attitude. It was unfair to Ray Emery at that time. He was a second goaltender, a young guy who didn't have stability. He had a compete level but not the stability in his game or life to allow him to lead a team to the Stanley Cup.

The Senators won Game 4 against the Sabres 2–1 but lost the series in five games when Jason Pominville scored a shorthanded goal in overtime.

Murray, who passed away in the summer of 2017 without having won the Stanley Cup, felt that 2006 season might have been his best chance, even considering that the Senators made it to the Final in 2007, when they lost to the Anaheim Ducks.

The Senators had a chance to bring Hasek back for that 2007 season, but Murray famously said, "We've had enough of Dominik." Hasek went back to the Detroit Red Wings, where he had won the Stanley Cup in 2002, and was the backup to Chris Osgood when they won again in 2008.

"We felt he could have played, and at the end I made the comment, 'We've had enough of Dominik.' We could have had him for another year, and probably he might have made a difference in us going somewhere, but…he had let us down so much, and it was such a disappointment to all of us—the players as much as me," Murray said.

"It was a great chance. We had a really, really solid team. When he was good, he was really good. It's hindsight and guessing, but if we had him play goal for us down the stretch and in the playoffs, that was the year we probably could have and should have won the Stanley Cup."

82 The Game Changer

On a sweltering morning in Quebec City in June 1993, Alexandre Daigle, 18, rode in an open calèche alongside the immaculately dressed Jean Beliveau, the 61-year-old former captain of the Montreal Canadiens, who still owned the hearts of this city, Montreal, and the province. On that morning before the NHL Draft, in which the Ottawa Senators owned the first pick, the same kind of stardom was envisioned for Daigle.

They were part of a procession from an autograph signing at the Manège Militaire Grande-Allée to the draft at Le Colisée, the home of the Quebec Nordiques and the building that, after the previous barn burned down, was built on the back of Beliveau's talent and charisma when he was not much older than Daigle, gifts so great the Montreal Canadiens bought an entire league to get his rights. As it turned out, the NHL would *shut down* an entire league, in no small part because of Alexandre Daigle.

It was no coincidence Daigle and Beliveau had been sat at the same table at the autograph signing and attracted the longest line despite the presence of other Quebecois icons such as Maurice "the Rocket" Richard and Guy Lafleur and hockey legends Gordie Howe and Bobby Hull.

Outside, the sun gleamed on Daigle's slick hair, and in that moment, it was impossible for all those looking upon the scene not to think all the greatness that was forecast for him would be as sure and long-lasting as the love that was coming from hockey fans along the route. Daigle had been drafted by Victoriaville of the Quebec Major Junior Hockey League, where Beliveau had played, and was Rookie of the Year. His game was based on speed. It separated him from the competition. He had 110 points in 42 games in Midget AAA and 281 points in 137 games with the Tigres in Victoriaville, 137 points in 53 games in his draft year.

A few hours after the calèche ride, the Senators made Daigle the first pick in the draft—the first Quebecois to have the honor since Pierre Turgeon in 1987 and Mario Lemieux in 1984—and put in motion a series of developments that would forever change the NHL.

There had been weeks of contract negotiations between the Daigle camp, led by agent Pierre Lacroix and lieutenant Bob Sauve, and the Senators, led by president Randy Sexton. "It was more involved than the Paris Peace Talks," said one person involved. "'You come to Ottawa.' 'No, you come to Montreal.' We settled on a restaurant near Hawkesbury that was halfway."

On that Saturday in June, Daigle would sign an unprecedented rookie deal: a five-year, $12.25 million contract, $4 million of which was for his marketing rights, which the Senators were sure they would recoup and more. Those marketing expectations were based on Daigle's Elvis Presley–type swagger, his telegenic presence, and an engaging personality tinged with a biting sense of humor.

Later on that Saturday, at an evening party to celebrate the Senators' franchise-defining day, Senators owner Bruce Firestone told a group of reporters a plan had been in place to make sure the Senators finished last, behind the San Jose Sharks, and secure the first pick. The story broke in August, a couple days after Firestone had sold his remaining stake in the team to partner Rod Bryden. The revelations of a possible plan to throw the Senators' final game of the regular season led to an NHL investigation that found no evidence such a plan was in place but resulted in Firestone being fined $100,000 for his "intemperate" remarks.

Despite a fine rookie season in which he had 51 points (20 goals and 31 assists), Daigle would go on to be branded a flop—unfairly to a large extent—but the impact he had off the ice in the earliest stages of his career resonates in the NHL to this day.

The idea that a team would intentionally lose to nail down the first pick led to the NHL introducing a draft lottery in 1995 that opened the door for any of the five lowest-ranked teams in the standings to win the No. 1 pick (the odds were weighted in favor of the last-place team, but those odds were changed for 2015, giving the team finishing last even less of a chance of winning the top selection).

Daigle's contract, which immediately had an impact on other rookie contract negotiations, drew outrage from the rest of the NHL. How could a team pay that kind of money to an unproven rookie? The Hartford Whalers took Chris Pronger second and wound up in a contract battle with him. Whalers acting GM Paul Holmgren said his conversations with other general managers revealed the impact Daigle's unprecedented deal was having on negotiations with other rookies. "Daigle's contract has obviously thrown things out of whack," Holmgren told the *Ottawa Sun*. "I know from talking to [Bob] Clarke in Florida and [Phil] Esposito in Tampa that they are certainly upset about it."

The escalation in rookie salaries was one of the reasons NHL players were locked out in 1994–95. The work stoppage took out half the season. One of the big concessions won by the owners?: a rookie salary cap.

83 "Stop Looking at the Clock"

The public persona of Senators coach Jacques Martin, who took the team from doormat to perennial contender after taking over in 1995, was pretty much summed up by Irish Tom, a frequent crusty caller to radio station TSN 1200.

Irish Tom wasn't a fan of the coach. "Stop looking at the clock," Irish Tom would say disgustedly, unhappy with Martin's placid demeanor behind the bench. During critical, heated moments, Martin might have once or twice been seen looking up at the clock, hands tucked in his pockets.

While that was the public face Martin presented, there were times when, behind closed doors, he could bring the heat. One such incident occurred near the end of the 1996–97 season, Martin's first full season behind the bench, as the Senators were pushing hard to make the Stanley Cup Playoffs for the first time in the franchise's modern history.

After a 3–2 win over the Florida Panthers in Miami on March 27, there was no charter aircraft available to take the Senators home that night to prepare for a key game against the Montreal Canadiens two nights later. With the team flying home on a commercial flight the next morning, arrangements were made for the players to be fed and have a few beers back at the club's hotel, the Biscayne Bay Marriott, just across the MacArthur Causeway from South Beach.

"I knew how players liked to go to South Beach," Martin said. Having food and drinks for them at the hotel would mean they didn't have a reason to go out, right? "In [Martin's] mind, he was saying 'We're going home [back to the hotel] and we're staying in the hotel,'" remembered Senators goaltender Ron Tugnutt. "Well, I guess quite a few guys didn't get that. A lot of guys didn't get that."

After having the postgame meal, Martin went up to his room with his video coach, Randy Lee, and broke down the tape from that night's game, doing the scoring chances. Martin recounted:

> I think it was about a quarter to one when we were complete, so I thought I'd go downstairs and take a walk outside a little bit. I ran into [assistant coach] Craig Ramsay. He had coached in Florida and went out with some friends. A couple of players, Shawn McEachern, they had gone for a walk. No problem.
>
> About 1:15 I walked back, and there was a couch and a newspaper [so I sat down]. I kind of hid by a potted palm. I sat down and looked at the paper, and then suddenly, I get one guy coming in; I think it was a quarter to two. Then 2:15, a quarter to three. I stayed up until 6:00. I made the list up. Oh, was I frustrated. Disappointed is really the word.

The next morning as the bus loaded up to go to the airport, Martin told Ramsay and Perry Pearn, his other assistant coach, "I don't know what I'm going to do yet. Let me think about it."

When the plane landed in Ottawa and the players were around the baggage carousel, Pearn told them to be in the dressing room at

7:00 PM that night. Martin let them sit in the room for 15 minutes before he entered and then stopped in front of each player.

Tugnutt, who was battling a sore knee, hadn't gone out after the game against the Panthers. Now he sat in the dressing room wondering what was going to unfold when Martin stormed into the room. "And he starts. 'You fucking guys,' and I was like, 'What the hell happened?' And he starts going around the room," Tugnutt said. "'What time did you get in last night?' A guy goes, 'One.' 'How's 2:35 sound?' He starts going around the room, each guy, one by one. I'm wondering, *How many guys went out last night?*"

Both Tugnutt and Martin laughed recalling Swedish forward Andreas Dackell's answer. "He had an accent, and he says, '1:30?' And I looked at my paper and I said, 'More like 2:30,'" Martin said. "And he said, 'Oh, yeah.'... I kind of gave them a spiel about commitment and [how they were] letting the organization down and their teammates down," said Martin.

Chorske remembered Martin's rant: "'We're in a race to make playoffs, and this is how you guys are going to treat it? Hundreds of employees are relying on this team to make the playoffs, what this is going to mean to the organization, and you guys don't care enough.' He was not wrong."

"He's just giving it to us," Tugnutt said. "'You better win the next one,' and he storms out of the room, just livid."

"I finished by saying, 'Tomorrow night you're playing Montreal, and if you don't win the game tomorrow night, you'll never forget Sunday's practice," Martin said. The Senators beat the Habs 5–2.

"We blew out Montreal. We blew them out," Tugnutt said. "Guys were scared. I remember clearly we took it to them. In the first period, the game was over. People didn't see that side of Jacques. He didn't get like that very often. I think he was strategic when he did it. He didn't suspend anyone. At the end I don't know if he was even that upset the guys went out. He used it as a motivator."

Martin came into the room after the win over the Canadiens. "He comes in and says, 'Sunday is a day off. Nice job,' and starts to walk out," Chorske said. "[Defenseman] Sean Hill says, 'Hey, Jacques.' He stops. 'Do we have the green light to go out tonight?' We felt bad. I felt bad. The end result was good. We ended up making the playoffs."

84 "Crooks with Taste"

On the eve of the 2011 Stanley Cup Final, Vancouver Canucks associate coach Rick Bowness led me back through the stands and into his office at Rogers Arena. In what seemed like a previous life-time, Bowness, the Senators' first head coach, had hired a young assistant from the Hull Olympiques, across the river from Ottawa, giving Alain Vigneault his first coaching job in the professional ranks. Now Vigneault was the Canucks' head coach. Bowness and Alain Vigneault were back together again and at the pinnacle of the game after having spent those early years looking up from the basement in Ottawa.

The third man on the staff in that first year in Ottawa was E.J. McGuire, a former assistant coach to "Iron" Mike Keenan with the Philadelphia Flyers and the Chicago Blackhawks. McGuire's was a different voice, and not just because of his Western New York accent (he was a native of Buffalo). McGuire's was often the voice of calm practicality in that first season in Ottawa.

They won 10 games that first season, 33 in the first three years, with a roster of hardworking castoffs, most quite beyond their best-before dates. "Sometimes you would go weeks without a win," Vigneault said in an interview that day—the eve of the 2011

Stanley Cup Final—for a piece I wrote for Sun Media. "When I look back at it, I tell myself it made me a better coach to go through that stuff. It was more challenging than people think. Whenever a player got good, we'd trade him to get draft picks. It was a real tough environment for a coach. How we all got through it was by support, and E.J. was probably the one there out of the three guys who was the most upbeat and positive. He made it bearable."

"We would all come in the next day and E.J. would be ready to go. Enthusiastic. Never down," said Bowness. "He could have been a professor at a university teaching sports psychology. We'd be in the middle of some of those losing streaks, and I'd say, 'E.J., you can be a professor. You can do whatever you want in life and enjoy it, and we're going through hell here,' and he would say, 'No, this is where I want to be.' This is exactly what he was and who he was, and that's a hockey lifer."

On that afternoon in Vancouver, I settled into a chair across Bowness's desk, and the talk turned to McGuire, who had lost a shocking, brief, and ferocious fight with cancer just a couple months earlier. He was diagnosed in December 2010 with leiomyosarcoma, a terminal and rare form of cancer that attacks the body's involuntary muscles. He passed away five months later. We had tears in our eyes that day.

We recalled the day burglars had broken into the Senators' office at their suburban rink and stolen the club's extensive collection of video equipment. (Back in those days, there weren't near the number of games on television that there are now. The Senators had racks of videotape recorders hooked up to a satellite dish to pull in the games of upcoming opponents for scouting purposes.) Six video recorders, a television, and a satellite receiver were gone.

That was an area of McGuire's responsibility, and after taking stock of the situation, McGuire pointed out that the tapes of the hapless Senators games had been left untouched. "Crooks with taste," he deadpanned. That was classic E.J.

In 1992–93 the Senators' first season in the NHL, Vigneault was a 31-year-old rookie coach in the NHL. He said:

> I was younger than half the players we were coaching then. With E.J.'s experience, his personality, such an easy guy to talk to and be open with, it just made my integration into the NHL so much easier.
>
> E.J. was one of the hardest-working guys I ever met in my life. He'd spend hours and hours at the rink making sure all the bases were covered, making sure he had as much feedback and positive input as he could for Rick.
>
> I really learned from him. I was coming out of junior hockey and really learned from him the demands of the NHL. He was great to me.

Everybody in the Senators' entourage in those seasons learned a lot about hockey thanks to the willingness and passion of Professor McGuire to share his knowledge and insight, often over a beer, shifting the empties around the table to make a point or illustrate a play. The Beer Bottle Breakout became a running joke among the media following the team.

After his coaching days, McGuire went on to affect the lives of hundreds of others as the director of NHL Central Scouting. He was marvelously articulate, passionate, and knowledgable and was in constant demand by the media heading into every NHL Draft.

NHL commissioner Gary Bettman summed up the place McGuire occupied in the hockey world at the time of his passing. "I think E.J. had four important things in his life—his wife, Terry, the girls [his daughters, Jacqueline and Erin], and hockey. But as important as hockey was, I know his family always came first," Bettman said. "Everybody liked E.J. He was so respected and so admired. He was a great people person, and I don't think anybody had a bad word to say about him. People always talk about the game of hockey and how different hockey people are. Well, I think E.J. was emblematic of how good hockey people really are."

After his passing, the NHL introduced the E.J. McGuire Award, presented at each year's NHL Draft to a player who exemplifies commitment to excellence through strength of character, competitiveness, and athleticism.

McGuire's passion and knowledge for the game impressed Bowness when Bowness was the head coach of the Boston Bruins and McGuire was the coach of the Bruins' farm team in Maine of the American Hockey League in the early 1990s. "He was the most intelligent man I've ever been around. Intelligent and well-versed on every aspect of life and certainly one of the hardest-working and most loyal people I've ever met," Bowness said. "I think about him every day. He had a tremendous passion and he was a knowledgeable guy, intelligent guy, and you knew he was going to be a hard worker, very loyal, which was the main reason I hired him in Ottawa. We all work hard. I've said this before: we all work hard… every coach, every player. Then there's E.J. He takes…he took it to a whole other level." Bowness believed it was an otherworldly level.

After Vancouver's Kevin Bieksa benefited from a lucky, crazy bounce in double overtime to score a goal and eliminate the San Jose Sharks in the Western Conference Final, after the celebration, Bowness stopped by Vigneault's office.

"When everything died down, Bones put his head in my office and said, 'That was E.J. looking after us.' He was right," said Vigneault. "He was right."

85 Hoss and the Heater

Two players who will always be linked in Senators history are forwards Marian Hossa and Dany Heatley, two gifted players who were traded for each other. Their talents and personalities make for one of the great "What might have been?" discussions about the Senators.

The background: Hossa was the Senators' first pick (No. 12) in the 1997 NHL Draft, and after rehabbing a knee injury he sustained in the Memorial Cup with the victorious Portland Winter Hawks of the WHL in 1998, he played his first full NHL season with the Senators in 1998–99.

Under coach Jacques Martin, Hossa became one of the best two-way players in the NHL. Playing most of the time on a line with center Radek Bonk and wing Magnus Arvedson, Hossa started a string of four 30-goal seasons peaking with 45 in 2002–03, when the Senators won the Presidents' Trophy and lost in seven games to the New Jersey Devils in the Eastern Conference Final.

"I think Hoss, to me, was a workhorse," Martin said. "He played on a line with Arvedson and Bonk. Before Hossa joined them, it was a checking line. When Hossa joined them, it was a checking line but also a scoring line. He was so good at both ends of the ice. He's probably the best player I ever coached as far as tracking back and getting loose pucks, creating turnovers. Even in the last couple of years in Chicago with the Blackhawks, he's still one of the best doing that."

After a season of 36 goals and 46 assists for 82 points in 2003–04—the most points he had had in a season in his career—Hossa, like everybody else, sat around for a year because of the lockout of 2004–05 that wiped out the season. Hossa needed a new contract and had arbitration rights. A hearing was set for August 23, 2005.

Heatley was the Atlanta Thrashers' first pick, No. 2 in the 2000 draft. He was the NHL's Rookie of the Year in 2002 after a 26-goal (67-point) season. There was no sophomore slump for the 22-year-old, who had 41 goals the next season.

On September 29, 2003, Heatley and teammate Dan Snyder were returning from a team function in Heatley's Ferrari. Heatley was driving up to 82 mph in a 35 mph zone, according to experts, on a narrow road in suburban Atlanta when Heatley lost control coming out of a corner. The car went sideways and crashed into a brick and wrought-iron fence, according to court documents, hitting one of the brick posts. The car was sheared in half.

Snyder was thrown 30 feet from the car, suffered massive brain trauma, and never emerged from a coma. The 25-year-old died on

Marian Hossa celebrates after scoring a goal in 2001.

October 5, 2003. Heatley sustained a knee injury, a concussion, a broken jaw, and a bruised lung and kidney. He recovered to play 31 games in 2003–04.

In July 2004 Heatley was indicted on six charges related to the crash and faced up to 20 years in prison. During the lockout, in February 2005, Heatley pleaded guilty to four of six charges. A first-degree vehicular homicide charge and a charge of reckless driving were dropped as part of the deal, and Fulton County district attorney Paul L. Howard Jr. acknowledged the dropping of the felony charge of first-degree vehicular homicide was due to Snyder's parents, LuAnn and Graham, not wanting Heatley to face jail time.

Judge Rowland W. Barnes said the Snyders' compassion for Heatley played a huge role in the sentencing. "I am imposing this sentence because, first of all, the Snyders wanted it this way," he told Heatley, according to the *New York Times*. "Second, I don't think the community would benefit by you being in prison." He told the Snyders, "I don't know that I could do this if I were you."

"As a parent, it's hard to explain how you feel about losing your son. My pride in Dan was immeasurable," Graham Snyder said. "We will all miss him. So how do we move on from here? Forgiveness in our hearts has helped us move on. We forgive because Dany has shown remorse to his family."

Heatley was also required to deliver 150 speeches about the dangers of speeding and had his driving privileges limited. As part of the deal, the court could approve the type of car Heatley would be allowed to drive, and it would be equipped with a governor to limit its top speed to 70 mph. "The mistake I made that night was speeding," Heatley told the court. "This mistake will stay with me the rest of my life."

Two weeks before Hossa's arbitration hearing was set, Heatley requested a trade from the Thrashers, and the wheels were put in motion for the trade. Shortly after signing Hossa to a three-year,

$18 million deal, the Senators traded him and defenseman Greg de Vries to the Thrashers for Heatley. The Senators needed room under the new $39 million salary cap that emerged from the lockout. They signed Heatley to a three-year, $13.5 million deal and saved $2.16 million moving de Vries.

Senators GM John Muckler, after seeing his team eliminated by the Toronto Maple Leafs for the fourth time in five seasons in 2004, also hastened more change. Martin had been fired and goaltender Patrick Lalime traded after the latest loss. Hossa got swept up in that wave of change. "We let a good player go to Atlanta, but I felt it was time for a change," Muckler said. "We had two runs at the Stanley Cup, and in the last year we failed. The reason we failed has to be looked at and rectified, and that's what we've tried to do."

Muckler's move paid off to a certain extent: Heatley had two record-setting seasons with the Senators and helped them make the Stanley Cup Final for the first time in 2007, leading the playoffs in scoring with 22 points in 20 games (oddly enough, he led in assists too, with 15). He became the only Senator to score 50 goals—and did it in back-to-back seasons. He's the only player in club history to top 100 points twice (103 in 2005–06 and 105 in 2006–07). Heatley scored 80 goals over the next two seasons, but as the 2008–09 season wound down, a rift between him and Coach Cory Clouston over Heatley's "diminished role," as he put it, resulted in Heatley asking for another trade.

He vetoed a move to the Edmonton Oilers in July 2009 (reportedly for Andrew Cogliano, Dustin Penner, and Ladislav Smid), exercising his no-trade clause. (That led to another interesting debate: Should a player who demands a trade be allowed to decide to where he will be traded? Should he have his cake and decide where he will eat it too?)

Heatley was finally dealt to the San Jose Sharks on September 12 for Jonathan Cheechoo and Milan Michalek and a swap of draft picks, ending two of the more tumultuous months in Senators history. "There's some personal things that [happened], and I feel a change was the best thing," Heatley said after the deal. "I don't think I did anything wrong asking for a trade. I had my reasons, and if people think different of me, that's fine, but I feel I've done nothing wrong and I'm happy to move on."

After the three seasons following the trade, the careers of Heatley and Hossa went in staggeringly different directions. Heatley scored 39 goals with the Senators in the 2008–09 season and matched that in his first year with the Sharks. Then his output declined rapidly through subsequent seasons with the Sharks, Minnesota Wild, and Anaheim Ducks. He played his final game in the NHL in 2014–15 with the Ducks.

Hossa, the guy traded from the Senators because they didn't win, went on to play in five Stanley Cup Finals and won three Cups with the Chicago Blackhawks. He started the 2017–18 season on the long-term injury list because of a reaction to medication he was taking to combat his allergy to hockey equipment. He will be a Hall of Famer.

Would the Senators have been better off keeping Hossa? It's a great debate. Muckler clearly felt he was expendable, especially after being a key part of a team that had lost to the hated Maple Leafs again. And the salary cap crunch would have meant they likely wouldn't have been able to keep other key pieces that all came together to get to the Stanley Cup Final in 2007.

As bad as it ended with Heatley and the ill feeling that surrounded him when he asked to be traded, he did have a spectacular two seasons with the Senators and was a key part of them making it to their first Stanley Cup Final.

86 Du-Du-Du-Du-Duchesne

If there was a moment when the Ottawa Senators truly became a part of the emotional fabric of the city of Ottawa, it was on April 12, 1997. Five years in, that was the night it truly became real for a city and its hockey team.

The Senators had been so bad for so long, finishing dead last in their first four seasons, and now, after finally finding their stride in the final quarter of the season (9–4–2 in the final 15 games, backed by the performance of backup goaltender Ron Tugnutt), the Senators could make the Stanley Cup Playoffs for the first time. They needed a win against the Northeast Division–leading Buffalo Sabres and All-World goaltender Dominik Hasek, who was at the peak of his powers. "In the warmup I was watching," Tugnutt said, "and hoping Hasek wouldn't lead the march onto the ice."

There would be but one goal that night, scored by Senators defenseman Steve Duchesne, who had his own story of working his way up from hockey's fringes to ultimately win the Stanley Cup. Duchesne, a native of Sept-Îles, Quebec, wasn't drafted despite having 81 points in 1984–85, his final junior season with the Drummondville Voltigeurs of the Quebec Major Junior Hockey League. He was offered a free-agent tryout by the Los Angeles Kings, and I remember him saying in reference to the stamp he put on his letter accepting the Kings' invitation: "That 10 cents was the best investment I ever made."

After a season with the New Haven Nighthawks, Duchesne made the Kings in 1986–87 and was on his way. His offensive ability was a complement to the Kings and Wayne Gretzky, who arrived in 1988, and things went well for Duchesne, who wound up playing five seasons in Los Angeles. That was about the most stability Duchesne would have in his career.

In May 1991, Duchesne was traded to the Philadelphia Flyers along with Steve Kasper for defensemen Jeff Chychrun and Jari Kurri, Gretzky's old partner with the Edmonton Oilers, who was traded from the Oilers to the Flyers to the Kings on the same day, May 30.

After a season in Philadelphia, Duchesne was part of one of the biggest trades in NHL history as the Flyers dealt with the Quebec Nordiques for Eric Lindros. Going along with Duchesne were Peter Forsberg, Ron Hextall, Mike Ricci, Kerry Huffman and $15 million. The trade was infamous because the Nordiques traded Lindros to both the Flyers and the New York Rangers, and an arbitrator ruled in the Flyers' favor. Because the Flyers had in the meantime used a draft pick that was originally to be part of the deal, Chris Simon and another draft pick were later substituted as future considerations (the Nordiques used one of the picks to select goaltender Jocelyn Thibault and traded the other pick to the Washington Capitals, who used it to select Nolan Baumgartner to close the circle).

Duchesne had an All-Star season with the Nordiques in 1992–93 but was traded the next season to the St. Louis Blues and in August 1995 was shipped to the Senators for a second-round draft pick (which was traded to the Buffalo Sabres, who used it to take defenseman Cory Sarich).

After a tumultuous fall of 1995 that saw the Senators go through three coaches, two general managers, one president, and two buildings, the Senators started to hit their stride in the second half of the season under new coach Jacques Martin. Duchesne was the Senators' top-scoring defenseman that season with 12 goals and 24 assists for 36 points in 62 games. He was the top scoring defenseman again in 1996–97. He had 19 goals and 28 assists, and that stood as the record for most goals in a season by a Senators defenseman until Erik Karlsson scored 20 in the 2013–14 season.

Duchesne's final point of the 1996–97 season became one of the most significant in Senators history. With four minutes to go against the Sabres in the final game of the regular season, the teams were playing four-on-four hockey after Ottawa's Denny Lambert and Buffalo's Brad May were sent off for roughing at 15:23.

Alexei Yashin, the Senators' star center, who played one of the best games of his young career that night, burst into the Buffalo zone and bulled his way by Sabres defenseman Garry Galley, who fell. Yashin spun on his forehand, back by Galley again, and away from defenseman Alexei Zhitnik. Yashin passed the puck across the ice—just past the outstretched stick of Mike Peca—to Duchesne, who in one motion whipped a shot that went by Sabres forward Jason Dawe and beat Hasek to the stick side. The call by Senators play-by-play man Dave "the Voice" Schreiber was classic: "Steve Du-Du-Du-Du-Duchesne scores!"

When the final horn went, Tugnutt leapt into the arms of defenseman Wade Redden, the first player off the bench to greet him, and the city celebrated a return to the Stanley Cup Playoffs. "I was starting to believe we weren't going to get anything past Hasek," Tugnutt said. "It was frustrating, watching him. I'm not usually at a loss for words. Wow. We totally dominated them in the third period, and I was just trying not to let a bad one in. That was the motivation I was using."

In the dressing room after the game, Duchesne, the hero, planted a kiss on Yashin's cheek. "After scoring that goal if I had run for mayor I would have had a chance," Duchesne said in a feature the Senators put together highlighting the big moments in the team's history. "You know I never kissed a guy before, but I kissed a bunch of Senators that night and it was so much fun; we jumped all over the place."

That summer of 1997 Duchesne was on the move again. He was traded to the St. Louis Blues for defenseman Igor Kravchuk. He signed as a free agent back where he started with the Kings in 1998 and followed a familiar route, getting traded to Philadelphia again for Dave Babych and a draft pick at the trade deadline in 1999.

Just before training camp started in 1999, Duchesne signed with the Detroit Red Wings and in 2002 won the Stanley Cup with the Wings. The Red Wings' goaltender? Dominik Hasek. Duchesne retired a champion after that season.

In Ottawa, he will always be remembered for that goal against the Sabres and Schreiber's memorable call. "Other than winning the Cup," Duchesne said, "[that goal against the Sabres] is the most memorable thing in my career."

87 Redden

When I think about Wade Redden, the first homegrown star on the Senators' blue line, there are two pictures that come to mind: one taken near the beginning of his career and the other near the end.

In the first, he is leaping into the arms of Senators goaltender Ron Tugnutt under the bright lights of the Corel Centre on the night of April 12, 1997, celebrating the Senators' 1–0 win against the Buffalo Sabres, which propelled the young franchise into the Stanley Cup Playoffs for the first time. There seemed to be so much possibility in that photo. Redden, just 19, was part of a core of young players such as Daniel Alfredsson, Alexei Yashin, Alexandre Daigle, and Radek Bonk—stars-to-be who were just finding their

Wade Redden carries the Prince of Wales trophy toward the bench after Game 5 of the NHL Eastern Conference Final.

stride and would surely, before long, bring the Stanley Cup back to its home on the Rideau.

The other photo was taken in dim light of a minor league dressing room in Hartford, Connecticut, and showed a 33-year-old Redden just of the ice after practice with the American Hockey League's Hartford Wolfpack, leaning over in his stall, his head in his hands.

A lot happened between those two photos. There was a good stretch there when Wade Redden embodied what was well and good and hopeful about the Ottawa Senators. For about a decade, he was one of the best defensemen on one of the best teams in the league. He was obtained in a big three-way trade with the New York Islanders and the Toronto Maple Leafs by Senators general manager Pierre Gauthier in January 1996. Redden, the second pick in the 1995 draft after the Senators took Bryan Berard with the first selection, came from the Islanders as part of the deal that sent Berard, who had vowed never to play for the Senators, to the Islanders.

Redden was a star. "Best first pass in the game," was what everybody said about him. He was one of the Senators' first legitimate stars. He played for Canada at the World Cup of Hockey in 2004 and in the Olympic Games in 2006. Poised to become an unrestricted free agent in 2006, he signed a two-year deal for $6.5 million per season on June 30, leaving some money on the table as the Senators tried unsuccessfully to keep both Redden and Zdeno Chara, the future Norris Trophy winner who would go to the Boston Bruins for $7.5 million per season.

At the end of that deal, the changes in the NHL that opened up the game after the lockout had further exposed the weaknesses in Redden's game. Never the fleetest of skaters, the game was getting faster and he was going the other way. Senators GM Bryan Murray offered to keep Redden for $3.5 million a year, but the Redden camp correctly predicted there was still a big deal out there to be had. "It's always disappointing when you have a good player and you have to say good-bye," Murray said. "It's part of the new [salary cap] system, and you're going to see it more and more."

Redden, who had a no-trade clause, twice turned down the opportunity to be moved, once to the Edmonton Oilers in the summer of 2007 and to the San Jose Sharks in February 2008, near the trade deadline. Redden, who had been a fan favorite, ticked off fans because he wouldn't accept a trade and free up the cap space. There was a lot of bitterness around the Senators in that 2007–08 season. After losing in the Stanley Cup Final to the Anaheim Ducks in 2007, the team got off to a 15–2 start under new coach John Paddock, who had replaced Murray.

Goaltender Ray Emery had some distracting incidents; there were rumors of the players partying excessively, and the team slipped into a funk from which Paddock could not pull it out. He was fired on February 27.

Redden got swept up in the need for change, and his departure left a void on the Senators' blue line…and in the community. For instance, his work with the 65 Roses Sports Club, which raised money for the fight against cystic fibrosis, brightened the lives of thousands. "He never turned down a function that I know of," said 65 Roses past president Harold Moore in 2013, "and I asked for many."

There were also the unpublicized instances when Redden gave of his time. "He would show up and play ball hockey with kids for hours," Moore said. "It would be the highlight of their lives. How many players do you think would give up some hours on an off day to do that? That's the kind of guy he was."

The New York Rangers signed Redden to a six-year, $39 million contract on July 1, 2008. Within two years, he had been waived by the league and shipped to their AHL team in Hartford to become the highest-paid player in AHL history. He had played 994 NHL games.

Redden contemplated quitting but swallowed his pride and stuck it out in Hartford for two years. "[Quitting] crossed my mind," he told me during my visit to Hartford. "After thinking about it for a bit, I'm sure glad I didn't. I think there's more hockey left in me. Getting out of New York and getting a fresh start is the best thing for me."

As part of the new collective bargaining agreement in 2013, Redden was one of the first compliance buyouts, and the Rangers made him a free agent. He was signed by the St. Louis Blues then traded to the Boston Bruins. He wound up getting his 1,000 games in the NHL, winding up with a total of 1,023.

The NHL introduced what was dubbed the Wade Redden Rule as part of the 2013 collective bargaining agreement, which prevented teams from burying bad contracts in the minors. The deals would still count against the NHL salary cap.

Redden's place as one of the Senators' greats is secure, and that was confirmed on the night of December 29, 2016, when Alfredsson became the first modern-day Senator to have his sweater retired. Redden was selected to speak on behalf of Alfredsson's teammates. The warm ovation he received when he walked onto the ice that night showed the place he occupies in the hearts of Senators fans.

88 A Gift of Life

The plea went out on May 14, 2015: then–Senators president Cyril Leeder and team physician Dr. Don Chow sat at a dais at Canadian Tire Centre and made an announcement that stunned Ottawa hockey fans: if Senators owner Eugene Melnyk, 55, did not receive a live liver transplant within weeks, he would die. "It's urgent," Leeder said that day. Within days, 2,000 people had contacted a makeshift call center at Canadian Tire Centre to see if they would be a match to save Melnyk's life.

Leeder said Melnyk was on the official donor list and was not jumping the queue but did benefit from having a public platform and high profile in the community to make a plea. Within a week, a successful match was found and Melnyk underwent an eight-hour surgery. The Senators announced both Melnyk and his anonymous donor were doing well. Melnyk recovered as the liver transplant grew into a functioning organ, and two years later, he revealed more details about what he and his family went through, the controversial decision to go public, and a request from his anonymous donor.

Melnyk wrote an article for the *Players Tribune* in April 2017. "Liver transplant. Those were two words that I just never expected to hear. There wasn't much room for interpretation anymore," Melnyk wrote. "My first thought—my immediate gut reaction— was to dismiss it all. Like, come on, this has to be some kind of joke."

Melnyk said he was against a public plea even as he was told he had a matter of days to live without a transplant. "To me, it didn't seem worth it to ask. I'd kept everything private up to that point, and I didn't want to court sympathy," he wrote. "The whole process had taken such a toll on me physically and emotionally that it had sapped me of my will to live. So I prepared to die. I began making arrangements to sort out my estate with my lawyer. And for the first time, I thought about how I was going to say good-bye to the people I loved. All of this was taking place at the same time that my beloved Ottawa Senators went on a wild winning streak to make the playoffs in 2015. Did I care? Absolutely. Could I stay up to watch the games? No. All my focus was on getting a liver."

Finally, it was his daughters Anne and Olivia who convinced him to go public. "If all the decisions had been left up to me, I probably would have died shortly after that. But my life wasn't just about me," Melnyk wrote. "When they found out I wasn't going to go public searching for a donor, they did something that made me very proud. They took control of the situation. I'll never forget lying there while a 12-year-old girl was admonishing me. Olivia said, with tears in her eyes, 'Dad, you can refuse to ask for help and die, or you can try to live and raise us. You need to choose to be our dad.'"

Melnyk chose to be Anne and Olivia's dad, and after his health had returned, he decided to pay back the debt that was worth his life. Melnyk created the Organ Project (theorganproject.net, @theorganproject) in February 2017. It's an initiative to assist people on the waitlist in their search for a living donor and to drive donor registration. An annual gala in Toronto (the first featured country star Carrie Underwood) raises money to fund the project.

In addition to the Organ Project, Melnyk has another goal after his life-changing experience. "Before the surgery, I was informed that my donor had told the surgeon to send me one [remarkably Canadian] message: 'I'd like to remain anonymous, but please tell Eugene I want him to bring a Stanley Cup to Ottawa,'" Melnyk wrote in his *Players Tribune* article. "To whoever saved my life, I just want you to know that your kindness has touched me in a way that I feel I can never repay. But I'm working on it."

89 Three $2,000 Pies

One of the admirable things Ottawa Senators general manager Bryan Murray did after he was diagnosed with terminal cancer in the summer of 2014 was set about using his high profile to raise money and awareness in the fight against the disease. Some of that was done behind the scenes, such as giving advice or an encouraging word to fellow cancer patients, which brightened their lives and gave them inspiration. Murray was a charismatic man whose small-town roots in the Ottawa Valley enabled him to insantly connect with people on a personal level.

One of the biggest events in which he allowed himself to be involved was an Evening with Bryan on June 15, 2016: a celebration of Murray's 34-year NHL career that raised $100,000 for the Ottawa General Hospital, where Murray received some of his treatments. The money raised went toward a molecular oncology diagnostics lab, and Murray said he welcomed the opportunity to take advantage of a negative situation to do something positive in the community.

Murray said:

> It means a great deal. Being from the area, being able to include by brothers and sisters and their spouses as well, it's a real honor for me to be recognized in this way.
>
> [The hospital] is a very important place to me. I've been treated so well by the doctors and nurses. I go every other week pretty much for chemo. It's not just Bryan Murray. I look around, I talk to a lot of patients, I [spend] a lot of time there. The treatment has been outstanding. When they ask me to help in a little way to give back, that's

what I'm trying to do. It's not about anything other than if we can help the foundation in Ottawa, who really do a good job for other people coming down the line, that's what I'd like to do.

I talked about going to other, bigger cancer centers at one time, but I don't know if I could be looked after better [or by] more compassionate people.

One of the highlights of the night was a live auction that—in addition to other items, such as a road trip on the Senators' charter aircraft—collected $2,000 each for three strawberry and rhubarb pies baked by Murray's sister, Darlene, who used the Murray family recipe.

The guests for the evening were treated to dinner on the floor of the Canadian Tire Centre, the silent and live auctions, and a then a hot-stove roundtable with Murray and many of the people with whom he connected over his career. They included a former boss in Nashville Predators general manager David Poile; guys who got their start under Murray, such as Minnesota Wild general manager Chuck Fletcher and former Columbus Blue Jackets GM Doug MacLean, who was hired by Murray to work with the Washington Capitals, Florida Panthers, and Detroit Red Wings; and some of his players: Daniel Alfredsson and Chris Kelly. Senators general manager Pierre Dorion also spoke.

Much of the commentary focused on the lessons they had learned about how to treat people. MacLean said:

> It was an unbelievable honor to work for 10 years with Bryan Murray in the National Hockey League. I wouldn't have been in the NHL if it wasn't for Bryan Murray. There's absolutely no doubt about that.
>
> One of the greatest lessons I got from Bryan Murray was he said, "You know, Doug, you don't have to be hated

to be a coach in the National Hockey League. You can be tough on your players, you can be fair with your players, but you don't have to be hated." I think that was a great lesson for a young coach.

Murray said he learned much about coaching from his mentor, Bob Pugh, the athletics director at McGill University's Macdonald College, who gave Murray his first coaching job. "The one lesson Bob taught me and I tried to carry around with me…he showed me that you can coach, make demands, [and] get performance while treating players with respect, which he always did when I was around," Murray said. "And I always tried to do it with the people I was associated with."

Alfredsson was a part of the 2007 Senators team that made it to the Stanley Cup Final for the first time in the Senators' modern era. On this night, Alfredsson said Murray empowered his players by making them feel he was squarely in their corner:

He just gave you a feeling no matter how good or bad the team was playing, you could win every game. You just had that feeling. You go back to Bryan yelling at the referees all the time; I think there was a bigger plan behind that. He always had the players' backs.

Looking back, that's probably the biggest thing why our team did so well, was because he was like the big father figure, and no matter what happened during the game, no matter what was happening, he was backing you up, and that was very powerful.

So was the way Murray used his illness to make things better for those who would unfortunately come behind him.

90 Grizz

You can argue what your favorite feel-good moment in the 25 seasons the Senators have been around might be, but you would have to come up with a pretty good case to beat what went down on April 15, 2017. Actually, it was a case of what went *up*.

At 10:57 of the second period of the Senators' first-round Stanley Cup Playoff game against the Boston Bruins, Ottawa forward Clarke MacArthur dropped to one knee and snapped a shot over the left shoulder of Bruins goaltender Tuukka Rask to tie the game 1–1. But it was so much more than a goal that tied a Stanley Cup Playoff game. MacArthur turned and started to skate toward center ice, sweeping his arms up over his head once and then twice.

The crowd at Canadian Tire Centre exploded, for the fans knew this goal, as big as it was at that moment, was even bigger in the life of the 32-year-old MacArthur. "When he raises his arms," Senators coach Guy Boucher said, "I think the whole city did at the same time."

After missing almost two years because of concussions (four in an 18-month span, the last in training camp in 2016 when hit by Patrick Sieloff), after having Senators general manager Pierre Dorion announce three months earlier that MacArthur would not play again that season, and after briefly retiring, MacArthur returned to score what he said was the biggest goal of his life. "Just because of the length of time it took to get that one," he said. "Definitely never going to take my last goal for granted, that's for sure."

On January 20, after announcing MacArthur was finished for the season, Dorion said: "Clarke is devastated by this news. He felt he didn't have any symptoms, but I think in the long term of this process, we always said that the doctors would decide if Clarke was going to play. They all feel that Clarke should not play this year."

After he couldn't get clearance to return, MacArthur briefly retired to Florida but was haunted by the thought he was giving up too early. He returned and started skating with his teammates, taking part in the practices, doing extra work, coming into the dressing room and being the good teammate that he was, if in name only. (Speaking of names, Grizz was his nickname, and as far as hockey nicknames go, it was better than most. He was named after Clark Griswold, Chevy Chase's character in the National Lampoon's *Vacation* movies.)

MacArthur put in the hours with no guarantee his efforts would lead to anything but the knowledge he had done everything he could to try and come back. Maybe that was the point of it all. Then on April 4, during the day the Senators were to play the Detroit Red Wings, Dorion announced MacArthur would play. He hadn't played since October 14, 2015. MacArthur played 9:44 that night and played three more regular-season games, clocking 16:33 in the last, against the New York Islanders.

The Senators faced the Bruins in the first round of the playoffs and lost the first game at home, 2–1. In his colorful way that made him a media favorite, MacArthur likened the Senators' offensive struggles to "banging the ketchup bottle here, waiting for it too ooze out." He added, "I'd love to get one. That would help." He helped.

MacArthur took a pass from Bobby Ryan and scored his first goal in two years and six days. "Seeing everything it took for him to come back is one thing, and then seeing him play that good is another, but to actually get a goal in the playoffs?" Boucher said. "One of the most special moments I've lived as a coach, because it's everybody in the rink and the players and the organization celebrating something that must have been very, very tough to live all year. And it comes at a perfect time."

Senators defenseman Dion Phaneuf scored in overtime to win Game 2, and also had two assists. "He's one of my best friends in the game, and to see what he went through to find a way to come back and continue to push, continue to stay in shape, and to continue to work toward coming and helping our team—just an incredible story," Phaneuf said. "You could see our whole building, our fans, were behind him, and I think the whole city is." MacArthur said that ovation in Game 2 would probably stand up as the best moment he would have in hockey.

In Game 6 against the Bruins, MacArthur scored the series-clinching goal in overtime. "There's nothing like living in the NHL and living in these playoffs, and [the end is] something everyone is going to have to deal with one day," MacArthur said. "But I want to stretch it out as long as I can, obviously, and with the staff and our whole organization helping me get back and sticking with me, it's just a great feeling."

In the second round against the New York Rangers, in Game 2, MacArthur took a big hit from Rangers defenseman Ryan McDonagh near the end of the first period. He came back for a couple shifts but didn't finish the game. He said it didn't have anything to do with his head.

MacArthur played the next game and all the rest after that until the Senators were eliminated in overtime of Game 7 of the Eastern Conference Final against the Pittsburgh Penguins.

But on what they call Garbage Bag Day, when a season is over and players clean out their lockers and do exit interviews with the media and their bosses, there was the first hint something wasn't quite right. After the high of his return and the club's playoff run, MacArthur didn't commit to returning the next season. He said he played with a sore neck after the first round and wanted to confer with doctors before deciding on his future.

As training camp approached near the end of the summer of 2017, reports started to surface that MacArthur might not get the green light to participate in training camp. On September 14 Dorion made it official: MacArthur had failed his medical and was not cleared to play the 2017–18 season.

In November 2017, in an interview on radio station TSN 1200, Dorion said he believed MacArthur had moved to Florida but did not completely close the door on a return at some point in the future. "You know what? If he wants to come back next year [2018–19] and try, we'd definitely look at it," Dorion said. "Clarke was a big part of our playoff success, but I think health [and] family come before hockey any day…. I couldn't be responsible for allowing him to play after doctors said that he failed his medical."

If that's it for MacArthur, he went out on close to his own terms. He came back, he scored, and he got to raise his arms again…and a city raised its arms with him.

91 The Shawville Express

A smart pillar of the Bring Back the Senators campaign, launched in 1989, was drawing the connection between Ottawa's rich hockey tradition and this new initiative to revive NHL hockey in Canada's capital. At every opportunity, the bidders from Terrace Investments reminded the NHL governors that Ottawa had something none of the other bidders had: a previous connection to the origins of NHL hockey and the Stanley Cup itself.

Frank Finnigan was a living connection to Ottawa's last Stanley Cup era. Finnigan had played for the 1927 Stanley Cup champion Ottawa Senators, and he made frequent appearances on behalf of the Bring Back the Senators campaign. He was there, in a No. 8 sweater with the Senators Peace Tower logo on the front, for the first press conference at the Château Laurier Hotel when Senators founder Bruce Firestone and the rest of the Terrace team launched their campaign.

Nicknamed the Shawville Express, Finnigan was so named because he used to take the train from Shawville in the Ottawa Valley into Ottawa to play hockey at the University of Ottawa, according to the *Ottawa Citizen*. He joined the Senators in 1923–24 and spent the next seven seasons with the team. When they won the Stanley Cup in 1927, Finnigan had scored 15 goals in 36 regular-season games and three more in six playoff games.

He followed that up with seasons of 20, 15, and 21 goals playing between 38 and 44 games per season. When the Senators suspended play after the Great Depression, he wound up being selected by the Toronto Maple Leafs in a dispersal draft for 1931–32 and won another Cup with the Leafs.

He returned to Ottawa for two seasons and scored the last Senators goal in 1934 before they moved to St. Louis. The Eagles sold him to the Maple Leafs in February 1935, and he played in Toronto until he retired in 1937. He joined the air force, where he played for the Ottawa RCAF Flyers. After the war, he managed hotels in Ottawa and Shawville.

When the Bring Back the Senators campaign was launched, it was a brilliant move by Firestone and his team to have Finnigan around as the campaign's unofficial mascot. Finnigan accompanied the Bring Back the Senators campaign to Florida for the presentation to the NHL governors. "He was the spirit of our group," wrote Firestone in his book about the Senators campaign.

On December 18, 1991, Finnigan suffered a heart attack and was hospitalized. At the same time, the Senators were working to close their deal to become official members of the NHL. On December 19 the Senators completed all the conditions: they had paid the last installment of the $50 million expansion fee, sold

10,000 season tickets, and started work on the Palladium. The Senators were no longer an unconditional franchise.

Firestone said they were sending regular updates to Finnigan's son, Frank Jr., who was updating his dad. Finnigan dictated a message under the date Dec 20/91 and a printed headline, HOLIDAY GREETINGS: "Congratulations Bruce to you and all your dedicated staff. Your hard work has certainly paid off! I am proudly looking forward to the first Ottawa Senator N.H.L. game in October '92. Sincere best wishes to all, Frank Finnigan."

Finnigan passed away on Christmas Day. The Senators honored him on their return to the NHL. On opening night against the Montreal Canadiens at the Civic Centre the team retired Finnigan's number and raised a banner with his No. 8 on it. The banner now hangs in Canadian Tire Centre, a tribute to a man who spanned the generations of NHL hockey in Canada's capital.

92 Paging Dr. Chow

The motorcyclist was facedown on a gurney at the Ottawa Civic Hospital, his face unrecognizable under his helmet and behind a mask of blood. A trauma team worked to assess the extent of his injuries, and Dr. Don Chow, a trauma specialist who had for years worked for the Senators as their orthopedic surgeon, would later recite the grim inventory: a concussion, 15 broken ribs, a complete right wrist dislocation with damage to the ulnar nerve, and serious heart and left lung contusions. The list of injuries was so extensive and severe that the patient's family would be asked about the possibility of organ donation.

The injuries were the result of the rider colliding with a car that had pulled out in front of him. The motorcyclist T-boned the car, his head bouncing off the window, the collision propelling him almost 100 feet from the point of impact.

Dr. Chow is a respected sports medicine specialist who, in addition to being a Senators team doctor from the beginning, had worked 28 Toronto Indy car races, been the chief medical officer at the 2009 IIHF World Junior Hockey Championships in Ottawa, and worked for the NHL at the 2010 and 2014 Olympic Winter Games. He was on call that day as a spinal specialist in the trauma unit.

The head of the trauma team was concerned the rider had sustained some kind of spinal injury, so he instructed a member of the staff to summon Dr. Chow. Moments later, the injured motorcyclist's pager started to buzz. "Answer that," said the head of the trauma unit. "It could be a family member. Who is it?" A member of the team looked at the incoming number and replied, "It's us."

It took but a few moments for the quizzical looks on the faces of the members of the trauma team to disappear as they realized the situation: the broken man on the table in front of them was Dr. Chow. His motorcycle boots were finally a giveaway. He wore them everywhere.

It was August 30, 2010. An enthusiastic rider, he had mounted up and was on his way to the hospital on another call—he was substituting for another doctor who was attending his child's soccer game—when the accident happened on Fisher Ave. in Ottawa near Kintyre Private. The car came to a stop on the southwest corner of the intersection. Chow landed on the northwest corner. The trauma team saved Dr. Chow's life, and he was in an induced coma for a couple weeks to allow his internal injuries to heal.

It was serious stuff. Leave it to former Senators captain Daniel Alfredsson to play a key role in snapping Dr. Chow out of his coma. One of the first things Chow remembers—his memory was impaired by his concussion—is waking up and Alfredsson being the first voice he heard. Alfredsson had stopped in to visit.

On the Senators' opening night of the 2010–11 season in October, Dr. Chow was on hand to be introduced to the crowd. He received a standing ovation. There were probably a few people in the building that night whose lives, or those of a loved one, had been touched by Dr. Chow, who had fixed thousands of broken bones and given the gift of health to people who had been horribly damaged.

What followed was a long, painful, and dedicated rehabilitation for Dr. Chow, who never gave up his goal of returning to practice surgery. He looked through his MRIs and realized he would have given a patient with the same injuries a 50/50 chance of survival.

On May 3, 2012, Dr. Chow worked his first official Plaster Room Clinic at the Ottawa Hospital. When Senators captain Erik Karlsson had his Achilles' tendon cut by the skate of Pittsburgh Penguins forward Matt Cooke in February 2013, Dr. Chow was the lead surgeon to repair the damage.

It was a remarkable comeback. "My right hand was completely dislocated off my wrist...the four bones that make up my hand came off my wrist joint," he told the CBC at a fund-raising dinner for the Senators' Hopes and Heroes Foundation.

Incredibly, almost three years to the day after his horrible accident, Dr. Chow was involved in another accident when a car made an improper left turn not far from where his life was almost ended. Another Sunday. This time at 4:00 PM, an hour later than in 2010. He was "lucky" this time: a concussion, a broken ankle, and cracked ribs.

Dr. Chow was diagnosed with prostate cancer in 2016 and had successful surgery. In May 2017 Dr. Chow was back on a Harley riding in the TELUS Ride for Dad, a fund-raising ride to raise money to fight prostate cancer. In case you were wondering, Dr. Chow no longer *owns* a Harley; a sponsor provided one for him for the Ride for Dad.

93 He Said What?

There have been a lot of great quotes over the Senators' first 25 years, and you've read most of them through the course of the first 92 chapters of this book, which is surely one of the finest literary works you have ever been privileged to read.

There are some other wonderful quotes, but they didn't really fit into any of the previous wonderful chapters. So here is what we've got—the best of the remaining quotes from the Senators' first 25 seasons:

"Look, if I'd known Mullen was open, I never would've passed it to Stevens."

> —Senators defenseman Ken Hammond, the king of the one-liner, after he turned over the puck against Pittsburgh Penguins forward Kevin Stevens, who passed the puck to Joey Mullen for the Penguins' third goal in a 6–1 Penguins win on January 16, 1993

"Playing for Ottawa is not like playing for Boston or Chicago. They get some offense from their defensemen. How many pucks go off the glass? Alexei would have to play jai alai."

> —Mark Gandler, the agent for center Alexi Yashin, explaining how tough Yashin had it playing for the Senators and why he deserved a raise in April 1994 (that must have gone over really well with Yashin's teammates on the blue line)

"All I know is he makes more than I do, and I do more than he does."

> —Senators forward Brad Lauer on March 9, 1994, after Canadian Prime Minister Jean Chrétien said members of parliament deserved their pay because they only made half of what the worst hockey player on the worst hockey team made

"My dad said, 'Man, you could be a trivia question for life. If you've got a chance, get in the record books.' Mom said, 'Don't give him a sniff.' I was on the bench when Ron Hextall scored a goal. That's enough trivia for me."

—Senators goaltender Mark "Trees" Laforest before facing Wayne Gretzky and the Los Angeles Kings with Gretzky three goals away from tying Gordie Howe's 801 goals (Laforest got pulled but didn't give up a goal to the Great One)

"It's like having a new girlfriend. It's always pretty exciting at the start."

—Senators forward Phil Bourque after the Senators turned over their roster after an 18-day road trip in 1994. With eight different faces in the lineup than in their previous game at home, they beat the Detroit Red Wings 5–4

"This is a men's league, and he's still a boy."

—Senators coach Jacques Martin on the decision to send 18-year-old center Jason Spezza back to the Windsor Spitfires of the Ontario Hockey League after training camp in 2001

"You honor your contract. I'm sure I'm not the only one who has a problem with what Yashin did. I think he let the whole team down, not just me. If he cannot play for $3.6 million, OK, no one is holding a gun to his head, but he was not thinking about the team. He was thinking about himself. And at the time he was the captain. There's no captain in the NHL that lets his team down like that."

—Senators forward Vaclav Prospal after Yashin held out for the 1999–2000 season

"I really couldn't give a shit what you people have to say."

—Senators goaltender Tom Barrasso in an interview on *Hockey Night in Canada* after a Battle of Ontario playoff game in 2000

"Do you want me to stop the ones that are going wide too?"

—Barrasso, after the game, when asked about
getting some help from his posts

"Mother Teresa would have a bad reputation in Ottawa. You can't
go down the street and so much as sneeze without something going
wrong."

—New York Islanders general manager Mike Milbury on why he wasn't
worried about Yashin's reputation after trading for him in 2001

"Crunch, crunch."

—The sound of Emery eating a cockroach that appeared in
the Senators dressing room in Carolina in 2005; he won a
$500 dare from Senators captain Daniel Alfredsson

94 Marshy's Big Night

There was not much to bring a smile to an Ottawa Senators fan's
face in the winter of 1993. It was extraordinarily cold and there was
lots of snow—almost 120 inches, a total that was exceeded only
four times in the following 23 winters.

The losses for the expansion Senators piled up faster than the
snow. By the time the 1993 All-Star Game in Montreal rolled
around in early February, they had won only 6 of 56 games and
were still looking for their first win on the road.

When the best of the NHL's best convened in Montreal for
what would be the final All-Star Game in the venerable Forum (it
would close up for good three years later), there were two Senators
who made the trip. Given each franchise had to be represented,
goaltender Peter Sidorkiewicz got the nod (maybe because he was

used to being bombarded). Veteran defenseman Brad Marsh, 34 and in his final season, was a commissioner's selection. He had been invited to one previous NHL All-Star Game as an injury replacement when he was 23, but a snowstorm marooned him in Calgary and he watched the game from a barstool.

A decade later, Marsh would never be mistaken for one of the NHL's most talented players, but he was one of its most respected. He was a stay-at-home defenseman in every sense of the word. He lumbered around the ice, helmetless, and many a goal scorer's aspirations died in the grip of his big, thick hands.

He scored but 23 goals in his 1,086-game NHL career, a good couple months' worth for Mario Lemieux or Wayne Gretzky in that era. Marsh scored a personal high of three goals in a season three times in his 15-year career, and he was shut out three times, including his season with the Senators.

But here he was at the All-Star Game, on the same ice greats such as Maurice Richard, Jean Beliveau, and Guy Lafleur had called home, teammates with some of the greatest scorers the NHL has known.

In the skills competition the night before the game, Marsh was selected to participate in the accuracy shooting, in which players took passes in the slot and tried to smash foam targets. He had taken out the four in eight shots in Ottawa earlier in the season. "They didn't know it was luck," he said. Marsh took 10 shots and missed with 10 shots.

Only one defenseman would get a goal in a game that had 22 of them (the Wales Conference won 16–6 over the Campbell Conference). Playing for the Wales (who didn't love those old uniforms?) Marsh saw an opportunity in the third period. He got his tree trunk legs churning for the net, Kevin Stevens put a pass right on the tape of his broad wooden blade, and Marsh tipped it home. The Forum crowd loved it. Cheers rained down. His teammates rubbed his helmetless head. Marsh gathered the puck from referee

Dan Marouelli. In a game that had 22 goals, Marsh's was the one people would remember.

"Pinch me. I can't believe it," Marsh said afterward in the Montreal Canadiens dressing room, which served as the Wales Conference room for the weekend. The faces of the Canadiens greats peered down from the walls. "I've gone seasons without a goal. I've only scored 23 goals in 15 years, so goals are few and far between. Let's face it: anytime I score, it's a big celebration."

"When Brad Marsh scored, we knew things were really bad," sniffed Calgary Flames goaltender Mike Vernon.

"I'm just delighted to be here," Marsh said. "This is such a big, big thrill for me."

For the Senators and one of their good guys, it was a feel-good moment in a season that had very few of them.

Marsh was one of the most popular Senators for the startup franchise. He was a folksy, down-to-earth soul. On those rare nights when he was named one of the three stars, he would dash out to center ice (as much as Marsh could dash) and throw up a blanket of snow with a spectacular stop on the center-ice dot.

A native of London, Ontario, he stayed in Ottawa after his playing days and worked for the Senators and opened a couple bars. He led the Senators alumni, helped raise thousands for charity (he once biked across Canada to raise money for the Boys and Girls Club, and cycling has remained a passion), and made Ottawa a better place.

In 2015 he moved back to Philadelphia, where he had played with the Flyers for seven seasons during the heart of his career, and has remained active with the Flyers Alumni and cycling. That All-Star puck? It remains a treasured keepsake, displayed over Marsh's basement bar.

95 Visit Lord Stanley's Gift

Since Lord Stanley of Preston donated a decorative punch bowl made in Sheffield, England (cost: $50) in 1892 to be awarded to the champion hockey team of the Dominion of Canada, what came to be known as the Stanley Cup has resided in 24 cities. But there is only one city that can be called its home: Ottawa.

Frederick Arthur Stanley, Lord Stanley of Preston, Earl of Derby, accepted to become the sixth governor general of Canada in February 1888 and arrived in Canada in June. Lord Stanley and his family fell in love with the new country. With Rideau Hall in Ottawa as their base, they traveled the country from coast to coast and embraced its culture and traditions.

Stanley's sons, particularly Arthur, enjoyed the game of hockey, and in 1889, a junior team, the Rideau Hall Rebels was formed. In 1890 Arthur was a founder of the Ontario Hockey Association.

On March 18, 1892, Lord Stanley had this to say in a letter read at a dinner for the Ottawa Amateur Athletic Association at the Russell Hotel, according to the *Ottawa Journal*:

> I have for some time been thinking that it would be a good thing if there were a challenge cup which should be held from year to year by the champion hockey team in the Dominion. There does not appear to be any such outward sign of a championship at present, and considering the general interest which matches now elicit, and the importance of having the game played fairly and under rules generally recognized, I am willing to give a cup which shall be held from year to year by the winning team.

Until 1926 the Stanley Cup was competed for by amateur teams. That year, the Stanley Cup became the trophy awarded to the NHL's playoff champions. (The original bowl was retired in the 1960s because it was becoming brittle. It resides in the Hockey Hall of Fame.)

On October 28, 2017, a spectacular stainless steel monument that evokes the curves of the original bowl was unveiled on a misty night at the corner of the Sparks Street Mall and Elgin St. in downtown Ottawa, just steps away from where the Russell Hotel used to stand, where Lord Stanley first expressed his intention to create the trophy.

Late hockey historian Paul Kitchen had the idea for the tribute to the Stanley Cup. Lord Stanley's Memorial Monument, Inc.—a not-for-profit organization supported by the governments of Canada and the City of Ottawa—the NHL, and the Ottawa Senators made his idea a reality.

A competition was held for the privilege of designing the thing. The design competition was won by Covit/Nguyen/NORR of Montreal, and artist Linda Covit created a monument featuring Stanley steel bands that part to allow visitors access inside the bowl. A hockey rink forms the base with 36 granite pucks featuring the names of teams that have won the Cup in its 125 years. Ground was broken for the monument on March 18, 2017, the 125th anniversary of the Cup, with several Hockey Hall of Famers present.

Senators fans—or any hockey fans visiting Ottawa, for that matter—should step through those steel bands of the monument and allow themselves to be enveloped in the history of one of Canada's greatest icons.

96 Ryan's Dog Days

Senators winger Bobby Ryan, two kids, a puppy, and the Internet. Put them all together and you get perhaps the biggest viral moment in Ottawa Senators history.

Cole and Reece Jansen wanted a dog. Their dad, Warren, didn't. So there was a deal: if Senators forward Bobby Ryan scored that afternoon against the New York Rangers, they could have a puppy. If not, the debate was over.

So on January 24, 2016, as the Senators prepared to play the Rangers, the Jansen kids showed up with a sign they held against the glass during the warmup: Bobby, Dad said if you score, we get a puppy! Ryan skated by in the warmup, took note of the sign, and winked. It was on. The sign quickly made the rounds on the Internet.

After being blanked in the first period, Warren Jansen might have thought he was going to skate free for the second period too, but Ryan scored on a rebound with 20 seconds left in the second period. "I saw the dad's face when they announced the goal, and he wasn't too impressed, but the kids were, and that's all that matters," Ryan said after the game. "If they want a rescue [dog], I'll rescue one for them."

"They've been bugging me for months to get this dog, and I thought, *Hey if I make a bet and they lose, at least I'm scot-free,*" Warren Jansen told TSN. "I just shouldn't have picked such a talented player like Bobby Ryan; I should have picked someone else."

When they realized it was Ryan who had tucked in the rebound behind Rangers goaltender Henrik Lundqvist, Warren walked into the aisle, arms crossed, and laughed ruefully while the boys celebrated.

"It's hard to believe. It was just a sign. I made a bet kind of last-minute, just to get the kids off my back a bit, and it turned into this," he told CBC Radio's *Ottawa Morning* the next day. "I was a little bit shocked [and thinking], *How am I going to get out of this? And then it was all over TV, and I was like, *There's no way out.*"

"What a silly decision," joked Warren's wife, Amber. "He's one of our top scorers."

Representatives from PetSmart also provided the family with dog food, a grooming certificate, a chew toy, and a $100 gift card. Pizza Pizza presented the family with a year's supply of pizza.

The Jansens adopted a 40-pound husky mix that they named, of course, Bobby.

97 Get to Know T.P. Gorman

The National Hockey League is the fiefdom of millionaires, and with the way things are going, they will soon be relegated to the bench. If you can't start your net worth with a *b*, it's getting tougher and tougher to be a player. In December 2017 *Forbes* estimated the value of four NHL franchises at $1 billion or more: the New York Rangers at $1.5 billion, the Toronto Maple Leafs at $1.4 billion, the Montreal Canadiens at $1.25 billion, and the Chicago Blackhawks at $1 billion.

The expansion fee to get in the door for the Vegas Golden Knights in 2016 was $500 million (the Ottawa Senators and the Tampa Bay Lightning paid $50 million in 1992). The price tag for the next expansion team, possibly in Seattle, is projected to be $650 million.

The idea of somebody making $10 a week becoming a 50 percent owner of an NHL franchise, even 100 years ago, seems preposterous. Never mind inflation and what a dollar was worth or any of that stuff; the idea of a guy making the equivalent of two coffees at Starbucks buying an NHL team is just hard to get your mind around. But that's what Ottawa's Thomas Patrick (T.P.) Gorman did in 1917.

As the NHL celebrated its centennial in December 2017 and the Ottawa Senators and the Canadiens met in an outdoor game to celebrate the first game in NHL history, Gorman's story was told nicely by Ken Warren of Postmedia.

Granted access to Gorman's memoirs, Warren painted the picture: Gorman was a 31-year-old making $10 a week at the *Ottawa Citizen* newspaper. George Kennedy, who owned the Canadiens, suggested he buy the Ottawa franchise, which was for sale for $5,000. Gorman didn't have that kind of money, but Kennedy loaned him $2,500 and Gorman partnered up with Ted Day, and they were NHL owners. Warren wrote that Gorman paid back the loan within a year.

The Senators won the Stanley Cup in 1920, '21, and '23. In the Ottawa Senators' bid book they assembled when chasing a franchise, they had this passage on one of the introductory pages about the 1923 champs: "The Ottawa Senators, their ranks thinned by injuries, went west for the Stanley Cup Playoffs and eliminated Vancouver in four games and then took Edmonton in two straight to clinch it. After watching the gritty show put on by the undermanned Senators, Frank Patrick, president of the PCHA, called them the greatest team he had ever seen."

Wrote Gorman: "It is doubtful if ever a team carried on under such adverse conditions and went through so many trials to triumph as the Senators did in 1923." The Senators had been ravaged by injuries in the Eastern playoffs, and Gorman wrote they "only had about eight solid players left." Frank Clancy played every position, even replacing goaltender Clint Benedict when he was penalized.

Gorman sold the Senators in 1925 and went on to coach the Chicago Black Hawks to the Stanley Cup in 1934 and the Montreal Maroons the following season. Gorman turned his smarts to the floundering Montreal Canadiens in 1938. "Every player on the Canadiens except Toe Blake was waived out of the NHL, after which we had to tackle a terrific rebuilding job," Warren quoted Gorman. "Had we not been successful, the [Montreal] Forum would have been transferred into a garage or warehouse, so discouraged were the directors."

In 1946 Gorman won his seventh Stanley Cup with the Habs. He returned to Ottawa and continued to work in sports and entertainment, including owning the Connaught Park Racetrack in Gatineau. His son, Joe, owned the track when the Senators launched their Bring Back the Senators campaign in 1989. The team reached an agreement with T.P.'s surviving heirs, Joe and daughter Betty Ahearn, for the rights to the Senators' name and kept alive a connection between the modern-day Senators and their original owner in the NHL.

98 That Time Chris Kelly Saved Alfie's Career

In November 2006 Senators captain Daniel Alfredsson was contemplating retirement. Seriously. He was coming off the most productive season of his career, with 103 points (43 goals, 60 assists) in 2005–06, the only time he would have more than 100 points in a season.

He scored in the first game of the 2006–07 season against the Toronto Maple Leafs and then went the rest of the month without a goal—10 games. He was miserable. He was examining every part of his game, talking with his dad, Hasse, back in Sweden, and other confidantes, wondering what to do.

Turns out the answer wasn't with his head but his feet. Alfredsson was constantly changing his skates: The size of the tongue. The number of eyelets. The angle of the boot. He was especially experimental in 2006 when Bauer was making changes to its Vapor line of skates and there were issues with durability. The good side of that was the break-in period was next to nonexistent. Alfredsson went through 30 pairs, varying sizes and specs. He would break a pair out of the box, wear them for the morning skate, and see if they had the magic that night.

Alfredsson would always be looking in other guys' stalls, checking out their skates. The weight of his struggles was growing greater each day. As legend has it, he had given himself one more game to see if he could get things on track or he was going to tell Coach Bryan Murray and general manager John Muckler that he was done. He had gone four games without a point and was a minus-4 in the previous game against the Montreal Canadiens at Bell Centre.

Before a game against the Carolina Hurricanes on November 4, he passed by the stall of Senators forward Chris Kelly. He stopped, took a look at Kelly's skates, pulled one off the hook, and tried it on. It felt good. Alfredsson wore Kelly's skates. He scored that night against the Hurricanes…and in the next game against the Washington Capitals and the next game after that against the Atlanta Thrashers. "Those skates saved my career," Alfredsson said years later.

On the occasion of the retirement of Alfredsson's No. 11 on December 29, 2016, a couple reporters hung around Kelly's stall. He had returned to the Senators as a free agent that summer after six seasons with the Boston Bruins, during which he won the Stanley Cup in 2011.

Kelly was a great role player, a solid penalty killer, the captain of the Senators' AHL farm team, and a teammate who was well-liked because of his dry, often self-deprecating wit. That came through as he talked about his role in helping resurrect Alfredsson's career. After Alfredsson discovered the magic of Kelly's skates, Kelly would wear a new pair every two weeks before passing them over to the captain. They probably wouldn't have been retiring Alfredsson's number without Kelly's skates. "That kept me around for a few more years," Kelly joked that day in the dressing room. "They couldn't get rid of me. Alfie always needed those skates."

In 2011 Murray was general manager by that point, having replaced Muckler. Murray was instructed by owner Eugene Melnyk to embark on a teardown to shed payroll, and Kelly and Mike Fisher (traded to the Nashville Predators) were sent packing. (It didn't turn out too badly for either of them. Nashville was the home of Fisher's wife, country music superstar Carrie Underwood, and Kelly, as mentioned, got a chance to win a Stanley Cup.) "I heard [Alfie] was devastated when Bryan traded me," Kelly deadpanned. "Bryan tried to work into the deal that I would send skates back for him every two weeks."

After putting on Kelly's magic slippers, Alfredsson had 81 points (28 goals and 53 assists) in 66 games. He helped the Senators advance to their first Stanley Cup Final at the end of that season. Alfredsson, playing with Jason Spezza and Dany Heatley on the Pizza Line, tied for the playoff scoring lead with 22 points each. Alfredsson went on to play another seven seasons.

Kelly didn't do too badly himself, carving out a 14-year NHL career. Who would have known his most important contribution to Senators lore hinged on the size of his feet?

99 One Last Great Night

Until April 15, 1999, all the big nights at what is now known as Canadian Tire Centre were firsts: the Ottawa Senators' first game in their new building in 1996, the first time they made the Stanley Cup Playoffs in 1997, the first Stanley Cup Final game in 2007, hosting their first NHL All-Star Game in 2012, the first number retirement of a modern-day Senator when Daniel Alfredsson's No. 11 was cranked to the rafters in December 2016. I'd say the biggest night in the rink's history was a *last*: Wayne Gretzky's final NHL game in Canada.

Ottawa hockey fans and millions more watching on television took away great memories from the night. Senators defenseman Igor Kravchuk, a former Gretzky teammate with the St. Louis Blues (18 games in 1995–96) came away with much more than that.

The rumors had begun to grow in the lead-up to the New York Rangers' visit to Ottawa that Gretzky would announce his retirement at the end of the season, four days away. That would make the game against the Senators the last in his native Canada. What made the night so special was it was so spontaneous. In keeping with Gretzky's modest personality, there was no long farewell tour. There was the rumor, then the arrival of Gretzky's family in Ottawa, and the realization that this was it: the greatest hockey player and arguably the greatest athlete in Canada's history would play his last game on native soil. It would be up to Senators fans to put voice to what all Canadians wanted to say: thank you.

The 18,499 fans in the building (capacity was 18,500, but 18,499 seemed more appropriate) didn't disappoint: There were signs that said Gretzky Is Hockey and The Greatest One

FOREVER. There was a long ovation during a TV timeout in the third period, and the crowd began to chant, "One more year! One more year!" Gretzky stood sheepishly by the Rangers bench, tapping his skates together and glancing down at the ice.

A tearful Janet Jones Gretzky looked on with the couple's children as the crowd chanted and players from both teams saluted Gretzky by tapping their sticks on the boards. His father, Walter, looked on as well.

Gretzky was on the ice for the final shift, of course, and when the horn sounded to end the game, Kravchuk was the closest player to Gretzky. I caught up with Kravchuk on the telephone in Vladivostok in the 2017–18 season. He was visiting the eastern Russian city with Beijing's Kunlun Red Star hockey club (playing mostly out of Shanghai) in the Kontinental Hockey League, where he was an assistant coach.

I remember Kravchuk was the first guy to congratulate Gretzky when the horn went to end the game. Kravchuk was the smartest guy on the ice: He tapped Gretzky with his glove and asked him for his stick. Brilliant. Gretzky handed him the stick and patted him on top of the helmet before going to Rangers goaltender Dan Cloutier.

Kravchuk was also the first Senator to head over and shake Gretzky's hand as he lingered near the gate to the Rangers bench. Senators Bruce Gardiner, Wade Redden, and Chris Phillips all lined up to shake the Great One's hand.

Kravchuk, like all good players, read the play as time wound down. "A coincidence, whatever, you name it. It happened accidentally, I believe, but I guess it happen[ed] for a reason," he said. "I ended up playing the last shift as he did, and he was just beside me. The final second went off, the game was stopped, and he was just beside me. I didn't really realize he was going to give me that stick. I thought he was going to keep it, but he was so overwhelmed and excited."

Kravchuk said he was fortunate to have called Gretzky a teammate but had never asked Gretzky for any kid of souvenir when they played together. Not until the big night and the moment was right. "I played with him in St. Louis, and I never asked him for anything. Being in the same dressing room, being in the same city, traveling in the same bus or plane, I have not asked him for an autographed stick or a hockey puck. Ever," he said. "I asked. I did. I don't know if I ever prepared to do that, because first of all I didn't know I was going to end up playing the last shift with him, being on the ice. Whatever happens, happens for a reason, usually. That's the way I describe it."

When asked what Alfredsson could expect on his retirement night, Gretzky told Bruce Garrioch of the *Ottawa Sun*, "I'm not

The Great One gets a standing ovation from the Ottawa crowd before playing his last NHL game in Canada.

trying to compare myself to him in any way whatsoever, but one of the greatest nights I ever had in my career was my last road game in Ottawa." Gretzky added, "I just truly knew that it was going to be my last game. I just took it all in. I just enjoyed the entire experience and took it in."

Gretzky was named the first, second, and third star, and after the crowd pleaded, he came out for two curtain calls.

Kravchuk said it was a highlight of his career to have been a part of the historic night. "The whole stadium was cheering for him, personally for him. Both teams. 'One more year!' I know Wayne was having tears in his eyes. I almost cried too. Every player who played in that game, it was one of a kind. It was just a privilege to be on the ice against him. That's the way I look at it."

It wasn't the first time Gretzky and Kravchuk had been involved in an iconic Canadian moment. In the waning minutes of the final game of the 1987 Canada Cup, Kravchuk was on the ice for a faceoff in the Canadian zone. Kravchuk jumped up and tried to make something happen on a 50/50 puck against Mario Lemieux and wound up having Lemieux and Gretzky jump by him and start the most famous three-on-one in Canadian history. Lemieux scored and Canada won at Copps Coliseum.

Things turned out better for Kravchuk at what was then the Corel Centre, with Gretzky giving him the winning pass—in this case, his stick. "I wanted him to sign it, but I don't think I'm ever going to because it's really hard right now to catch up with Gretz. It is a Wayne Gretzky stick. Everybody knows that. It's a very, very special one and very special to me and for the whole country of Canada, I believe," Kravchuk said. "I've got a feeling the Hockey Hall of Fame is going to come after me soon. You never know."

100 On Top of the Hill

It would be difficult to imagine a better scene for nostalgic Ottawa Senators fans: the greatest player in Senators history standing in the falling snow on the Canada 150 Rink on Parliament Hill on the night of December 15, 2017, the fans who had watched the first Senators Alumni Classic still chanting Daniel Alfredsson's name as he took in the setting.

The snowflakes that fell and swirled were illuminated by the lights around the rink and gave a soft glow to the face of the clock on the Peace Tower. "Just a fabulous day with this surrounding and the weather. It's perfect, I thought," Alredsson said. "It's a great memory."

It was a great memory for the thousand or so fans who filled the frigid metal bleachers to watch the players who had created the highs and lows over the first 25 years of the modern Senators franchise.

Alfredsson and former Senators defenseman Chris Phillips drafted the two teams that met on Parliament Hill as part of the celebrations on the eve of the 2017 Scotiabank NHL100 Classic between the Senators and the Montreal Canadiens at Lansdowne Park, a celebration of the centennial of the first game in NHL history.

It was an awesome list of players and personalities who were responsible for making many of the people in the stands into fans of the Senators. Team Alfredsson, led by four goals from Alexandre Daigle, the No. 1 pick in the 1993 draft, defeated Team Phillips 12–3. Team Alfredsson was loaded up with skill. Team Phillips had the grit. "I think Phillips made a lot of emotional picks," Daigle joked. The 42-year-old was flying. Daigle, who runs a television studio in Montreal, said he played hockey a couple times a week, and it showed.

"We had the younger legs and were maybe quicker at times, and the guys made some great plays. Daigle was fantastic today. It was fun to watch him. He still has the speed and the finish," Alfredsson said.

"We may have lost to team Alfredsson on Parliament hill last night but team @CPhillipsFour was hand picked for being better and much more fun in the room!" tweeted defenseman Jason York.

Alfredsson and Mike Fisher had two goals for Team Alfredsson, and Laurie Boschman, Magnus Arvedson, Alexei Yashin, and Randy Robitaille also scored. Martin Havlat, Bryan Smolinski, and Chris Neil scored for Team Phillips.

Goaltender Patrick Lalime was strong in goal. "The best pick was Patty Lalime, no question, hands down," Alfredsson said. "Chris was nice enough to give me first pick, and we started with the goalies. I went with Patty, and it paid off big time today. He was outstanding. He made the saves on breakaways, two-on-ones, penalty shots."

Neil, who had announced his retirement the day before, tried his best to rally Team Phillips. He bumped his old friend Fisher along the boards and forced Alfredsson to sidestep some contact. Neil scored the last goal of the game, and even Team Alfredsson goaltender Patrick Lalime joined the post-goal celebration in the corner.

As Alfredsson clomped into the dressing room after the game, he said the official score was 12–2. "Neil's goal doesn't count," he said. "They had six skaters on the ice."

It was a night filled with that kind of competitive jabbing back and forth. "That's what it was all about," Lalime said, holding up his hand and tapping his fingers against his thumb, mimicking someone talking. "The guys were jabbing each other pretty good."

The Lineups for the Senators Alumni Classic, December 15, 2017, (Team Alfredsson 12, Team Phillips 3)

Team Alfredsson	Team Phillips
1. Damian Rhodes	31. Ron Tugnutt
40. Patrick Lalime	33. Pascal Leclaire
7. Curtis Leschyshyn	2. Jim Kyte
7. Rob Zamuner	2. Lance Pitlick
9. Brendan Bell	4. Chris Phillips
10. Shean Donovan	6. Wade Redden
11. Daniel Alfredsson	7. Randy Cunneyworth
12. Mike Fisher	9. Martin Havlat
14. Radek Bonk	17. Rob Murphy
16. Laurie Boschman	21. Bryan Smolinski
17. Denis Hamel	21. Dennis Vial
17. Filip Kuba	22. Shaun Van Allen
19. Alexei Yashin	25. Chris Neil
20. Magnus Arvedson	27. Janne Laukkanen
22. Norm Maciver	28. Denny Lambert
27. Randy Robitaille	28. Todd White
91. Alexandre Daigle	33. Jason York
	37. Brad Smyth

The alumni were culled from the first Senators team in 1992–93, which had won just 10 of 84 games through the 2016–17 team. "I didn't play for the 1992–93 team," Team Phillips forward Shaun Van Allen said, "but after tonight I know how they felt."

"Not the outcome we wanted, but had an amazing time with friends and old teammates on one of the coolest rinks I've ever played on," tweeted Phillips afterward.

In the dressing room after the game, the players thawed out old bones. "That's the first time I've had the pads on since 2005," goaltender Ron Tugnutt—who helped lead the 1996–97 Senators to their first playoff berth—said. "It was just a great night."

"That's it, that's the last game I'll ever play," defenseman Lance Pitlick, a solid stay-at-home defenseman from 1994 to 1999, said in the hallway under the stands. "My hip is done." The 50-year-old said he underwent physiotherapy on his degenerating hip for two months just to get it well enough to be able to play in the game. That's what the chance to come back and see their teammates and play one more time meant to some of these men.

Said Lalime: "I just wanted to hit the pause button so I could keep enjoying it."